Playing It by Heart

Playing It by Heart

Taking Care of Yourself
No Matter What

Melody Beattie

HAZELDEN®
INFORMATION & EDUCATIONAL SERVICES

Hazelden
Center City, Minnesota 55012-0176

1-800-328-0094
1-651-213-4590 (Fax)
www.hazelden.org

ISBN: 1-56838-338-X

03 02 01 00 99   6 5 4 3 2

Cover design by David Spohn
Typesetting by Universal Press

This book is based on actual experiences. In some cases, the names and
details have been changed to protect the privacy of the people involved.

Contents

Acknowledgments

First, I wish to thank and acknowledge God, my Higher Power, for all the gifts and grace, and for helping me write this book.

The following people deserve more than a thank you. They deserve a purple heart.

My mother, for all she's been through, for all her gifts, for her continued love and concern, and for bringing me into this world and seeing me through to maturity, whatever that means.

My father, for his gifts and love, and volunteering for the challenge of being my dad.

My children, who now live all over the place, for their invaluable support, encouragement, and love: Shane, Nichole, and John and his family—Jeanette, Brandon, and Courtney.

Kyle Mathews, my best friend and ex-partner in the bookstore (may it rest in peace) for his essential daily, sometimes hourly, support, encouragement, prodding, pushing, insights, validation, and belief in me and this book and for listening to me moan and whine every day. "Just write the little stories," he kept saying. "They'll all link together in the end."

Francisco, for his prayers and spiritual support and for introducing me to the Babalawo.

The Babalawo, for opening his heart to me and for all he taught me.

Louie, for believing in me and helping bring me and this book to life.

The Bodines—Mae, Echo, Michael, Katie, Bianca, and my beautiful godson Blake—for their love, support, and continued friendship.

David, for being the father of my children and for volunteering to teach me about my codependency.

Scotty, for his love and all he taught me.

Andy, for his patience and determination to teach me to skydive—and all the staff at Skydive Elsinore.

Michael, for introducing me to skydiving.

Becky, Karen, David, Joe, Vickie, Clay, and all the staff at Hazelden Information and Educational Services, for welcoming me back with open arms and for their patience, belief, skills, integrity, and dedication. This has truly been a team effort, and I'm honored to be on their team.

And finally to Ann Poe and Elizabeth Poe for coming in with their heightened, honed, sharpened editorial skills at the eleventh hour and for more than occasionally propping me up as we screamed to the finish line with this book

Dedication

I suppose that many readers skip by the dedication page without a glance, unless the writer has informed them that their names will appear correctly spelled in print on that page. For a slightly (I sincerely hope and believe the word *slightly* applies here and for the most part it does, depending on which hour of the day you catch me) neurotic and still codependent author/writer such as myself, the dedication page looms in magnitude. Understanding to whom I am writing helps me clarify what I have to say; more important, how I am going to say what I have to say; and most important, gives me a reason to crawl across the hot coals of anxiety, fear, confusion, self-accusation, ego, moodiness, laziness, accusatory voices from the past, a habitual tendency to cling to distractions and other people's dramas, apathy, insecurity, general tight-lipped uncommunicativeness, and murky thinking that most writers have to force themselves across in order to write a book.

Many years ago at a county fair in Stillwater, Minnesota, I attended a pig race. Little pigs were let loose at the beginning of a track similar to a horse-racing track only smaller. The motivation to get these pigs to bolt through the starting gate, run fast, and compete with each other was a plate of Oreo cookies. The winner took all. Although the reasons the pigs ran were perhaps more complex and influenced by a multitude of forces, pigs are simple. They thought they were running because they wanted the cookies, and that was good enough for them. On a subtle but profound spiritual level, that's what defining my ultimate reader, the dedicatee, does for me.

Writing eleven books including this one and that many dedication pages has measurably thinned my list of nominees for that honor.

While searching for the key to unlock the writing of this book, I stumbled into the Fat Lady in the pages of J. D. Salinger's book *Franny and Zooey*. Franny was an actress, who didn't want to act anymore. She couldn't figure out why she should devote her life to what she now saw as an egotistical and meaningless career.

Her brother Zooey was trying to convince her that working in the arts really wasn't about her—it was about her audience.

"An artist's only concern is to shoot for some kind of perfection, and on his own terms, not anyone else's. You have no right to think about those things, I swear to you," Zooey said.

Then Zooey reminded Franny of what their brother Seymour had taught them, while he was alive—Seymour had since committed suicide—when all three of them, Zooey, Franny, and Seymour, performed together on a weekly radio show.

The lesson occurred one day when Seymour had told Zooey to shine his shoes before going on the radio show. Zooey became furious. He told Seymour that the people in the audience were all morons, the announcer was a moron, the sponsors were morons, and he damn well wasn't going to shine his shoes for them because nobody could see his shoes anyway. Seymour told Zooey to shine his shoes for the Fat Lady.

Zooey didn't know exactly who the Fat Lady was but he pictured her as a woman sitting all day on her porch, swatting flies, with her radio blaring from morning to night. He figured she probably had cancer too. So he went ahead and shined his shoes for her that day and from then on.

Franny remembered the day Seymour had told her to be funny for the Fat Lady. Franny didn't know who the Fat Lady was either. She pictured her as a woman with thick legs, sitting in a wicker chair, listening to the radio while she recuperated from cancer.

"But I'll tell you a terrible secret—Are you listening to me?" Zooey said. "There isn't anyone out there who isn't Seymour's Fat Lady. Don't you know that? Don't you know that . . . secret yet? And don't you know—listen to me, now—don't you know who that Fat Lady really is? . . . Ah, buddy . . . It's Christ Himself."

The Fat Lady instantly became the key, the winning nominee, and my plate of Oreo cookies.

I dedicate this book to her.

A Date with Destiny

The first story I want to tell you concerns the day my destiny bracelet broke and what that meant to me. And what it might mean to you.

I was standing in one of those do-it-yourself car-wash stalls in Espanola, New Mexico. I was watching Scotty, *or what was left of Scotty,* as he valiantly and dutifully washed my car, a burgundy Infinity four-wheel drive, rearranged the contents of the back for at least the twelfth time in the three days we had been together, then vacuumed the seats and floor mats.

Espanola is a town of about eighty-three hundred people, and it is situated about ten miles west of Chimayo, New Mexico, which is about twenty-five miles northwest of Santa Fe. About twenty-seven hundred people live in Chimayo, a small town that contains a church, the Santuario de Chimayo, that is renowned throughout the world for its healing powers. It's also called the Lourdes of America, and I often go there when I need to connect with spiritual power. Scotty had joined me there, and his presence had been as sudden, as unexpected and yet natural, as it had been throughout the twenty-five year course of our on-again, off-again relationship.

I had suggested we drive through one of those car washes that does everything for you, but Scotty said no, pull in here. In the past, I would have argued with him.

"That's codependent," I used to say. "You don't have to do it the hard way."

"Everything's not *codependent*," he would answer. "You use that word to describe me when it doesn't describe why I'm doing what I'm doing. I like to wash the car and keep it organized and in order. It's a male thing, and I feel good about myself when I do it that way."

We had had that argument so many times that we didn't need to have it again. I just ran it through my head and kept quiet. I was having another argument with myself, anyway. I felt so guilty watching him work, pushing his frail body around as he washed, sorted, and vacuumed. I knew that every step he took, each time he used a muscle, it took all his reserve and concentration. *If he insisted on us doing it ourselves, at least he could sit quietly and let me do the work. Melody, be quiet, I hushed myself. You know how important it is to him to feel needed and useful. Let him have his dignity. And cleaning the car right now, doing that for you, is giving him dignity and purpose.*

It was so easy not to need anyone for anything—to just shut down and do it myself. Instead of saying anything, I deliberately clamped my mouth shut.

That's when I looked down and noticed my destiny bracelet was gone.

I felt its absence from my left wrist.

A rush of fear, like a gust of wind, rose from my belly into my throat.

My right hand involuntarily touched the spot where the bracelet had been. I didn't want it to be gone, didn't like it that it was gone. I had been wearing it for nine months now, and it had made a place on my body. Scotty was engrossed in vacuuming the driver's side of the car. I walked from the passenger door, which was open, to the rear of the car.

There on the oil-spotted cement ground, in the city of Espanola, lay the tiny yellow and jade-green translucent beads. Some of them were still threaded on the thin white string. The rest were spattered around.

I started to bend down, then remembered the words of the Babalawo. "If it breaks, leave the beads where they fall," he had said, as he tied the strand around my wrist. "Don't touch them. Don't pick them up. Just walk away.

"Don't forget to duck," he added. "When the bracelet breaks, it means death is near. But it also means you're protected. It's done its job."

I walked around to where Scotty was standing and showed him my wrist.

"My destiny bracelet broke," I said. "I'm a little nervous. I don't know what that means." I paused. "If anything."

That had become our standing joke, one that kept us from making too much out of incidents before we understood what they meant. It stopped us from obsessing about understanding what we were learning before it was time to know, before the lesson became clear. It kept us out of our heads—a favorite place for both of us—and into the experience.

He finished the task he had set to, then turned his frail body to me. "Maybe it means it's time to get a new bracelet," he said.

"Or a new destiny," I added, under my breath.

Scotty handed me a rag, motioning for me to get inside the car and begin wiping. I got in the car and started working on the window, glad to have something to do. I didn't want to start crying again, which I had been doing for three days every time I looked at Scotty, really looked at him, and stayed open to what I saw and felt.

Scotty stood watching me try to clean the inside windows for a while. The more I wiped, the more they streaked. Finally, he took the cloth from me. "When you use this kind of cloth, you have to dampen it first, otherwise it won't work," he said. "That's one of the rules." He started to walk away, then turned back. "But then, like you say, *there are no rules.*"

"I didn't say that," I said.

"Yes. You did," he said.

I remembered that conversation too. It was more of an ongoing argument that had begun between us when he came back into my life about a year after my son Shane had died. Scotty kept insisting there were rules. I interpreted that, as I had most of my life, to mean a strict code of right and wrong—a rigid, stifling course of conduct that no human could adhere to. I said I couldn't function when I judged myself that way. It kept me in a perpetual state of hating myself.

"There are no rules," I'd insist, "only lessons."

"Yes there are rules," he'd say. Now I understood. He was talking about how this world worked, talking about the universal laws, the ancient codes. I didn't know what I was learning back then when he made his grand reentrance into my life. It had taken me eight long years to begin to understand. He was teaching me those laws.

Scotty was saving my life too. I had quit, given up, shut down at that deep, almost impenetrable level that people sometimes reach.

Scotty had brought me back to life. Resuscitated me. Then through our discussions, our times at the beach, at the mountains, in the desert he had breathed new life into me. Even fighting in the car—and being trapped in the car with him for a cross-country trip was a hellish experience—had been part of my revival.

"You like fighting with me," he'd say. "I'm the only one who has the guts to do it with you. And it makes you feel alive. It makes you feel."

He was right.

He had been my friend, my lover, and my spiritual teacher.

And now, he was deteriorating.

I couldn't do anything about it except watch, listen, and let him wash the car himself, if that's what he wanted to do.

There was a time, not so long ago, when his strapping 185-pound frame and cropped wavy hair made people stop him on the street, asking him if he was Robert Redford. Now, he looked seventy-five years old. He had withered to 135 pounds. His muscles had withered and disappeared, except for a few hardened knots on his arms. He was a walking skeleton, with skin. The Guillain-Barré syndrome, a neuromuscular disorder similar to polio, had caught up to him. Hepatitis had caught up to him. Twenty-five years of periodic relapse from the disease of alcoholism had caught up to him. These periodic times of sobriety would come upon him as suddenly and unexpectedly as his drunken ones—those times he would be walking down the street on his way to the grocery store or a meditation class and find himself sitting on a bar stool in a sleazy cheap barroom with an empty beer glass in his hand.

Life had caught up with him.

Now death almost had him too.

Ebby Thacher, one of the original participants in Alcoholics Anonymous, the Twelve Step organization that helps many people in all countries of the world recover from the disease of alcoholism, was Scotty's role model. Ebby had helped begin this organization, but had not been able to achieve consistent sobriety himself. The message of hope had come through him, but he never quite got it himself, not in a way that *took*.

In an odd way, Ebby's story gave Scotty dignity, hope, and purpose. Ebby's story helped Scotty make sense out of his life. "It's the message, not the messenger," Scotty would hammer at me. "When are you going to get that?"

It took me a long time to understand that not all destinies are the same.

In the twenty-five years that I had known Scotty, I had only seen him drunk a handful of times. I didn't like seeing him that way, being around him when he was like that. It changed him from a strong yet gentle man into a monster, from the most intelligent, brilliant teacher I'd met yet into a slobbering senseless jackal, from a man I loved into a man I didn't recognize. Scotty didn't like me seeing him that way. I don't think he liked seeing himself that way. So he went away from me, or I from him.

I didn't like seeing him this way either, an almost unrecognizable shadow of who and what he was. Sometimes I would blink my eyes and try to picture him the way he used to be. There were moments when I could feel him, feel the Scotty I had known and loved—still loved even now—if I relaxed and didn't look too hard or too closely.

The memory would only surface for a second. Then the walking, withered skeleton would reappear.

Right before I had left my home in Malibu on this trip, when I was rummaging through some papers, sorting, filing, and throwing away what I no longer needed, I had come across a postcard Scotty had mailed me a few years before. On the front was a picture of Stephen Hawking, acclaimed by many to be one of the most brilliant physicists of our time, and author of *A Brief History of Time*. Hawking, who suffers from the degenerative and crippling disease of ALS (Lou Gehrig's disease), was sitting all gnarled and bent in his wheelchair. On the back of the card, Scotty had written a note to me paraphrasing one of Hawking's quotes. Over time that quote had become one of Scotty and my favorite little sayings, one of the little codes that people who are close throw back and forth between each other to tell each other a story, to communicate a feeling, to sum things up.

"You have to be awfully sure you are to die on the gallows before you put to sea in a small boat during a storm," Scotty had scrawled. "Everything is (pre)determined, but you may as well behave as if it isn't."

ॐ

I received my destiny bracelet in the spring of 1998 in Los Angeles, California. My friend Francisco took me to get it. He wanted me to meet the Babalawo, the ranking position in what Francisco often mysteriously referred to as The Religion. In that religion, a Babalawo is like a priest, or minister, or rabbi is in other faiths. Francisco knew that over the past years I had been studying world religions. I had been to Egypt, and worshiped, prayed, and meditated with the Muslims, learning of their love and respect for Mohammed. I had traipsed about Israel, visited the tomb of David, and peeked at the beautiful, ritualistic religion of Judaism. I had wandered into the city of Safed, stumbling through the home and roots of the Kabbalah, the mystical sect of Judaism. I had waded in the Dead Sea, so salty you could float cross-legged on it and read a newspaper. I had sat by the Sea of Galilee, and wondered what it might have been like to look out and see Christ walking across its surface. I had walked down the Via Dolorosa inside the old city in Jerusalem, now a narrow cobblestone road that ran through a marketplace crowded with small shops. Two thousand years ago on this same street, Christ had carried his cross, knowing he was soon to be nailed to it. I didn't want to study these religions by reading books, although that was part of it. I wanted to go to the home of these religions, talk to the people, eat with them, listen to them tell me about their lives, their pain, their struggles, their prayers, their hopes, and their beliefs. That's why Francisco thought it would be interesting and helpful to me to talk with the Babalawo.

"In my religion," Francisco said, "we believe that there is one God, and one God only. And we believe in Jesus Christ. We also believe that God has put special powers or forces in the universe and on this earth. The Babalawo has special rights. He is a holy man, and the only person allowed to communicate with the force or power that people call *destiny* or *fate.*"

At first that morning, I had dressed in casual street attire for my appointment with the Babalawo. I put on dark slacks, a light sweater, and a pair of black shoes. I was ready to walk out the door and wait outside for Francisco, but something didn't feel right. A nagging thought crossed my mind, causing me to change my mind and my clothes. In my travels I had learned that dressing in white was extremely important to certain religions. Before I had gone into the pyramids to meditate on my first trip to the Middle East, my friend and teacher there, Essam, had insisted that I wear all white if

I wanted to receive what he had called the *special powers*. I had felt ridiculous and self-conscious, especially when I had to place a white hanky on top of my head, but later I realized that dressing in white was a way people showed humility, purity, and respect in some religions. Dressing in white had been an act of love, even if I hadn't understood it clearly at the time.

I quickly changed clothes before Francisco arrived, carefully putting on all white garments from my underclothes to my shoes. Instead of putting on pants, I dressed in a long white skirt. Then I covered my head with a white scarf, tying it in back with a knot. I checked myself in the mirror on my way out the door. I looked strange, oddly ancient and old-worldly, presenting an entirely different image from the one I normally portrayed. I shrugged my shoulders, then left. This meeting was important to me but it wasn't a date. How I looked wasn't as important as the message my appearance conveyed.

After almost two hours of driving, we arrived at the Babalawo's house, a simple house with a large, well-tended frontyard in an area of Los Angeles I had never visited before. "It's an honor and a privilege for you to meet the Babalawo," Francisco said, as we got out of the car and walked up to the gate. "People in my religion don't often open their hearts or their homes to outsiders. You're one of the lucky ones."

We rang the doorbell. Moments later, the door opened. I instantly relaxed and felt grateful for how I was dressed. The Babalawo, this man who was reportedly connected to so much power, looked far different than I had imagined. He had dark, chestnut brown hair. He was short, slightly rotund, with an innocuous, sweet but almost handsome face. And from his shoes to his socks, pants, and shirt, he was dressed completely and immaculately in white.

Maybe this was a date, after all.

He led us back to the interior of his house, a small comfortable room containing a large wooden desk. We made small talk for a while. The Babalawo said he had been born in Cuba, then later as a boy had made his way to the United States. He lived in Florida for a while, then some years ago, moved to Los Angeles. His mother, an elderly woman whose demeanor conveyed both frailty and power, served me a demitasse filled with a few thimblefuls of thick, black liquid. It tasted sweet, warming my throat as it went down.

"Cuban coffee," Francisco said. "Isn't it good?"

I nodded.

Then, the Babalawo cleared his throat. I felt slightly intimidated. I didn't know what to expect. "I'm very impressed that you dressed in white and wore a skirt," the Babalawo said. "It respects my position, my religion, and me as a man. Many people come wearing shorts. That's a strange way to dress to come to talk to the spokesman for the power of destiny or fate. White is the color to wear when you want to receive spiritual power."

His compliment relaxed me some. But I still wasn't completely at ease. I felt like I was in a different world, a different country, another time and place, even though I hadn't left California. Then the small talk ended and the reason for our meeting began. The Babalawo asked me to spell my full name, including my maiden name. Then he handed me two stones, asking me to shake them, put one in each hand, then hand them back to him one hand at a time so he could see the stone that each hand held.

He asked no questions. He was hard at work. Each time I shook the stones and held out my hands, he consulted a book and made some notes. He looked more confused with each notation he made.

He talked in Spanish to Francisco for a while, and then he began talking to me. "I checked the records," the Babalawo said. "At first I couldn't believe what they said about your life, about the things that have happened to you. So I checked again. It looks like it's all true. The records say you were abused as a child. You had a broken marriage. Then it appears your son, whom you loved deeply, died at a young age. Even the man who was your spiritual teacher had his own demons and dark side."

The Babalawo leaned toward me. "There's such a slim chance

one of these things could happen, but it appears that many did. How come you didn't go crazy? How come you didn't lose your mind?"

His question ignited questions in me. Was he confirming one of my deepest fears? Had God and destiny forgotten about, overlooked me? And who said I hadn't gone crazy? Some of my behaviors had been downright absurd.

After watching his look of concern and disbelief about the events in my life, after he said he had to double-check the records to make certain what he saw was true, I had one pressing question on my mind. I had to blurt it out.

"What are you saying?" I asked him. "Are you saying that my whole life has been a mistake?"

He checked the records again. "It had to be that way," is what he calmly said. "It was your karma. Your fate."

"What's karma?" I immediately asked. It wasn't that karma was a new word to me. I had been hearing about karma for years. Some people say it means what comes around goes around, and lands right back at your door. Other people, especially those who believe in reincarnation, believe that karma is a universal balancing act. If we have any unfinished business with people—unresolved emotions, or an abuse or imbalance in power—we'll meet with those people again and again until the business is finished and the power scales no longer tip. We owe them a debt or they owe us. The unfinished business might be from this lifetime or another, but we'll run into that person again and again until our debt with them, or theirs with us, has been paid off. What we owe that person may be as simple a debt as compassion or the truth. Often, karma implies guilt on the side of one person or the other, as if someone had done something wrong. So when the Babalawo said *it was your karma*, I wanted to know exactly what he meant.

"Your karma is what you had to go through," he said. "Karma means bringing the past into the future. Using past negativity to create."

What he was saying was almost more than I could take in. All these twists and turns in my life had been twists and turns of fate, the hand, or, as one friend says, the finger of God?

"The records also hold a special warning. I've seen it in people's lives before. You need to stay away from alcohol. And don't smell the flowers."

I turned to Francisco with a confused look on my face.

"Don't smell the flowers means stay away from drugs," Francisco explained. "The Babalawo is saying that if you drink alcohol or use drugs, with the markings you've got and your destiny this life, you'll go crazy. You'll go nuts."

"What's your work?" asked the Babalawo.

"I'm a writer," I said. "I used to write for a newspaper. Now I write books."

"Oh, I see," he said. "Do you write stories about romance, books about love?"

I had intended to write romance novels when I began my writing career, but that part of my life had twisted too. When I sat down to write my first book on love, I realized that I didn't understand it, at least not the romantic kind. So I had written books about something else. I couldn't explain the whole codependency thing to this man, tell him that it was not only how I had coped—my codependency was how I had gone insane.

"I write books about spirituality, about the pain and loss I went through, and what I learned from each experience and what helped me heal," I replied instead.

The Babalawo peered at me intently. "You have an obsessive spirit," he said. "You have to watch out for that."

I sat forward on my chair, ready to defend myself, explain that obsession is closely connected to passion, and how it helped me get things done. Then I relaxed. Maybe this ruler of fate and destiny understood codependency better than I thought.

"Do you believe in past lives?" he asked me. I said I didn't know whether I did or not. As far as I was concerned, it was theory and hadn't been proven.

The Babalawo said the concept of past lives is true.

"All this loss and negative energy surrounding you needs to be cleansed," the Babalowo said. "It's passed down from your father's grandmother, to his mother, to him, and then to you. And from your mother's mother, to your mother, to you. It's like a curse."

I followed him into another room, a smaller special room he had built out back, next to a garden filled with exotic flowers and herbs. He sat on a straw mat on the floor, working intently on a round wooden table covered with sand. I sat in front of him on a small turquoise stool. I opened my hands, palms up, resting them on my knees—a sign to him and God that whatever good came, I was willing to receive.

This spokesman for the power of destiny and fate then began working intently and with great devotion on the table of sand. He said this round table, with markings all around the edges and the sand spread evenly throughout the center, represented my life. He made markings in the sand and sent audible prayers to God the entire time. He had a small paper bag filled with something and tied with a string. Every so often he'd pause for a moment, touching the bag to my forehead, my heart, and my shoulders, making the sign of the cross. Then he'd touch the bag to my feet, my knees, my hands, and the crown of my head, connecting my body to the series of incidents, events, people, and strange happenings I had come to call *my life*.

Despite my resistance, I began to feel hypnotized, drawn back in space and time to another world. I could almost hear the beating of drums, the heartbeat of the universe, keeping time as I became transported to this other place.

For the next three hours, the Babalawo talked with me about everything under the sun, the moon, and the stars. He told me things nobody could possibly have known about my life and me. I said I had a few questions. Well, more than a few. Then this mystical force, this ruler of destiny, patiently explained some of the mysteries of life—including why things had to be the way they were, the way they are, and the way they would be.

At the end of our visit, the Babalawo fastened the delicate beaded bracelet around my wrist. "Make a pact with death," he said. "Solemnly swear not to go before your time."

This was destiny talking, so I immediately agreed. I still didn't know whether I believed in past lives, but the slimmest chance that I would have to come back and repeat the same experiences with the same people was enough threat to keep me alive.

"There's another loss coming but it can be averted," the Babalawo warned as I got ready to walk out the door.

I turned back to him in confusion. "Just a minute," I said. "You just said that my destiny, my karma, had to be. Now you're telling me that some things can be avoided? I don't understand. Does that mean we have more than one destiny?"

"That's right," he explained. "Two parallel destinies stretch out before us, all the time. One is positive. One is negative. In any situation, you can choose either one. Parallel destinies aren't that far apart. Just keep looking to the right."

In that moment, I got a glimpse, a glimmer of it. Parallel universes. Time wasn't what I thought. For a second, my limited thinking about time, space, the future, and how this world worked expanded, exploded, and I touched the edge of possibilities, probabilities, and free will in the universe. Nothing could happen that hasn't been written. But all wasn't written in stone. One reason we can't see the future clearly is because we are co-creating it as we go along. We could take as much time as we needed to understand the lesson in a particular story. We could learn it many different ways. Or we could hide our heads in the sand and wait until clarity was forced when our lives blew up in our face. Sometimes we need this blowing up, this inevitable and consequential explosion, to help us learn our lesson and to take us to the next place.

"The bracelet will protect you," the Babalawo said, walking me to the door. "Don't take it off for anyone. If it breaks, it means it has done its work. You'll survive."

‚ ᗁ

Nothing bad happened the day my bracelet broke in Espanola, New Mexico. Scotty finished washing the car. I got in the driver's seat. He got in the passenger side. And I drove away.

We stopped at the church in Chimayo on our way out of town. We said some prayers, touched the holy dirt, the dirt people said was so powerful it could cure illnesses and emotional pain on the spot. Then we stopped by the priest's office on the way out of the church and asked for a blessing. The priest, a man in his late seventies, made the sign of the cross on each of our foreheads, touching our skin with his thumb.

We got in the car and headed toward Phoenix. For the past few days, I had been urging Scotty to go to the hot springs with me, get some acupuncture, really focus, pray, try to get God to heal him, try to heal himself. When I realized what I was doing, trying to control even this part of his process, I let go and instead asked Scotty what he wanted to do. It now seemed more important than ever to let him decide for himself. He said he wanted to return to Phoenix. I said I'd drive him there, then I had to go home.

Later that night at a motel, I curled up in bed next to Scotty. "Will you be my girl again?" he asked.

"Sure," I said. "If you get well."

"Will you marry me?" he asked.

"We tried that," I said. "It didn't work. I think we should stick with a nontraditional relationship, like the one we've had over the years."

"What's that?" he asked.

"When I really need you or you really need me, we call to each other and then we're just there. And when it's time to leave, we each go home."

I thanked him for all he had taught me and for helping me heal from my son's death. "But you've ruined me," I said quietly. "You're my soul mate and the love of my life. I won't be able to settle for anyone else."

"That's not true," he said. "You're not *ruined*. You just can't hide from what you know anymore. You can't stick your head in the sand."

His legs were aching that night. He said he was tired of being in pain. Then he looked at me. "I know you've lived every day with a lot of pain too," he said. "Maybe my death will bring you full circle. Maybe it will be the final missing piece."

Each time we had come together over the years, we had unfinished business that drew us back together again. It was part of our dance. Now, I wasn't angry anymore. I wasn't resentful that I couldn't get what I thought I wanted from this man. I wasn't vengeful that although Scotty had come along and helped me heal from the loss of my son, he had become another loss too. I wasn't angry with God because I had to let Scotty go. I wasn't angry with myself for not being the person Scotty wanted me to be. Those old familiar but uncomfortable feelings weren't eternally lingering in the air.

When I dropped Scotty off in Phoenix, it didn't feel like we were saying good-bye. We had said that a lot over the years, and I didn't know if or when I'd see him again. Instead, it felt like we finished an important piece of karmic business. I stopped holding Scotty and my son responsible for the belief that I would never love again. I took back my power, stopped being a victim, and left him without a broken heart.

Slowly I began to understand what the Babalawo had been talking about the day he first fastened the destiny bracelet around my wrist and talked about reversing the curse.

Codependency is and can be many things—low self-esteem, a haunting sense of incompleteness and victimization, abandonment of emotions and power, fear of loss of control—but essentially it operates like a curse. Generation after generation hands down limitations, weaknesses, tendencies, thoughts, beliefs, emotions, and patterns that limit our ability to see clearly, feel emotions authentically, be happy, fulfill our purpose, function autonomously, and own our power. Often by the time we get in a relationship, whether it's with a parent, child, friend, business associate, or lover, we've inherited so much dysfunctional *stuff*—as has the other person—that both people can feel like they're under a *spell*. We can feel tortured, held hostage, stymied, and speechless with an almost uncontrollable desire to get even, pay back, and teach the other person what we most need to learn.

The Babalawo calls it cleansing the energy. Some people call it family of origin work. What I was learning about was the power of healing the past.

I stand back and smile to myself when people tell me that they took a two-day seminar and completed their family-of-origin work. What I realized from the Babalawo was that healing the past, or family of origin work, runs much deeper than that. Two or three days examining the roots of our behaviors is extremely important. But it only touches the rim.

The day my destiny bracelet broke, I asked myself an important question. If I had known how things were going to work out—with Scotty or with my son, Shane—would I have done anything differently? Would I have held back, kept my heart closed, refused to love them because I knew loving them would bring pain? My answer was clear and immediate.

In a heartbeat, I'd do it again.

Like Scotty said, "Wouldn't have missed it for the world."

Promises, Promises

"Codependency, or whatever you want to call it—the tendency to be attracted to alcoholics, addicts, people with lots of problems, to get involved and stay involved, no matter how bad it gets—is an embarrassing affliction. It has no glamour, no dignity whatsoever. Its causes, its symptoms and manifestations are rooted in the sort of hurt, weak, childish impulses nobody wants to admit: fear of abandonment and authority, the desire to pacify and to please, low self-esteem. At its heart is the struggle to control the uncontrollable, to ensure love and security, to make the unsafe safe; it's the powerless striving for power in devious, circuitous ways."

Mary Allen wrote that definition of codependency in her book *The Rooms of Heaven*, her story about falling in love with Jim, who was addicted to cocaine and later stuck a gun barrel in his mouth, pulled the trigger, and committed suicide instead of going to treatment, attending Alcoholics Anonymous or Cocaine Anonymous meetings, and marrying her. She said she never saw it coming, *it* meaning her getting stuck in the flypaper of his addiction, then his suicide, and all. Well, she admits, she did see it coming in that half-conscious way we see things, but at the same time we don't. She met Jim in Iowa, of all places, and by the time it sunk in that he was an addict, she said it was *too late*. She was seated, strapped in, and along for the ride.

She was in love.

This is a story about mountain climbing, the hard way. It's a story about event horizons, points of no return, and getting in so deep that the only way out is through.

℘

Mount Sinai is a peak, actually it's a group of mountains or peaks located on the barren Sinai Peninsula, a stretch of land belonging to Egypt. The peninsula is bordered on the west by Egypt, the east by Israel, Jordan and Saudi Arabia, the North by the Mediterranean and the south by the Red Sea, just to give you a sense of placement. *A thousand square kilometers of nothing* is the description given in one tourist book. *The wilderness of sin* is another phrase used to describe the peninsula.

Lifeless was the word that came to me as I traveled across it.

It is said that many, many, many years ago, in the cluster of time we now call B.C., before the time of David, an eighty-year-old man named Moses led a large number of Hebrew people (called the children of Israel) out of Egypt and across this peninsula to the land of milk and honey, a place called the *Promised Land*. The children of Israel, for reasons unclear to historians, had been enslaved in Egypt for hundreds of years. Over this period, they had worked their way into the societal and cultural positions of craftsman and tradesman. The slaves were the bulk of Egypt's industry workers. They kept the country's economy alive.

One day, according to the story in the Bible and the Torah, God spoke to Moses. God told Moses that Moses was to go to the ruler of the Egyptian people, a man called the Pharaoh, and tell the Pharaoh to "let my people go." Being a sane man, Moses argued with God. Moses knew the Pharaoh. The Pharaoh's daughter had raised him after she found the baby Moses tucked away in the weeds in the river. (Moses' real mother had hid him there to keep him from being killed during an era when the Pharaoh had mandated that all male Hebrew babies be killed immediately upon birth as a form of population control—birth control.) The Pharaoh had a reputation for being harsh. Because the Hebrew people were an essential part of the daily operations and economy of Egypt, Moses knew the Pharaoh would resist the idea of freeing the slaves. The country's economy would collapse. And Moses knew the Pharaoh would be resistant to the idea if Moses, someone the Pharaoh knew well, suggested it. To complicate matters, Moses had a speech impediment. Some people suggest it was a lisp. Nope, Moses didn't want to be the one to tell the Pharaoh, in a lisp, to let the people go.

Moses said he didn't think he was cut out for this work and suggested to God that a man who could speak clearly would be a better man to get the job done. But God insisted, telling Moses exactly how things would unfold.

It's not that I think you don't know the story of Moses. And the story of Moses isn't the story of this chapter. But part of the story I want to tell you is connected to this part of history.

God then told Moses that Moses would become empowered to do certain magical, supernatural deeds—signs and wonders—to get the Pharaoh's attention. Moses would succeed in catching the Pharaoh's eye. God also said there would be a trick, a twist. Each time Moses would do something to get the Pharaoh's attention, the Pharaoh would start to open his heart and free the slaves, then at the last minute the Pharaoh would change his mind. That would be Moses's cue to do another eye-catching act.

Moses thought about all this, then asked God how he should break the news, and whom he should tell the Pharaoh that this message was from.

"Tell him you were sent by the I AM," God said.

Moses did as he was told. He threw down his rod in front of the Pharaoh. The rod turned into a snake. The Pharaoh raised his eyebrows slightly, but the magicians in his court were able to duplicate the act. The Pharaoh was not impressed.

Moses turned the rivers into blood. But the magicians of the day were able to manifest that trick too. The Pharaoh remained unimpressed.

Upon God's command, Moses sent a plague of frogs, lice, and then flies upon the land. The magicians were able to duplicate the frogs, but couldn't keep up with Moses any longer after the lice and the flies. Each time before sending a plague, Moses would tell the Pharaoh what God was about to do. The Pharaoh would ignore the warning until the plague actually came. Then when it did, he would beg Moses to reverse the plague, promising to let the people go. But each time that God ended the plague, the Pharaoh would go back on his word.

This dance between God, Moses, and the Pharaoh went on for a while. The cattle in the land were killed. The locusts came and devoured the crops. A brutal hailstorm pelted the land. Each time a plague appeared, the Pharaoh would beg Moses to beg God to stop torturing the land, promising to do whatever God wanted of him. But the minute the plague ceased, the Pharaoh had a change of heart.

Moses wasn't surprised. God had predicted this part of the story too. God told Moses that He was the one that each time hardened the Pharaoh's heart.

Even the twists and turns were part of the plan.

Finally, God had enough. The ultimate torture was about to cross the land. Moses told the Pharaoh that God said all the first-born male children in the land would be killed in one stroke if the Pharaoh didn't let the people go. The Hebrews were told to sacrifice a lamb and mark their doorposts with its blood. If they did that, the Angel of Death would pass over their homes. Their children would be spared.

The Hebrews did as they were told, but the Pharaoh ignored the warning. That night, the Angel of Death swooped over the land. All first-born male children in houses not marked with a lamb's blood died—including the Pharaoh's beloved son.

The Pharaoh was finally beaten. The battle, the dance, between him and God was over. God had won. The Pharaoh told Moses to take the people and go. He even agreed to load the Hebrews with all the gold, silver, and supplies they needed for their trip.

"Just get out," the Pharaoh said in heartbroken disgust. "I never want to see your face again."

It happened just as God had promised Moses it would. That's how the ritual of Passover—still celebrated today—came into being. That's how God got the Pharaoh to set his people free.

But the journey to freedom had only begun.

Moses still had to lead his people, a large lot who had only known life as slaves, out of the land of Egypt and across the Sinai Peninsula to reach the Promised Land. But before Moses and his group could reach the peninsula, the Pharaoh again changed his mind. The Pharaoh was infuriated, in a rage, about what had taken place. He ordered an army of chariots to kill the Hebrews or bring them back.

When Moses and his people heard and saw the Egyptian chariots approaching, they became concerned. The pursuing Egyptians were directly behind them. In front of them was the Red Sea.

The frightened Hebrews complained to Moses. "At least when we were slaves we had food, we were comfortable, we were warm, and we knew exactly what to expect. Now you've led us out of safety directly into our death."

God then told Moses to pick up his rod, the one he had used all along to perform the wonders and signs. Moses pointed the rod toward the sea. The Red Sea opened. It parted, creating a safe passageway from slavery to the Promised Land. The Hebrews stopped grumbling and began trekking through this path created between walls of water on each side. When every last Hebrew passed through, reaching the land on the Sinai side, the temporary walls of water collapsed, drowning the Egyptians who were in hot pursuit.

"I want them to know that I am God" is what God had said.

Moses and the slaves were safe on the Sinai side of the sea, but they hadn't yet reached the Promised Land. When they looked around, all they could see was this barren, lifeless thousand square kilometers of nothing. That's when the real worrying and complaining began.

How were they going to eat? What were they doing here?

As the story goes, God had already anticipated and graciously, often miraculously continued to fulfill their every need. When the Hebrews were hungry, manna and roasted quail came down out of the sky to feed every last person until they were filled. When they were thirsty, fresh water sprang out of the barren rocks. But the catch to getting their needs met was that God only gave them what they needed each day. If they tried to hoard, food and water that had miraculously appeared just as miraculously disappeared. The Hebrews were fearful about this new way of life, one that depended on them trusting God. So they did what people do—they complained each step of the way.

Finally, Moses and his grumbling group reached the peaks known as Sinai. They stopped and made camp there. Moses climbed one peak to talk to God, then came down to tell the people what God had said.

Moses told the people that everything was going to be okay, but there was one thing, actually ten things, the people had to keep in mind. The people had to obey these rules. The people promised they would and then asked Moses what these laws were.

1. I am the Lord your God. Thou shalt have no other Gods before me. (Don't worship or put first anything or anyone but me.)

2. Thou shalt not take the name of God in vain. (Don't call on God foolishly or with contempt.)

3. Remember the Sabbath day to keep it holy. (Take one day off from work each week. Rest. Take a break.)

4. Honor your father and your mother. (It's good to do your family-of-origin work but respect your ancestors too. It's where you came from and they're part of you.)

5. Thou shalt not murder. (Play nice, kids.)

6. Thou shalt not commit adultery. (If you're married, don't fool around.)

7. Thou shalt not steal. (Don't take anyone's things without asking and getting permission, first. If it belongs to someone else and they didn't give it to you, it's not yours.)

8. Thou shalt not bear false witness against your neighbor. (Don't lie and say people did things they really didn't do. Don't hurt people with your words.)

9. Thou shalt not covet your neighbor's wife.

10. Thou shalt not covet anything that belongs to your neighbor. (Don't spend your time and energy envying and wanting what isn't yours, whether it's a person, place, or thing.)

"If you follow these ten rules," Moses told the people, "you'll be able to live peacefully in the Promised Land."

Hold on. This part of the story isn't over yet.

After Moses gave the people these first ten rules, he went back up on the mountain for forty days and forty nights. During that time, he was busy meeting in person with God, and God inscribed these and hundreds of other rules on stone tablets. God then gave Moses the prescription for how things were to be done, all the laws of the land—613 to be exact.

But by the time Moses came down from the mountain, the people had gotten bored, restless, and forgetful. They had an accident. A slip. They had reverted to their old ways, and had already begun making golden images of calves to worship as idols or gods. Moses wasn't able to get the first ten laws in writing before the people forgot and broke the first one.

I understand. I've had accidents too. According to one survey, over half of the Americans questioned can't even name what five of these rules called the *Ten Commandments* are.

Moses got upset. He had an episode, a fit. He threw down the stone tablets, broke them, and had to go back up on the mountain and have another meeting with God for forty more days and nights. God and Moses wrote all the rules again, in stone. When Moses descended Mount Sinai for the second time, the rules remained intact. These rules carved in stone still live today. They became the Five Books of Moses. They comprise the first five books in the Torah, the Holy Book of Judaism, the rules drilled into young rabbis in the synagogues of Israel, and the first five books in the Old Testament of the Bible, the Holy Book of Christianity. Muslims also honor and acknowledge Moses for the important work he did.

Moses was eighty years old. He had a speech impediment. He was raised by foster parents. He didn't want the job. But he became known as one of the greatest prophets in history. He embodied the spirit of the law. He also gave us a metaphor, an example of what it feels like to take the journey from being enslaved to being free.

❦

For all these reasons, plus a few more, I decided to climb Mount Sinai myself. There exists some confusion about which peak in this cluster is the mountain Moses climbed and upon which God appeared. That doesn't matter. I climbed all of them one cold January day. I didn't mean to, nor did I intend to. Things just worked out that way.

I was tromping around the Middle East, not certain what I was looking for or what I'd find. I was on a spiritual expedition in that part of the world. But I was getting tired of seeking enlightenment. I was hoping to find inspiration that would help me write something different from a self-help book. I thought I had a plan. But my plans went afoul. I ended up firing my tour guide in Egypt and getting ill with a virus that put me in bed in a hotel in Cairo for ten days.

I considered going home, but I was too sick to fly on a plane. I had no expectations at all by now. I didn't know where to go next. I was traveling blind. My agenda, however weakly formed it was, had expired. I didn't know what I was looking for, or why I was here.

I headed across the Sinai Peninsula by car. I hired a driver from the village of Giza, a suburb of Cairo situated by the pyramids, to take me as far as Mount Sinai. We drove for hour after hour across this barren wilderness. I intended to stay at a tourist compound at the foot of Mount Sinai for a few days and rest, then head for Israel and soak in some of the healing mineral waters there. As long as I was here, in this part of the world, I would check out the Promised Land. It felt like my destination, the next place to go.

When I checked into the compound at the foot of the mountains, the manager started urging me to climb the mountain as long as I was there. "It's a great spiritual experience. Do it at sunup or sundown," he said. "You'll remember it all your life. You don't have to go with a tour group," he said. "I'll get you your own personal guide."

The manager caught me in a weak moment. I agreed to climb the mountain. Yes, it was my choice. But I wasn't excited about it. I was sick, weak. I felt lost and confused. I wasn't a victim, but I was vulnerable. I believed him. I gave in. I acquiesced.

At noon the next day, I showed up in the lobby to meet my guide. The plan was to climb the mountain the easy way, going up the back—not the route of the tourist traps. I'd sit there for a while, gaze at the scenery, and then return to the hotel later that afternoon for a wonderful Egyptian feast. A few minutes later, a boy appeared in the lobby. He talked to the manager for a minute, and then the manager brought him to my side. The boy was short with dark wavy hair, piercing dark eyes, and a wide grin that made his face light up. I would have guessed him to be about eleven or twelve years old; I was surprised to learn he was fourteen.

"His name is Shobin," the hotel manager said. "He'll be your guide."

I looked at the energetic, beaming boy. "I'm not sure I'm up to this trip," I said. "I don't feel great."

"Don't worry. You're going to take a shortcut," the manager promised. He talked to Shobin in Arabic for a moment. "He'll take it easy with you," the manager said. He turned to Shobin. "Right?"

"No problem," Shobin said.

I purchased an inexpensive linen tote bag, a backpack, and Bedouin jacket from the gift shop. I put the jacket on over my turtleneck. I bought a pair of black sweat pants—there was a K-Mart tag inside—for nine dollars and put them on over my black stretch pants for additional warmth. I purchased a bottle of mineral water, put that and some tissues into my bag. It was cold outside. My nose was running. But I was ready. I turned to Shobin. "Let's go."

I trudged along, trying to breathe and keep up with Shobin as he led me down streets and through desert fields to the foot of the mountains. By the time we reached the mountains, we had already walked at least a mile. What had looked like regular mountains from the distance now turned into clumps—huge piles—of rocks. I looked back. The tourist compound had already turned into a small speck. I looked ahead at an endless pile of rocks and peaks. *I don't know about this*, I thought. *Maybe I should go back now while I can still get out.*

Shobin headed into the rocky expanse.

I didn't want any more adventures. I had had enough.

I followed him anyway.

For the next hour, I scrambled up the rocks behind Shobin. *Any minute we'll be there*, I thought. *Any second, we'll reach the top.* Shobin climbed like a mountain goat. I didn't, gingerly trying to place each foot on solid ground, and hoist the other one up, sneezing and coughing, and yelling at Shobin to wait. Rocks, piled on one another, were all I could see ahead and all around me. Behind me too, I thought, plopping down and pulling out my water bottle. I thought about going back, but I felt like I was already in too deep to get out.

"How much farther?" I asked Shobin.

He furrowed his brows in a quizzical look as though he didn't understand a word I'd said.

"I'm tired, Shobin." I pointed to the rocks ahead. "How much farther do we have to go?"

He smiled. "No problem" is all he said.

It dawned on me that those might be the only English words he knew.

Maybe I should turn around, I thought. Make him take me back. I looked back at the rocks we'd already climbed. By now, going back—turning around, going down all those rocks we had climbed and walking back that mile to the hotel, looked and felt like more work than going ahead.

Anyway, I thought as I stood up to follow Shobin, how much farther could it be?

We hiked and climbed one rock at a time. I noticed the sun was midway down in the sky. I figured it to be about three o'clock by then. Shobin pointed in the distance. A scraggly goat was nibbling on a branch. Not far away stood a Bedouin goat herder, a woman draped in a long dress. Shobin waved and yelled to her. She hollered back. Then he headed toward her and I followed him.

When we reached her, he sat down. The woman goat herder eyed me suspiciously while picking her teeth with a hunting knife. I sat down anyway, eager for any excuse to rest.

We visited for a while, in that odd way that people communicate when they speak different languages. I think she told me she had children. I think I told her I had some too. And I think she said Shobin was a good boy. Then our rest was over, and we started back up the peak.

We climbed, and climbed, and climbed. I kept trying to remember what my sensei in aikido, the Japanese martial art I had been studying, had said. Don't use force. Relax. Breathe. Use the chi, the energy around you, to do what you need to do. I had a hard time relaxing, though, worrying about all the climbing I still had left to do. When we finally neared the top of the peak, a place where I couldn't see anything higher, I began to relax. *Good. This is almost over*, I thought.

But as soon as we got to that peak, another higher one loomed in the distance. I couldn't even see the way down the hill. The only way was up

We reached a plateau, an oasis in the rocky terrain. A green velvety moss covered the ground, and a tree similar to an olive tree flourished in its midst. Shobin scrambled up the tree then ran back to me. He held out his hand.

"Eat," he said, offering me one small, hard, red berry.

I scrunched my face.

"Eat," Shobin said again. "For energy."

I popped it into my mouth and began to look around.

I started to wonder about the spiritual significance of this location, how it stayed green, then I pushed those thoughts from my head. I didn't care who did the watering up here. All I wanted was to go home—well, at least back to my room at the hotel.

We headed back into the rocks, climbing peak after peak after peak. Each time we reached a peak, I'd think, *That's it. We're ready to start our descent.* But we just kept climbing higher. There was no other way out.

Once I had written a meditation about mountain climbing and getting to the top. "You don't just think it has been hard; it has been hard. You have been tested, tried, and retested on what you have learned," I had written. "You have been climbing a mountain. It has not been easy, but mountain climbing never is. Now you are near the top. A moment longer, and the victory shall be yours....There will be more mountains, but now you know how to climb them. And you have learned the secret of what is at the top."

Yes, I thought. *I have. What's there is another peak.*

My entire life had felt like climbing this mountain. I'd just get through with one tough uphill climb, then another peak would appear. No wonder I spent so much time feeling lost, confused, and full of dread.

As we approached yet one more peak, the sun was setting in the sky. The sunset might have been breathtaking, but I barely noticed. My head was so stuffed up from the virus, I scarcely had any breath to take away. It was cold. I had to go to the bathroom. I was sick. And by now, I was getting mad

"Shobin, you must tell me how much farther we have to go," I said. "You're young. I'm old and I'm tired."

Shobin pointed at the next peak and smiled. "No problem," he said.

I looked around. I couldn't see the place we had begun this mountain climb. I didn't want to be here. I didn't know where we were going. It was way too late to turn back. The only way out was through. An event horizon—an event looming and beckoning in the distance—had turned into an experience taking place. I had passed the point of no return.

℘

Now, on the top of that mountain—or at least hopefully getting near to the top—I got it. I finally understood what karma was all about. Karma meant getting into something so deeply, you couldn't just get out. We don't like where we are, but we can't just go back or walk away— pretend the whole thing isn't happening and wish it away.

My drug and alcohol addiction had sneaked up on me. Started when I was twelve, sneaking shots of whiskey from the cupboard under the sink. By the time I got my bearings, realized what was going on, it was too late. I was addicted to drugs.

When I was twenty-seven, I got married. By then, I was recovering from my addiction to alcohol and drugs. I thought the man I married was recovering too. By the time I realized he wasn't recovering, it was too late. I was married with two children, no money, and no car. I wasn't living happily ever after. I was a full-blown codependent and soon to be a single parent too.

After my recovery from codependency, I found myself involved in situations that seemed and felt beyond my control. A new relationship with a friend. A dating experience. Even the success from writing *Codependent No More* sprung up overnight, creating a whole new environment in my life. It's not that all these incidents were bad. It's just that events rarely ever felt like how I had imagined they would feel.

"How would you define codependency?" a reporter would ask. I'd take a deep breath, look around, and wonder how and why I became an expert on this, of all things. I'd stumble for words, trying to get clear, all the time thinking that success was much different than what I thought it would be.

Then, after Shane slipped on an icy patch skiing at the slope, I can remember thinking, *God, I don't want to go through this.* But it was too late then too. The accident had already occurred.

My relationship with Scotty had hit a point of no return early on, when he came back into my life. I knew I could walk away when it wasn't right to be with him. And I did. But I couldn't shut off my heart.

My dream all my life had been to have a family. But by the time I recovered from Shane's death, Nichole was grown. It was too late again. She was an adult and had moved away from home.

Each time I got into a circumstance, it twisted and turned. The way I thought things would be turned into something else. *Promises are made to be broken* became a strong theme in my life. None of the promises I thought life held seemed to manifest. By the time I got my bearings and realized where I was, it didn't matter if I wanted to be there. I was in it, like it or not.

People often think they have so much control, so much say in their destinies. And to some degree, we do. But up there on that cluster of rocky peaks called Mount Sinai, I began to understand for the first time about event horizons, karma, and points of no return.

We think we're going to see a few sites. Then before we know it, we're knee-deep into an adventure. Suddenly we're pulled into the experience up to our neck. We can remember the beginning and how it came about, but there's no going back. We can only push ahead.

Like the Babalawo said, when I asked him about my life, "It was what you had to go through."

Karma means you're seated, strapped in, and along for the ride— even and especially when the ride turns into something different than you thought it promised to be.

An event horizon is what we see coming, before it happens, whatever it is. We can almost see it and feel it. We might even know in our heads that it's something we're going to do or try. But we're still on the edge of the experience. We haven't entered into it yet. The energy is present but we can still make a choice.

I have hit the point of no return many times in my life. In my addiction. With my codependency. In business. In love. With my children. And once you hit the point of no return, turning back is no longer a choice. The energy of the experience takes on a life of its own.

ℭ

Shobin started up the trail that led to the top of the next peak. I followed begrudgingly. My stomach hurt. The soles of my feet hurt. Everything hurt. My hands were numb from the cold. I didn't think I could keep going, but I didn't have a choice. I just kept putting one foot in front of the other, trying not to get too mad.

Finally we reached the top of a peak and were able to look down. I saw a trail. On it, people were riding camels. Shacks, little roadside stands, lined the trail. At the bottom of the trail, almost seventy-five hundred feet below us, was St. Catherine's Monastery, which I had visited the day before. And somewhere in the distance, one of the clusters of sparkling lights—for by now it was nighttime—was the hotel that housed my bed. We were there. We had arrived!

We started down the trail. Shobin was merrily skipping down the path. I stumbled behind. After a few minutes, we reached the first roadside stand, a concession selling beverages and snacks with two camels tied at the shack's side. I dug some paper money out of my pocket. My fingers were numb from the cold. Then I slapped the money on the counter.

"I'd like a bag of potato chips and a bottle of water," I said to the man. "And I'd like a camel too."

"What?" he said.

"I'm too tired to walk all the way down that hill," I said. "I'm cold and I'm sick. I want to go to bed. Please rent me a camel. I'll take one of those," I said, pointing.

"I can't do that," he said. "People rode them up here. They're out looking around and they're going to come back for them."

I dug in my pocket, pulled out some more money, then leaned over the counter and got real close to him. "You're going to rent me a camel," I said. "I'm not walking down that hill."

He took a deep breath. "Well," he said, "if you wait around for twenty minutes or so, I think I've got a camel coming in you can ride. You can tie it in the parking lot by the monastery."

"Perfect," I said. "I'll wait."

The camel knelt. Shobin helped me mount. I leaned back, prepared for the backward jolt as the camel stood up. The man from the stand ran over to me and shoved a pair of thin gloves in my hand. "Here," he said. "These will help warm your hands."

Shobin, the camel, and I started the descent down Mount Sinai. I relaxed. This part should be easy, I thought. The words *no problem* might finally be true. Shobin skipped down the trail, holding the rein to the camel and leading the way.

He likes this, I thought. *Shobin really likes this. He's having fun.*

We were up in the air about 7,500 feet, 7,497 to be exact. The top of the camel's back was about six feet, more or less, from the ground. Sitting on the camel's back, my head and eyes were about ten feet off the ground. The camel didn't want to follow Shobin. It kept moving to the very edge of the winding path, an edge that dropped straight down 7,500 feet. As the camel clopped along, his hoofs slipped and slid on the edge. With each step, the rocks underneath his hoofs crumbled and fell down, down, down the 7,500-foot drop.

The camel's right legs weren't stable. Its feet slid around each time they touched the ground. What if a big section of that edge crumbled? The camel could slip. We'd fall!

"Shobin," I screamed. "Put the camel in the middle of the path!"

Shobin turned and looked at me with that same confused look that told me he didn't understand a word I said. I pointed to the middle of the path. "Put the camel there," I said.

"No problem," Shobin said.

About ten steps later, the camel worked his way over to the edge of the ledge and started doing that clumsy foot-slipping thing again. All I could see from where I sat was a long, painful drop down.

"Shobin," I screamed. "He's doing it again!"

Shobin turned around and looked at me. This time he didn't smile. His look was one of disgust.

"No problem," he said.

"Yes, Shobin, there is a problem," I screamed. "I'm scared. Get me down!"

I pointed to the ground. "Now!"

Up until now I'd been practicing patience and tolerance. It was time to let my feelings out.

Shobin started to make the camel kneel, right there at the edge. We started to jerk around. I was leaning over the edge.

"In the name of all that's holy, take him to the middle of the road first!" I yelled.

Finally Shobin understood. He led the camel to the middle of the path. The camel knelt. I got down. Shobin skipped down the path for the remaining, winding, distance—pulling the camel behind him.

I walked behind the camel, grumbling all the way.

Sometimes even the way out of our karma can be a disgusting, difficult task. Just because we learn our lesson and the end is in sight doesn't mean we're home free.

When we arrived at the monastery at the foot of the hill, I made Shobin go into the monastery dining room and find someone with a car to drive us back to the motel. I was cold and hungry. I couldn't wait to eat. But by the time we got to the hotel, it was too late, again. Dinner had already been served, eaten, and cleared away.

I went back to my room, a cubicle containing two twin beds and no heater. I pulled the blanket off the bed I wasn't using, wrapped it around me, then crawled in under the covers on the other bed and prayed for sleep and warmth. I was still fully dressed from my day.

The motel manager was right. I would remember this experience the rest of my life.

∾

Moses led his people out of slavery to the Promised Land. Many of us have taken a similar journey across the wilderness. What we were enslaved to might have been alcohol, drugs, or another person's addiction. Then we decided to take the journey to freedom too.

The mountain we had to climb wasn't as grueling as Mount Sinai or as barren as the peninsula. It only involved twelve steps. These Twelve Steps are the spiritual foundation for Alcoholics Anonymous and Al-Anon. They don't replace the Ten Commandants. They are suggestions. They were designed to give us a simple program that would be a spiritual way for fallible human beings to live.

We begin by accepting and admitting we are powerless when we have lost control. We recognize that our lives are unmanageable even when that is something we would prefer not to see. Then we believe as much as we are able to that a Higher Power can restore us to sane living, and we surrender our will and our lives to God's care.

We stop pointing the finger at other people and take a look at ourselves. Then we tell God, ourselves, and someone else all the dirty details of what we see. And we tell the truth.

These Steps aren't exactly self-help. We don't change ourselves; we become ready to let God change us. Then we humbly ask God to do that. We list the people we have hurt and go say sorry to them, except when doing that would cause people we had already hurt more pain. After that, we examine our behaviors regularly to make sure we don't get off track. Our goal is to become closer to God and ourselves. To do that, it is suggested we meditate and pray. By the time we have reached the last Step, the Steps say we will have seen the Light. So it is suggested we try to apply this process in all areas of our lives, then try to tell other people how we crossed the desert so they can join us on this journey to freedom too.

The law of the land is love for other people and ourselves.

"If we are painstaking about this phase of our development," the Big Book of Alcoholics Anonymous promises, "we will be amazed before we are half way through. We are going to know a new freedom and a new happiness. We will not regret the past nor wish to shut the door on it. We will comprehend the word serenity and we will know peace. No matter how far down the scale we have gone, we will see how our experience can benefit others. That feeling of uselessness and self-pity will disappear. We will lose interest in selfish things and gain interest in our fellows. Self-seeking will slip away. Our whole attitude and outlook upon life will change. Fear of people and of economic insecurity will leave us. We will intuitively know how to handle situations which used to baffle us. We will suddenly realize that God is doing for us what we could not do for ourselves. Are these extravagant promises? We think not. They are being fulfilled."

All our needs will be met. The Red Sea will part before our eyes. God will clear the path. Sometimes we grumble and complain but we can take care of ourselves no matter what—and some of us have a lot of *whats*. What we can't do, God will do for us, one day at a time.

At least not all promises are made to be broken. Some of them really do come true.

Jump

Nichole was driving. I was a passenger. We were on the short road that runs behind my home, on our way to get some food, when the car ahead of us, an older dark Mercedes, slammed on the brakes. The next or simultaneous thing we heard was the screeching of an animal piercing the evening air. The next thing we saw was a cat shooting through the air and into the bushes on the side of the road. The car started to drive away. Nichole stepped on the gas, driving around and in front of the Mercedes—effectively blocking it from moving forward. Nichole lowered the passenger window and leaned across me. The driver of the Mercedes, a dark-haired man with a high forehead—the kind that has worry wrinkles running all the way across it in parallel lines—rolled down his.

"What are you going to do about that cat?" she screamed.

He furrowed his eyebrows. "What cat?" he asked. He maneuvered the Mercedes around us and drove off into the night.

"Why do people do that?" Nichole said, turning to me in anger and confusion. "Why do people lie like that?"

I started to psychoanalyze the man. Then I cut myself short.

On my trip to the Middle East, I had faced that question too. It was one I had asked for many years in my life. Shortly after climbing Mount Sinai, I had gone on to Israel. I spent ten days in the Holy Land, then traveled by car to the country of Jordan. For some reason, I had it in my mind and heart that I wanted to visit Pakistan on this trip too. In fact, I was obsessed with getting into this country, even though I had been told that obtaining a visa was difficult, if not impossible. Undaunted, challenged, and determined, I traveled by car to Jordan, a small country neighboring Israel, and started working on the visa officer at the Pakistani Embassy there, trying to beg, coerce, or convince this man to let me in.

After I went back and forth with this somber visa officer for several days, he finally relented and agreed to let me visit Pakistan—for one week. I felt humbled, honored, and excited. It was the week before elections in Pakistan. They weren't letting foreigners, particularly writers, into the country. I felt special, like I had won a prize.

I felt blessed.

That evening, I went to a Jordanian supermarket and bought a shoe polishing kit. My black boots were dirty and dusty from all the walking I'd done. I stopped in the hotel lobby for a while, on my way to the room. It was the month of Ramadan in the Islam religion. For Muslims, that meant it was a holy fasting day—no smoking, food, beverages of any kind, or sex during daylight hours. I had tried to participate in the fast for just this one day—to honor the religion of this country and to see how it felt to participate. By lunchtime, I couldn't take it anymore. I was starving and thirsty. I sneaked up to my room and wolfed down a bag of potato chips and gulped a bottle of mineral water.

By now, the restaurant in the lobby was filled with an air of festive celebration. Once the sun went down, Muslims broke the day's fast by engaging in a virtual feast. I didn't feel festive. I felt guilty, remembering the potato chips and water. "I'm sorry," I said, offering a simple heartfelt prayer up to the ceiling and hopefully straight on through it to God.

What I heard and felt next I'll remember for a long time. Perhaps it was the intense spiritual ambiance created by the fasting and prayers of most of the population of the country I was in, filling the air with words, thoughts, and devotion the way incense does with its scent. I don't know if it had something to do with me, that altered state that happens to me when I'm scurrying about the world with my antenna up to see what I can see, hear, and find, protecting myself, and trying to discern where to go next. Or maybe it wasn't about me at all. Maybe it was about God.

But I swear I heard these words: *You tried. That was good enough.* It was a still, small voice—a gentle nurturing one—whispering to my heart. Then the strangest feeling washed over me, from my head down to my toes. It was gloriously blissful, loving, accepting, and cleansing at the same time.

Oh, I said, remembering. *So this is how God's unconditional love and forgiveness feels.*

I went up to my room, removed my boots, carefully washing and polishing each one. I didn't know what was coming next, what this trip to Pakistan would bring, but I wanted to put my best foot forward. As for now, I was riding high. I had just tasted heaven, right here on earth.

I knew I was in trouble when I entered Pakistan and boarded the plane heading for Lahore. A young girl was clomping about the plane wearing heavy men's shoes that were too big for her feet. I couldn't use the bathroom for the entire flight. A man locked himself in for almost an hour; I refused to be the one to use it next. All around me, people were prostrating themselves on prayer rugs on the floors of the aisles of the plane. I had experienced this before in Islamic nations. But something felt different here. The recitations of the prayers in other countries had been like soothing, spiritual, music—a mantra to my heart and ears. Now, it felt like flies buzzing, a moaning, despairing sound—like people locked in a dungeon begging, pleading to get out.

When I got to the airport, I headed for the outside door to get a breath of fresh air while I waited for my luggage. Throngs of people, some whining, some begging, some screaming pushed against the metal bar separating the inside of the airport from outdoors. Something different, something I had never felt before permeated the air. "Don't go out there," one of the airport guards said, grabbing me. "It's not safe outside. You'll get hurt. And don't take a taxi. If you do, you'll get robbed." He paused. "Or killed."

I took a deep breath, looked around the airport, trying to figure out what to do next. A large poster on the wall, ripped, with one side hanging loose, boasted the attributes of a hotel. "The only hotel in Lahore where everything works," it proudly proclaimed.

I walked to the side of the airport and leaned against the wall. I would have to think carefully, very carefully about how to proceed and where to go next.

If what I had felt in Jordan was a taste of heaven, then I was now standing at the gates of hell.

The concept of waiting in line for your turn hadn't been discovered in Pakistan yet. I learned that at the hotel where I stayed, the one where everything worked, well almost everything. The only way to get a turn was to force your way into a mob and insist that you were next.

The women of Pakistan were beautiful. The hotel guards were kind too. An employee scrambled up the outside of the building to my third floor balcony, then tried to break in while I lay in bed reading a book, the guards responded immediately and effectively as soon as I jumped naked into the hallway and screamed.

On my day trip to Islamabad, the nation's capital, the route the driver took was a two-lane highway. Except each lane went both ways. Like cars playing the old game of chicken, the loser was the one that swerved first. Once, when we slowed down going through a small town, a man whose hands had been severed ran up to the car and began pounding on the hood with his stumps. Along the road, as if trying to keep pace with the trucks and cars, men whose legs had been severed galloped along propelling themselves with their arms. I finally went to sleep, passed out from stress, emotional exhaustion, and disgust. This was an adventure, but not the exciting kind.

This was more than I wanted or needed to see.

I had visited the Children's Holocaust Museum in Israel, a darkened room arranged with mirrors to create the illusion of one twinkling candlelight flame for each child that had been killed. The wall in the corridor in a building close by featured a picture of a man holding a toddler, a little boy. The boy's eyes followed the man's hand. He was pointing toward the sky. "He's telling his son that's where they're going—up to Heaven to be with God," my tour guide said.

After touring the Holocaust Museum and now this—Pakistan—I couldn't run from it anymore. I'd been confused, depressed, and fighting the idea since I was three or four. I couldn't deny it, or hide from it now. The lesson I was learning became disgustingly and depressingly clear. Though we'd like to believe differently, everything on this planet and in our lives is not sweetness and light.

Evil in all its forms—lying, pain, suffering, sickness, oppression, corruption, and injustice—is an active and present force in this world.

And evil has been around for a long, long time.

Some people use the idea of evil to question or diminish their belief in the power of God, asking how a loving God could allow the Holocaust to take place—and many have occurred. I don't know why God, particularly a loving God, would allow a holocaust or the situation in Pakistan.

Maybe it's part of the plan.

"Monotheistic religions, religions that believe in one God have more in common than most people believe," my guide in Israel told me the day we visited a holy site shared by three religions—Judaism, Islam, and Christianity. "I don't understand why they have to fight all the time."

"What is it you believe they have in common?" I asked him. I really wanted to know what this educated person, this 65-year-old Jewish man thought.

"They all believe in the resurrection," he said. "They believe in Heaven. And they believe in . . ." He was too polite to even say the word.

"Hell," I finally said.

I knew something else that these three religions had in common. I had run into it repeatedly as I traveled across the world, looking at people's homes, the things they had on the walls, the souvenirs sold in stores, and by perusing through these three religions' good books. In Judaism and Islam, artists symbolized the concept by shaping and painting—in metal or glass—a single open eye. It's talked about in the Bible too. All three of these religions caution about the power of the evil eye.

They believe that evil isn't just something people do. They believe that people's thoughts, intentions, and motives—from jealousy, to hatred, envy, revenge, greed, and rage—are powerful vehicles that actually affect and harm people in the world and that these evil intentions are transmitted through the gateway to the soul—the eye.

"They found the Dead Sea Scrolls," my tour guide said, moments later. "The Scrolls talk about the prophecies for the world, the things coming to pass. They predict the final battle between Darkness and Light."

"Who wins?" I asked.

"Vell, the Light does," he said. "H'ov corz."

Heaven and Hell are real and both forces are present right here on earth.

On the way home from this particular trip, when I had a layover to change planes in Kuwait, I was browsing through a travel magazine. An article in it said that some people believe that the Garden of Eden may have been located right there, in Kuwait.

The story of that garden is another thing these three religions have in common. It's presented in all three holy books, books that members of each of these religions read.

Back then, way back there in that garden, when that serpent made his appearance, that's when evil began. The serpent talked Eve into eating the apple. She plucked it off the tree, disregarding what God had said. "You can have anything that's here," she had been instructed, "except for the fruit from those two trees."

"Oh, don't listen to that," the serpent chided. "The only reason God doesn't want you to eat that fruit is because if you do, then you'll be like Him. Go ahead," he said, "take a bite. You'll see."

Instead of trusting that God was protecting her by warning her to stay away from this tree, Eve thought God was depriving her of something that might be good for her—something that would give her more power than she already had. She bit into the apple, chewed, and swallowed. The Knowledge of Good and Evil is the name of that tree.

Before that, everything was innocence. It was all sweetness and light. We've known—and *known* is used here to mean "been intimate with, experienced, been consciously and excruciatingly aware of, seen, felt, heard, smelled, tasted, sometimes aligned ourselves with, participated in, and been affected by"—good and evil ever since.

Not only is evil present in this world, like good it can affect and come through us. In *Star Wars*, it's called "the dark side of the force."

In the early hours one morning, on my trip to Israel, I couldn't sleep. I got out of bed, dressed, and walked down the sidewalk that ran alongside the Sea of Galilee. I spotted a deli with an outdoor patio. The lights were on. People were milling about. I walked over, purchased a cup of coffee and a Danish roll, and went out to the patio to sit. The sun hadn't yet begun to light the morning sky. It was peaceful, calm, and serene. A good-looking young man with dark tousled hair walked over to my table, pulled out a chair, and asked if he could sit down. He made small talk for awhile, asking where I was from, what I was doing here, didn't it look like the beginning of a beautiful day. Then he asked me if I wanted to walk over to the beach and smoke a joint with him.

"No thanks," I said.

"Why not?" he asked. "Don't you like to smoke pot?"

"I like it very much," I said. "I just don't do it anymore."

"We could sit on the beach stoned and watch the sun come up," he said, giving it one more try. "It could really be a beautiful thing...."

"No thanks," I said, getting up from the table, preparing to leave and go my own way. "I don't need to be stoned to enjoy a beautiful sunrise or a beautiful day."

After this lengthy introduction, I'm ready now to tell you the story of this chapter, the one I really want to tell. It's a story about a battle between Light and Darkness, it's why I turned that man in Israel down, and it's what people mean when they point to someone and say, "There but for the Grace of God go I."

ℭ

The deputy matron, a burly-looking thing with short dark chopped-off hair and dark, thick-rimmed glasses, unlocked my door and handed me a dress. It was pale blue percale with short, slightly puffed sleeves.

It was one of my good-girl dresses that I kept in my closet for times like these.

I thanked her and waited for her to lock my cell door and leave so I could change clothes.

She stood there looking at me, staring, waiting. I put the dress down on the thin cot, covered by the brown wool blanket stamped "Ramsey County Correctional Services," sat down next to it, picked up the book I'd been reading, and deliberately ignored her.

She locked my door, making a rattling noise with the keys. "You've got half an hour," she barked. "I'll be back for you then. Be ready."

"I'll be right here waiting," I said, without looking up.

When I heard the door close to the small outside walkway that lined the cells, I got up, took off the khaki uniform dress, stepped into the blue dress, and buttoned up the front. There wasn't a mirror in the cell. It wasn't allowed. We might break the glass, slit our wrists—or someone else's. Luckily my hair was short and fell easily into place.

I chain-smoked Pall Mall cigarettes until I heard the outside door clank open again. I threw the cigarette I was smoking into the toilet, stood up, and walked over to the cell door. The deputy matron opened my door, eyed me up and down, and then fastened the handcuffs around both my wrists.

"Good luck, girl," Sherelle yelled out as I passed by her cell. Sherelle was a rail-thin black woman, about ten years older than I was. She was in for prostitution—again. Because she was so thin, I figured she must be a junkie too. She ran to the cell door and pushed a piece of paper through the bars.

"Write to me," she said. "Let me know what happened." Sherelle wanted to know more than what happened to me. She wanted to be my lover. She wanted me to be her girl.

"I'm not worried," I said. "It'll be fine."

That was a lie. I was worried. Even the thirty milligrams of methadone I had drunk earlier that day hadn't soothed my fears. Yesterday Yvonne, a beautiful young woman with long, dark hair and big brown eyes had gotten five years in Shakopee, the state penitentiary for women. Five years. And it was only her second offense. All she had done was write a few bad checks.

I had gotten busted for a felony—and I was already on probation for another felony and supposedly on a very short string. Even in my drugged stupor, I had a feeling that I wasn't going to just skate through this one like I usually did. When I had drunk my methadone that morning, that thick sweet liquid that sort of felt like heroin but without the ecstasy, I had felt a twinge of grief, almost like I was saying good-bye to a lover, like, *Times up, baby.* It was the oddest feeling. It almost ruined my high.

I could feel those old winds of change blowing again. It's like we can tell, like our soul knows, no matter how numbed and deadened that soul is.

I followed the matron through the maze of hallways, locked doors, elevators, and tunnels until we reached the section of the courthouse where court was held. She took off my handcuffs and deposited me in the holding room to the side of the courtroom until it was my turn.

After about twenty minutes, the door opened and the deputy motioned for me to come out. I stepped into the somber courtroom, buzzing with deputies, onlookers, and attorneys. I scanned the room. A short woman with dark wavy hair stood glaring at me. Yes, Mom was there too.

I averted her look and took my by now familiar place in front of the judge.

Mom and a gentleman—I assumed he was an attorney she had hired—came up to the front of the courtroom too. They stood just to the left of where I was standing.

The judge scanned the papers in front of him, scowling. Then he set the papers down, took off his wire-rimmed glasses, and peered into my eyes. "I usually ask people that come into my courtroom if they have anything to say. I'm not going to do that today. I have two full pages of your arrest records in front of me. I have pictures of your arms that are being used in drug prevention programs throughout the schools in this state. You are currently on probation for a felony. And what you have done, what you were arrested for last week, is an atrocious crime against the city. According to these records, they had to wrap you in chains from your neck down just to transport you to this jail."

The attorney standing next to my mother started to say something. The judge banged his gavel, stopping him in midsentence.

"Young lady," he said, "I don't care who you've brought into this courtroom with you today. I don't care if you've dragged your mother into court with you again. I don't care if you've got the best attorneys. I don't care that you graduated on the Twin City honor roll. I don't care how smart you are and who's with you and I'm not going to ask you what a nice girl like you is doing in a mess like this." He leaned toward me and spoke very deliberately, firmly, and slowly. "Do you understand that you are responsible for your own behavior?"

I reeled from his words. Responsible for my own behavior? No, I didn't know that. But I knew enough to lie.

"Yes," I said.

He sat back, and looked down at the papers on the desk again. He looked at me. "I'm going to give you a choice," he said.

Mmm, good, I thought.

"You can go to the State Correctional Institution for Women for five years." He paused. "Or, you can go to drug treatment at Willmar State Hospital—for as long as it takes for you to change." He paused again. "Which one will it be, Miss Vaillancourt?"

I couldn't speak. I couldn't get words out of my mouth. Prison? For five years? Or give up drugs?

Some people say that at the moment of death, a person's life flashes before their eyes. Right now, at this moment in time, I was dying. Melody Lynn Vaillancourt, born at 5:25 A.M. on May 26, 1948, prematurely, at 770 East Fourth Street on the kitchen table, assisted by Emma Kirschbaum, a smiling, rotund, elderly midwife who just loved bringing babies into this world, was dying. Melody Lynn Vaillancourt, who loved setting up an altar in the living room and reading from the Bible at age four and went from that to stripping in a sleazy nightclub on Hennepin Avenue at age twenty because she lied about her age and needed money to buy drugs, because heroin was as much a part of her blood and brains and the cells in her body as white and red corpuscles were, had just been sentenced to death.

℘

I was quiet, well-behaved, and most probably in retrospect a depressed child until I was twelve years old. I had a constant unspoken competition going with Richard Voss for being the smartest child in each class I was in. I knew the answer to every question that was asked. I loved raising my hand. I loved studying and learning. I had long dark hair that ran straight down my back, thick horn-rimmed glasses, and I loved being right.

In a world that constantly spun out of control around me, in the heart of a neighborhood where weird jackasses snatched children off the street, molested them, then made them lie on the floor while they played the theme song to *Davy Crockett* on the organ—books and learning were a place of safety.

After watching my father run—or did he stumble—out the door when I was three, a man who my mother described as an out-of-control alcoholic who wooed her long enough to get her pregnant with me, then abandoned her, leaving her with me and three older children by another man who had abandoned her by dying, and after watching my three older half-siblings follow suit by running out the door the second they turned eighteen, books and learning were a place of safety.

I knew my way around books. Books, I could figure out.

Mother would probably say I was contrary, obstinate, stubborn, moody, and refused to wear my glasses as I was told. She was outspoken about the idea that I was not wanted, and my birth and presence placed a burden on her life. She also maintains that I put her pet Chihuahua in the oven and baked it when I was three, but I don't believe that. I had no inclination to cook anything in the oven, much less dog, until I was in my thirties. I think I was a good child. With a certain amount of insight into psychology, I would probably say it was very Freudian and symbolic that the place I always threw my glasses away was in the alleylike pathway that ran alongside the church where the great offense occurred. I would probably bite my lip, say hmmmm, looks like the family and victim didn't want to look at what happened that day. But I didn't know any of that, back then.

I just knew I hated wearing those glasses. Besides, I had a secret that no one knew. I had prayed to God and asked him to heal my eyes so I didn't need to wear those hideous, ugly, horn-rimmed glasses. He had answered my prayers. I could see just fine without them. And I liked the way I looked without them much better. Mother didn't believe me though, about God healing my eyes, for years—until she took me to the doctor, demanded a thorough test, which then revealed I could see just fine.

I should have known I was in trouble that one particular day, shortly before my twelfth birthday, when I was playing in front of my house by myself. I had few friends. I wasn't allowed to play with most children, and as I had been chronically ill and bed-ridden for several years of my life, I didn't know many children. I hadn't needed a tutor. As long as I had my books, I could teach myself whatever it was I was supposed to learn, from mathematics, to English, to geography. Although I was totally lacking in social skills, my academic achievement and grades were superior.

That day I was playing a little game in front of the house. Cement steps led up to the front porch of the big two-story home where Mother and I lived together, alone. There was a cement wall on either side of those steps. I liked to jump across, from one side to another. The drop wasn't very deep. Only about three feet. But it was a fun, exciting little game I could play by myself.

I would get a run going on one side of the embankment, then leap across from one cement wall to the other.

On this day, I worked up to a run and leapt across through the air toward the embankment on the other side. But I missed by a few inches. Instead of landing on my feet on the embankment, my chin and head came crashing down on the cement wall, splitting my chin open. A searing pain cut through my body as bone met cement. Blood gushed down my face. I went into the house. Mother said it was my fault, I was being a careless child, go put a bandage on it and stop being a baby.

I stopped crying, went in the bathroom and stopped the bleeding. Then I went outside, looked at those steps, looked at them some more, then got back up on the embankment, ran toward the wall, and jumped again.

ᕯ

Scotty knows a lot about PTSD, the acronym that stands for post-traumatic stress disorder. He has it, because when he was eighteen years old and joined the U.S. Marines, on his way to Vietnam, Guillain-Barré syndrome, a cousin to polio, struck him down. For the next eighteen months, he was paralyzed from the neck down. They told him he'd never walk again. He did walk again, but only with the help of braces.

"People that have PTSD have three basic feelings," he told me once. "When something, anything happens, they feel afraid. Then they lash out in anger at what's frightened them. Then they go numb. Occasionally, they get so bored with being numb, they go out and do something that creates, or causes pain. That pain," he said, "is the only thing that can break through that numbness. It's the only thing that lets them know they're real.

"It's like that old saying," he said. "Pinch yourself to see if you're real."

ॐ

It was a Sunday morning, on the east side of St. Paul, Minnesota. My mother had awakened me early and sent me on my way to the Methodist church, about eight blocks from the house where we lived.

I loved going to church. I loved it more than Sunday school. I didn't understand the sermons, but I loved sitting in that pew and singing hymns. I couldn't carry a tune well, but that didn't stop me. I'd sit there and sing along to *What a Friend We Have in Jesus* and *How Great Thou Art*. Sometimes, I'd get the funniest feeling when I was singing and for no reason, I'd start crying too. So then I'd sit there singing and crying, not able to carry a tune, and it was the closest thing to happy I had ever felt.

I loved sitting at home and playing those songs on the piano too. I had been taking lessons since I was five. I'd walk the five or so blocks to old Mrs. Hudson's house once a week. I was good at it, playing the piano. I didn't have to practice all that much to convince Mrs. Hudson that I'd been practicing all week. Sometimes she gave me a cookie and a pat on the head for being such a good girl.

I'd have been practicing all week, all right. But I was playing all the songs I loved, the stack of music my father had left me when he walked out the door. Mama said that was about the only thing my daddy ever did well—play the piano. He was a jazz musician from New Orleans. Lately, Mama had been saying a lot that I reminded her of my daddy. I knew that wasn't a good thing, wasn't a good thing at all. All she said my daddy could do was drink, play the piano, and make her cry.

On this particular Sunday morning, I headed for church. When I got to the corner of the block I lived on, I had to pass by another church. I don't know who attended services there. There were a lot of churches in the neighborhood, and what went on in those other churches was a great mystery to me. Mama said we weren't supposed to affiliate with other religions. "If we were meant to be Catholics, we'd have been born Catholics," she said. And we'd been born Protestants. Secretly, I envied the Catholics. They got to go to confession each week and be forgiven. The rest of the week I was sure they got to party and do anything they wanted. I thought both ideas would be fun—getting to party and carry on, and be forgiven.

When I got close to the end of the block, I crossed over to the other side of the street, away from the church, even though it wasn't the direction I was going. To walk on that side of the street, I had to pass by the Krueger's house. They had a lot of kids; Mama called them brats running around with snotty noses and dirty pants. One day, one of them had even followed me home, dirty pants, snotty nose and all. I was so happy I just looked at Mama and said, "Can we keep it?" But Mama said no, we had to send it back. So we did. Mama didn't know I'd been praying to God to send me a little baby boy to take care of, one of my own, and I thought that one with the snotty nose was it, even if he did come from the direction of the Kruegers. Those Kruegers always had a car in the driveway with the hood up, and one of the Kruegers would be working on the engine or whatever was under the hood, usually the fat old dad wearing a dirty white T-shirt that didn't quite cover his belly, blue jeans that slipped down and showed the crack in his butt, and holding a dark brown beer bottle in his hand. They never hurt me, or did anything wrong to me, but Mama called them that horrible Krueger family, so I was scared of them too.

But not as scared as I was of that church on the corner of the block.

                        ℭ

I was only four years old that day I was playing with Wendy and Mary Lou. Wendy was the oldest, about six. Mary Lou was my age, four. They lived next door to me in a big house with a big family with a mom, a dad, and a grandfather. I wasn't often allowed to play with them or anyone else so that was a special day, that day. The three of us were being allowed to walk to the corner and back. So we just skipped and walked all the way from the middle of the block to the corner.

Well, almost to the corner.

We were skipping past the first door to the church, the one that people would go in for a potluck dinner or something, not the bigger door, farther down and closer to the corner that people entered for church services. It wasn't a Sunday that morning, so there weren't any people around. Just us.

The church door opened and a man popped out. He had blonde hair. He looked nice enough, but something about him scared me, made me feel creepy and afraid. Sometimes I had felt that way around my uncles.

I felt that way around one of my stepfathers too. His name was Otto. He only lived with us for a year. He worked the night shift at the big hospital in town as an orderly, whatever that was. I'd be in bed, sound asleep at night. All of a sudden I'd hear a noise and I'd look up and Otto would be standing in the middle of the room, staring at me, wearing a white uniform with a white mask over his face. Mama got rid of him. She said he was weird. Then he got arrested for raping a man at one of the parks by our house.

The man popped out of the church and held out a little box.

"Want some candy, little girls?" he asked.

Wendy said yes. He took a piece of candy out of the box and put it in Wendy's hand. Mary Lou stuck her hand out. He gave her a piece too. It actually looked like he gave her two pieces.

Then he looked at me. I shook my head and backed away. "No, thank you," I said.

The next thing happened so fast I really didn't have time to think. He grabbed my arm. Pulled me through that door and into the church. Locked the door. Then he whisked me down into the basement.

I barely remember what happened next. I felt like I wasn't even there or like I was dreaming. I can't remember feeling anything, feeling anything touching my body, nothing at all. I know he must have taken all my clothes off me, because afterward he told me to put on my undershirt and underpants. He wouldn't let me put on the rest of my clothes. He wouldn't even give them to me.

Then he sat down at the big pipe organ that was sitting in the corner of the room, put my clothes in his lap, and said that because I was such a good girl, he had a surprise for me. He turned on that organ and started playing and singing. "Davy, Davy Crockett, King of the Wild Frontier..."

When he finished the song, he looked down at me. I was lying quietly on the floor, listening to the music. "Did you like that?" he said.

Suddenly I heard banging and crashing and breaking sounds, then the next thing I knew I was sitting in the back of a police car next to Mama. She said the incident was done and over with. It was never discussed, not at all, not one more time that I can recall.

It may have been over and done with, but I remembered it each time I walked past that church on the corner of the block.

And I was remembering it again on this day as I passed by on my way to services at my own church, the Methodist church. When I got safely past the church, I crossed back over to the side of the street I needed to be on, and started walking down the hill. At first, I was hurrying. I didn't want to be late.

I had my own offering money. I liked putting it in the big plate they passed around. I worked hard to earn money. I was proud to say I had never gotten an allowance. By now, I had been working as a baby-sitter for over a year.

I babysat for one woman who had a little baby, but no husband. She lived around the corner from me. She'd leave her lipstick and mascara out and I'd be so happy being out of my house, playing with the baby, and putting on makeup. To top it off, I'd get paid.

I babysat for another family too. They lived in the other direction, about eight blocks. They had two children, a boy and a girl. The wife was real quiet. They'd stay out until midnight or one in the morning. After the kids went to sleep, I'd lie down on their couch and sleep until they came home.

The wife would wake me up. Then her husband would drive me home because he said it was too dark for me to walk and too late for me to be out alone.

The first time he drove me home I didn't understand it when he drove past my house and around to the other side of the block, then stopped the car. I watched him unzip his pants. Then the next thing I knew, he was lying on top of me. I didn't know what he was doing. I didn't feel anything then, either. Nothing. After a while, he'd sit back up, zip his pants up, and then drive me home. He'd put some money in my hand and I'd just walk up those steps, open the door, and go to my room, go to bed, and not think about things.

If I thought about anything, it would be my books. I could figure out mathematics. I could figure out English. I could figure all those things out. I just couldn't figure out this world I was living in when I wasn't reading my books.

I got to the bottom of the hill, turned the corner, and headed toward the Methodist church, hoping I wasn't late for services.

Then, for no reason, no reason at all, I just stopped walking.

I thought about all the little signs pasted up in that church, the ones that said God is Love. I thought about the way people looked at me all the time, like I was doing something wrong or I was bad.

I looked right up at the sky, almost directly into the sun. *God isn't real,* I thought. *Nope, God isn't real and if God is real, then He doesn't love me, because this sure doesn't feel like love to me.*

I spun around, and walked right back up that hill. Then I knocked on the door where I knew Sophie lived. She was older than I was and Mama said I wasn't supposed to play with her. We spent the next hour looking at true confession magazines.

Sophie told me I better get ready because I was getting old enough that soon I was going to have sex with men, just like the women in these magazine stories. I felt scared, wondering what sex was, and what it would be like to have sex with a man. Then I pushed the idea right out of my head and lit the cigarette she held out to me.

"How was church?" Mama asked when I got home.

"Fine," I said. "It was fine."

α

I didn't start drinking because I was sexually abused. I didn't start running home on my lunch hour from the seventh grade to sneak a drink because I had missed so much school because of medical conditions that I didn't know how to talk to my peers. I didn't start drinking because I couldn't get love and approval, or any kind of reward that felt significant, for being good but I could get a response—albeit disgust and contempt—when I misbehaved. I didn't start drinking because the first boy I had a crush on, the dark-haired boy with glasses who lived directly across the street from me, turned me down when I proposed that we be boyfriend and girlfriend and stood quietly waiting for my first legitimate kiss, a kiss based on love, not the way I had been kissed and touched so far—by men who snatched me off the street and did odd things to my body and then played the theme song to *Davy Crockett*, or by respectable men I trusted and worked for, men who had wives and children and still liked to take their *thing* out, as mother referred to it, and do strange things to me with it instead of taking me home, like they said they were going to do.

"Don't let men touch you with their *thing*," Mother had told me. Well, it seemed I didn't know how to stop them.

I didn't start drinking at age twelve because I absorbed, like a walking, talking human sponge, a dirty sense of shame from my family and from all these men.

All those factors helped, I'm sure, and contributed. But those are not the reasons I started sneaking home on my lunch hour and downing first one, then two, and three shots of straight Jack Daniels, instead of eating a peanut butter sandwich like the other children did.

I started drinking because it was love at first sip. Or gulp.

At first, I felt oddly superior when I returned to school, an old elementary grade school, grades kindergarten through eight, about four blocks from my home, for afternoon classes after sneaking a drink. I felt warm and glowing and nothing bothered or upset me. I had only one feeling: good. That good feeling lasted about four to six hours. And I got it every time I drank.

When it wore off, I would quietly do my homework, then go to bed and sleep.

Things changed that year, the year I turned twelve.

I started smoking cigarettes, L & Ms.

Mother stopped sewing beautiful, pink satin dresses for me, and taking me to piano recitals.

I stopped raising my hand in class, ready to blurt out the right answer. I started getting in trouble in school, rebelling against the teachers, even getting sent to the principal's office once, which both terrified and exhilarated me.

And the bottles of Jack Daniels underneath the sink began to get empty. I couldn't water them down much further.

I needed a connection.

ॐ

Sometimes we make a decision and that decision—that concrete string of words that turns into a sentence—alters our destiny. It swoops down into the fields of the universe and cuts us a clear path—for good or for ill.

God created a world with thought and belief.

That's how we help create our world too.

It is so rare that we see how A links up to B, the cause and effect, between our words, our beliefs, and the reality of physical events we find ourselves living in. It's only later, after the fact, that we see. Only then does the connection become clear.

My life changed irrevocably and not for the better the day when I was twelve years old and decided I didn't believe in God. I can't tell you the exact moment and day the changes began to manifest, but I can show you, if you'd like to look, where those changes led.

ᑐ

Each day on the way to school I passed a corner gas station where a group of men in their early twenties hung out. They played rock music. Smoked cigarettes. And drank beer. Some of them knew my older half-brother and two older half-sisters, all of whom had moved away from home by then.

I had an *in*.

One night, when I was thirteen, they invited me to a party. I told Mother I had to go to the library to study for classes. Instead, I went to the address I'd been given and knocked on the door. A man about twenty, whom I thought was good-looking at the time, let me in. I looked around. Everyone was drinking beer. They offered me one. I drank it like a glass of water. They offered me another. I downed that one. And another. And another.

This was good. I had friends. I had beer. I couldn't talk to the kids in my class, but these guys were talking to me. They actually seemed to like me.

One of them asked me to come with him, he had something to show me. He took my hand and led me down a hallway to a bedroom. He sat down on the bed and pulled me down next to him.

I had drunk a lot of beers by this time. I felt stupidly intoxicated. But the slimy feeling that began crawling into my stomach when he touched me was powerful enough to replace the intoxication and euphoria I had felt by drinking all those beers. I knew that feeling well. I felt that way when the man pulled me into the church. I felt that way when the man I babysat for drove me home.

I did what I had been trained to do. Nothing.

I thought I knew what was coming next, but I didn't. When this man, a stranger, finished with me and got up and left the room, another one came in. Then another, then another. By then, the beers I had drunk were wearing off. I stumbled out of the bedroom.

On my way to the door, a tall thin man with blonde hair and blue eyes grabbed me. "Not yet," he said, pulling me back into the room. I tried fighting him off. I was too drunk. He was too big.

When he finished, I got up and went home.

I walked timidly into the house. My job, my only job, was to walk a line straight enough to pass Mother, who sat in her chair by the door leading to her bedroom, and make it to the hallway leading to my bedroom.

I made it as far as the sofa in the family room. I sat down and stared at the television. Mother and I didn't talk much—she said I was uncommunicative—so I didn't have to worry about slurring my words. I sat there for a moment. Then I got up and started pacing my steps to my bedroom deliberately placing each foot firmly on the floor, forcing myself to be steady.

I made it halfway across the room. I was almost to the hallway when Mother's voice rang out. "Where have you been?"

Oh, God. I had to talk. "I told you," I said. "I went to the library."

"It's not open this late," she said. "Do you know what time of the night it is?"

I didn't. "I missed my bus," I said. The library was downtown. "Buses only come once an hour now."

She didn't say anything. She didn't have to. I felt that look, glaring, penetrating. It was the same look I could remember my father getting. It was contempt. It was disgust. It was my reward— for being bad.

I walked the rest of the way, opened my bedroom door, took off my clothes, put on my pajamas, and went to bed. A short time later, silence replaced the sounds of the television noise, and the lights in the living room turned to darkness. Mother had gone to bed.

It was over.

The room was rolling. I felt like I was in a boat, slightly nauseated and dizzy. But I was safe.

This was my first experience, my first bout with power.

I was in a battle to control the uncontrollable—the effects of alcohol on my behavior, my words, and my footsteps. I wasn't sure, but I thought that maybe I had won. I closed my eyes and went to sleep.

"Wake up." A hand was touching my shoulder.

At first, I thought it was mother.

I came to. A face bent down and kissed me. It was one of the men from the party. He had followed me home.

"How'd you get in here?" I said.

"The front door was unlocked. I walked in," he said.

What was odd, what was peculiar, what made me different, what made me stand out even then, what should have been a warning sign to the deepest places of my soul, was that it never occurred to me, not for one moment, to scream. To survive, to save myself, I believed I had to be nice, not cause trouble. And most of all, not wake Mother. I did, however, threaten to scream.

"If you don't leave," I said quietly, "I'm going to scream at the top of my lungs. I am underage and you are overage. My mother will wake up, call the police, and have you arrested."

He looked at me, then unzipped his pants and took out his thing. I pushed him away. He left.

Almost thirty years earlier the man my mother trusted, the man who was supposed to be her loving father—had walked over to my mother's bed. She was twelve at the time. He pulled the covers away from her little body, then crawled into bed next to her.

Mother didn't scream. She didn't call out for help. She took out the knife she was sleeping with and lashed out at his *thing*.

I didn't know about my mother's experience. I just knew that the man in my bedroom had left. I stared at the picture on the wall, hanging alongside my bedroom door—a small picture of the face of Jesus that glowed eerily in the dark. Finally I fell asleep.

All of this—the drinking, the men, the lying—hurt. But only a little more than the rest of my life had hurt.

This time, I had pinched myself hard. Maybe I was real.

Over the following months, I developed a relationship with one of the men from the party. I became his girlfriend. That meant that at night after Mother fell asleep, I sneaked out of the house and ran the two blocks to his house where he slept on the front porch. I climbed into bed with him, let him have sex with me, than ran back home and crawled into my bedroom window hoping and praying that Georgette, my mother's miniature dachshund, wouldn't hear me and start barking.

Occasionally, he passed me around to his friends at beer parties, but I considered that a small price to pay to have a boyfriend. I continued to get straight As in school. I studied hard during the day, acquiring typing, shorthand, and good English skills. I was the youngest person ever to be allowed to work on the school newspaper at Minnehaha Academy, the private Christian high school I attended that was located just over the bridge in Minneapolis. I continued to study classical music. I loved writing stories. I only occasionally had a friend my own age. I had many, many heated arguments with Mother. I drank alcohol almost daily. And I discovered, at about age sixteen, that if I swallowed a handful of diet pills, now known as amphetamines, I didn't get nearly as sick from hangovers the next day.

In 1961, my mother and I took a trip to California. It was our last mother-daughter trip while I lived at home.

I had gotten pregnant. She knew. She just knew. What she didn't know was that I had already bought a pill that was supposed to abort me. I had taken it, but nothing had happened.

We rented a car in Los Angeles and drove down to Mexico. She had the name and address of a doctor that was supposed to take care of my *condition*. When we got out of the car and knocked on the door of the clinic, a short fat man with a moustache and dirty fingernails answered the door and introduced himself as the doctor. I stared at this man's dirty fingernails, then I looked at my mother. We got back into the car.

A few days later, she took me to a doctor's office in Hollywood. He said he was giving me an injection for the pain, then he was going to inject some fluids in my uterus that would cause a miscarriage. We were to go back to the hotel. When I started bleeding, my mother was to take me to a local hospital and tell them I was having a miscarriage.

He tied off my arm with the string of rubber cloth, then stuck a large needle into my vein. A feeling went through me, a feeling like I had never felt before. I relaxed. Then he stuck the largest needle I had ever seen straight through my abdomen, into my uterus. I felt a searing pain.

When I was admitted to the hospital later that evening, the doctors and nurses questioned my mother extensively. She insisted that I was simply miscarrying.

We returned to the Twin Cities two days later.

In 1962, I graduated on the Twin City honor roll. My academic achievement was outstanding. I had enough credits, by then, that I only had to attend classes for three hours in the morning. And a large local company had hired me to work as a copy-writing assistant in the editorial department in the afternoons.

On my eighteenth birthday, everything was in place. Since I had been eleven, I had been counting the days, and crossing them off my calendar, waiting for this moment in time. I had saved enough money to buy myself a green, stick-shift, '56 Chevy. I had parked it a few blocks from home, taught myself to drive it, then passed my driver's test. I had searched the classifieds and found a cute little furnished apartment about half a mile from home.

On my lunch hour on my eighteenth birthday I went home from school. This day, I didn't get drunk. I walked through the house into my bedroom, packed a few items of clothing, and walked back into the living room.

My sister's ex-husband was living with Mother and me at the time. I didn't like him, but I didn't mind him too much. He had shown me his *thing* once when he was married to my older sister and she had left me alone with him. I had pretended I didn't notice and he never bothered me again.

When he saw me leaving with two brown paper bags filled with clothing he called my mother at work. "Your mother wants to talk to you," he said.

"I don't want to talk to her," I said.

He mumbled something into the phone.

"What'd she say?" I asked, on my way out the door.

"I should take a shotgun and shoot you," he replied.

I shrugged my shoulders and walked out the door.

Alone that night, in my new home, I made two decisions that would continue to alter the course of my destiny.

I was tired of letting men take advantage of me sexually. I was enraged. I was going to take control of my sexual life, my victimization. Second, I could no longer handle the effects alcohol had on my life and me. I couldn't stand the loss of control when I drank—the nausea, the blackouts, the way it left me vulnerable to whomever and whatever forces were around me.

So, I decided that evening to become a prostitute and a drug addict.

෪

The year was 1963. By then, LSD, pot, hippies,and the concepts of love, peace, sexual revolution, and getting high had infiltrated society. I had a good-paying job working as a typist in a publishing company in St. Paul. I still had my little apartment on the East Side, a studio with a couch that folded into a bed. But love, peace, and drugs escaped my reach. All I could find was alcohol and diet pills.

As I punched out from my 3 P.M. to 11 P.M. shift at the publishing company and got into my car that night, I had a plan.

I had heard about an after-hours joint in St. Paul. The guys I had been drinking with had pointed it out, told me where it was. Even with my high quotient for absorbing alcohol—made higher by the amphetamines that were easy to score then because many doctors were prescribing them to anyone who said they wanted to lose weight—I had an almost photographic memory. I was sure that if I went there, I could find a drug connection, a way to get *drugs*.

That meant I could stop drinking. I wasn't a social drinker. I wasn't a recreational drinker. I was as serious about consuming intoxicants as a person could be. Getting fucked up was my goal. And it was my only goal.

At 1 A.M. I parked my car outside the building, put the keys in my purse, got out, straightened my clothes, ran my hands through my hair, and walked up the stairs.

I was nervous. I didn't know what to expect. But I was on a mission. I had heard I could find Shelby O'Brian here. The talk among the beer drinkers in the back rooms of the bars that I now frequented was that this guy sold drugs. I had saved up my money. I didn't know what I was going to buy, but I was going to buy something.

I walked into a smoke-filled living room. The noise stopped, and all eyes followed me. I went over and stood in a corner of the room.

"Looking for someone?" a man asked.

"Shelby O'Brian," I replied. The man pointed to a short, stout, loud, balding man across the room. O'Brian was standing with a group of men, all of whom looked old to me, in their forties or fifties. I took a deep breath, and walked toward them. I was wearing a miniskirt, high heels, and long dangly earrings.

"Mr. O'Brian, my name is Melody Vaillancourt. I've heard about you, and it's a pleasure to meet you," I said, extending my hand.

There are moments in time when the world stops moving, fades into slow motion, then stands still. This was one of those moments.

The eyes of everyone in that group turned to me, then widened. Each man in that group, there were five or six of them, as if on cue, burst into laughter.

O'Brian shushed them. He looked at me with curiosity.

"Are you serious, kid?" He asked.

"Yes, sir, I am," I said.

He shook his head. "I don't know what she's about," he said to the men with him, "but I've got to get to know this girl."

O'Brian—Shelby—the raucous Irishman from the East Side of St. Paul, took me home with him that evening—along with the men who surrounded him when I first came in. When we got to his living room, he disappeared down a hallway, leaving me standing there alone. When he reappeared, he was carrying some bags. Out of one, he took something I immediately recognized as marijuana, or grass. Out of another, he took a handful of pills.

"How much will this cost?" I asked, digging in my purse and pulling out some bills.

"Oh, honey," he said. "I don't want your money. Not yet. But there is something you can do for me if you want to get your hands on these." He held out the grass and the pills.

I remember the drive back to my apartment. I didn't know which day of the week it was. It might have been three, four, five days later. It could have been a week or longer. But I left with a handful of pills and a joint.

I lit the joint then fought for control. Certainly if I focused, if I tried hard enough, I could control the effects from marijuana and drive at the same time. I felt a little woozy at first but then I got the hang of it.

My money was gone.

My breasts were covered with oozing cigarette burns.

And I was certain I had lost my job by now.

The men had given me pills, handfuls of them. It was different,

different than the alcohol. I had passed out, gone to someplace so deep, so dark, and so euphoric I didn't know where I had been or who had used my body. I didn't care. I remembered one man, a cab driver in his fifties with a loud, raspy voice. I remembered him holding his cigarette to my skin, and my surprise when I could hear my skin sizzling but couldn't feel any pain.

How much was it going to take now to know if I was real?

When I arrived at my apartment, the phone rang. It was Mother. She was frantic, furious.

"I've got the police out looking for you," she screamed. "Where have you been?"

"Why'd you do that?" I said, a rush of fear moving through me. "I wasn't lost. . . ."

I hung up the phone. Feelings I now know as shame, remorse, self-contempt, and self-hatred flooded through me. All I knew then was that something overwhelmingly dark overpowered me.

I could drive while smoking pot. I could maintain control. But I couldn't overpower the dark, nasty feelings flooding through me now. I couldn't even stand still.

I did the only thing I knew to do. I took a shower, got back in my car, and drove right back to Shelby's house.

I was ready to jump again.

I found another job. One of the more prestigious law firms in downtown St. Paul hired me as a legal secretary. I had excellent shorthand and typing skills and an appropriate, respectable demeanor during daytime hours. They fired me six months later.

I had met a nice young man named Tony, a friend of Shelby's. He worked out a deal with me. He would arrange for me to go on dates with businessmen. If I slept with them, they'd give Tony money and he'd split it with me. One of the clients of the firm must have reported that I was one of the prostitutes he had hired the night before.

It was about this time that I moved to Minneapolis and took LSD for the first time. I also met a man in his forties, a thin man who talked and talked and talked about cars and guns and women. He called himself "Dr. Ted."

Dr. Ted had bottles and bottles and bottles of every kind of pill imaginable. He had marijuana by the kilo. He pulled me away from O'Brian and that group. He wanted me to be his girl.

The rules were simple. Dr. Ted would buy my clothes and supply me with drugs. I'd sleep only with him or the men he directed me to. Then I'd take the money the men gave me and bring it home to him.

It was a step up, a step into respectability.

I can't remember if he ever told me he loved me. I wasn't sure it mattered.

It was close enough for me.

The first time Dr. Ted offered me a syringe full of Demerol, a synthetic narcotic used in hospitals for pain relief, I cringed and said no. A few months later, he again offered me a syringe. This time I grabbed the needle, stuck myself in the hip, pushed in the plunger, and waited.

I liked it. A warm feeling spread through me some minutes later. But it wasn't as much of a knockout high as when I took handfuls of pills.

I liked amphetamines, stimulants to keep me going, keep me full of energy.

I liked barbiturates, downers, and tranquilizers, to make me sleepy and relax.

I didn't care much for marijuana. It just made me feel sleepy and tired. But I would smoke it, if need be.

About once every four to six months, I'd take a massive dose of LSD, just to see where my head was at—a chemical psychological test to review and observe my state of mind.

I avoided alcohol like the plague.

ॐ

A few months after the first time I shot Demerol, I was at a friend's house. His name was Sammy. He was an odd little thing. He was perky, liked to talk a lot, and wasn't interested in having sex with me. We were sitting on the floor in his living room, listening to Jimi Hendrix and smoking pot.

"I've got something you'll like," he said. "I'll be right back."

When he came back into the room, he was carrying a tablespoon with an oddly bent handle, two syringes, and a glass of water. He pulled a tiny plastic bag out of his shirt pocket, opened up the packet, and sprinkled the powder from it into the spoon. He sucked water into the syringe, sprayed it into the spoon, then broke off a cigarette filter, ripped a tiny piece of the white cottony filter, rolled it into a ball, and tossed that into the spoon too. Then he took the needle from one of the syringes and gently stirred. He lit three matches at the same time, in one stroke, carefully picked up the spoon, and held the flame directly underneath the spoon, so the tips of the flame actually touched the metal. In seconds, the dark mixture bubbled.

He stuck a needle into the spoon, pulled back on the plunger, and sucked part of the dark liquid up into the syringe.

"Tie off," he said.

"What?" I said.

He took off his belt, wrapped it around my arm, tapped on the crease in my arm until a vein popped up, then stuck the needle into my arm.

He pulled back the plunger. Blood flooded into the syringe, mixing with the dark brewed broth. Then he slowly pushed on the plunger, pushing, pushing, pushing the dark liquid out of the hypodermic syringe and into my vein.

There was no waiting, this time, like there had been when I stuck the needle of Demerol in my hip. That had taken fifteen minutes or so. The next instant, the next moment, the heroin mixed with my blood, became one with me, reached my heart, and my brain. It exploded in me. Overcame me. It was sensuous. Overpowering. Caressing. Euphoric. All at the same time.

"Jeez," I said, lying back on the big pillow on the floor.

In nineteen years, it was the closest thing I had ever felt to love.

Nothing mattered. Nothing hurt. Nothing felt bad. Maybe, maybe this world was an all right place. This relief, this oblivion, this soothing, warm, comforting burst of synthetic love was what I had been searching for all my life.

Drinking alcohol, that first warm tingly musky burst of Jack Daniels in my stomach, was a mere crush. Puppy love. This was the real thing. It was more than love at first sight. It was a marriage with my soul mate—heroin and my blood. The wedding had just taken place.

Someone once asked me if there had been any bright spots in my life somewhere between drinking at age twelve and inserting heroin in my veins at nineteen.

"Nope," I calmly replied. "Shooting that syringe of heroin was the closest I had ever been to the Light."

There are codes of conduct among junkies.

There's the code of honor. On the streets, that's called being *stand-up*. Being stand-up means you don't steal from your friends; only businesses and strangers are fair game. If you've got some—and *some* could mean drugs, money, food, and shelter although it usually meant drugs—you share. You put what you've got on the table and let your friend take what he or she needs. Being stand-up means you don't sleep with the lover of a friend. It means you cover your friend's back—you don't let anyone hurt him. It means you don't snitch. You never, never tell the police what's going on, even if that means you take the rap and go to jail yourself. Being stand-up means you'll do whatever it takes to survive in a world of prostitutes, thieves, and junkies—but you won't cause harm to a friend.

It's also known on the streets as someone who has *heart*.

There's another code on the streets too. This is a code junkies use to measure the quality of junk, boy—or whatever nickname they call heroin—that they've just shot into their veins. There's the initial rush—that feeling that explodes into your heart and brain within seconds after you push the plunger in. That's an important test to pass, one measure of a good score.

But it's the quality of what follows after that first rush that counts, that really matters, to any good junkie's soul.

That measuring stick is called the *nod*.

Nodding is a strange, peculiar state where you're not asleep but you're not awake either. You just float off to someplace, a place people who aren't junkies don't know, haven't been, will never visit. I don't know how long it lasts—seconds, minutes maybe. If the junk is good, you can't tell. It's the place in the universe where time stands still.

If you're a casual observer, if you're sober and straight enough to have consciousness and can tolerate being around a junkie, this is what you'd see. The junkie sits, stands, or lies there. And it can happen sitting, standing, or lying down. The junkie will be talking. He or she will be midsentence, telling you something, explaining something. He might say ten words. Then he'll nod off midsentence. You might think he's asleep, or unconscious—not aware of what he's saying. Or you might think the conversation is over. That's not true.

He's just visiting the land of nod.

When he comes back, he finishes the sentence. He picks up on the very next word that comes after the word where he left off, as if he never went away. Because to him, he didn't.

Nod is a mysterious place. And it's annoying, if you're clean and sober and can stand to be around the junkie long enough to make conversation or get some sense out of him or her.

There are turning points in every person's life. These places mark the end of one stage and the beginning of the next. They take you around the corner, around the bend. They help you go in the direction you're trying to go.

The day I shot boy—the day I used heroin intravenously—was one of those points.

I entered a new world. I made new friends. Then I watched them die.

The pharmacist shot Billy Butler, my speed-freak friend, right through the forehead when Billy tried to rob that final drugstore. But then Billy always said they weren't going to take him away in cuffs. He said he was going *to hold court in the street.*

I began getting critically ill at times too. I got hepatitis. Turned yellow. Couldn't hold down any food. They stuck me in the hospital for a few days. But I couldn't take being separated from drugs—not for an hour or a day, much less the month the doctor said I had to stay. So I checked out. Started using again. The next time I got sick, it was worse. It took the doctors a week to figure out what was wrong. They had a team working day and night when they diagnosed my illness.

An infection from injecting drugs intravenously had settled on the coronary artery and the valve in the left side of my heart—probably caused by something the dope dealers had mixed with the junk, doctors later said.

That didn't stop me for long. I had to be confined to the hospital for six weeks with an IV bag full of penicillin dripping directly into my veins. They didn't know if they could save me. But I knew a secret. I had my salvation. I had my friends bring my drugs into the room and shoot them right into the IV drip.

Over the next few years I overdosed five or six times. I'd wake up—stunned into instant sobriety by the shot of Narcon doctors give you to neutralize the effects of any drugs in your system. I'd rip off the heart monitor and any other medical apparatus they had hooked up to my body, push my way out of the emergency room, grab a cab, and immediately use more drugs. The doctors thought what they had given me was a miracle.

What they didn't know was that the shot of Narcon they gave me, the one that reversed and cleansed the overdose, also gave me in an instant the two things I wanted least: sobriety and my life.

After one overdose, I opened my eyes in the emergency room

and looked first into the eyes of a priest, then into the saddened, hor-rified face of my mother. She was crying. The priest had just given me last rites.

I was furious. I was angry that I was still alive and even angrier that I was sober. I raced out of that emergency room, chasing my next high.

I spent the next five years chasing the high, that first blissful, euphoric burst of heroin in my blood, the one I got the first time I shot it at Sammy's house. I didn't know, couldn't accept, couldn't believe it would never be the same or that good again.

ൔ

The dark stretch of highway loomed before me, unlit by even an occasional street light. It was late at night, around midnight or so. I was struggling to stay awake, and get this old Cadillac, Dr. Ted, and myself to Duluth, Minnesota. I wanted to turn the radio on, crank it up loud, but I was afraid it would wake up Ted, whom I was glad had either fallen asleep or passed out from drugs. It didn't matter to me which one.

At least he had shut up.

When I had first met him, I found his amphetamine-induced speed freak monologue, in that medium-pitched, fairly well-educated male pay-attention-to-every-detail voice amusing, if only occasionally interesting. He was kind of a freak of nature, tall, thin, wiry, and meticulous. Had he not taken the route he did, turned to drugs, he might have been a doctor. He had gained his nickname because he always carried a large stock of drugs—drugs of every shape, color, kind, and assortment—with him in what looked like a doctor's bag. If you wanted to go up with amphetamines or down with barbiturates, he had the pill. If you wanted to mellow out and go sideways with a tranquilizer, he had those in his bag too. If you wanted to turn yourself inside out with LSD, see what you were made of, check out what was going on, he could scrimmage around and find some of that too. He had little vials of Demerol and sterile syringes. Whatever you wanted or needed at the moment, Dr. Ted could and would fill the bill.

He was older than me by twenty-three years, but at least he had taken me away from Shelby O'Brian and his group. He had what I needed most—a constant supply of drugs. He had been my ticket to a better life.

Lately, though, things hadn't been going well between us.

℘

There are many routes of ingestion, ways to get substances into the body. You can swallow something, in which case it will be digested by the stomach and absorbed into the blood stream. This is a slow way, sometimes taking up to forty-five minutes or an hour for the substance ingested to reach the blood, the heart, and the brain. What you have in your stomach, and the condition your stomach is in at the time, can considerably influence this process. If you have just eaten a big meal or if your digestive enzymes aren't working properly, this can be a tedious, slow, and inefficient method of absorption and ingestion. It does, however, work as a route to get pills such as amphetamines, tranquilizers, and barbiturates into the bloodstream.

You can also inhale a substance. That's called *snorting*. If you can crush up a pill and turn it into powder, you can suck it into your nose through a straw, a rolled-up dollar bill or a match cover, and the powder will be absorbed through the sinus or nasal passages. It will reach the bloodstream, heart, and brain more quickly than the stomach and intestinal route. But there's a price to pay for snorting. Many of the pills used by drug addicts are bitter, vile, and noxious. You can crush them up and snort them, but they burn like a son of a bitch. More than occasionally, this method of absorption will cause the nose and sinus cavity to burn, then bleed.

You can also smoke a substance. You can smoke marijuana; you can smoke heroin and cocaine. When you ingest a substance by smoking it, the fumes from the drug—whether it's pot, crack, or boy—are absorbed by the delicate tissue in the lungs and that's how it gets into the blood and to the brain. The drug turns into a puff of smoke and the lungs absorb that puff. It's a quick route of absorption but the drug is somewhat diluted by this process of turning it into smoke.

Drugs can also be put into the body by injecting them with a needle. But even this route—using a needle to take drugs from the outside world and put them inside your body—has different options too. You can insert a hypodermic needle with drugs into a muscle, or just under the skin—for instance in your hips or the muscle just under your shoulder on the arm. Then you just push the plunger in. In anywhere from five to twenty minutes, the substance injected will pass from the muscle into the blood. That's how it gets to the brain, causing the feeling of being high.

Or, you can take that same hypodermic needle, insert it directly into a vein—you know if you're there because when you pull back on the plunger, you'll draw blood—then push the drug into the vein. This way is instantaneous. In only seconds the substance will hit the brain in full force, undiluted by having to pass through muscles, intestines, or by being turned into smoke. You can also absorb drugs through your rectum, vagina, or skin. Skin is an organ too, the largest one we have.

What I am saying is this: If you have a mind-altering substance— a drug—you can sniff it, smoke it, swallow it, put it in a needle and shove it into your vein, your hip, or your arm. You can rub it on your skin, stick it in your vagina, or shove it up your ass. And you will to some degree feel the mind-altering effects of that substance.

You'll get high.

At one time or another, I used all these routes of ingestion except for skin absorption because patches weren't invented yet. One route fast became my favorite, my compulsion, and that was shooting drugs directly into my veins. I loved the ritual of preparing the drug—turning it into a liquid then drawing it into the syringe. I loved tying off, and the moment of joy I felt when I drew back the plunger, saw blood, and knew I had found a vein.

But most of all I loved what came instantly next—the moment of oblivion, pure intoxication, the overpowering feeling when the drug undiluted in any shape and form flooded through my heart and brain.

That was the way I preferred to get high.

But my preferred route of ingestion was causing problems between Dr. Ted and me. He liked to pop (swallow) pills. He liked to smoke grass and only occasionally would indulge in a syringe full of Demerol injected into the muscle or under the skin. He was worried and concerned that I seemed obsessed with putting drugs into my veins. It was causing tension in our relationship. A rift.

I was also refusing to have sex with men for money, then bring the money to him. Ted wasn't a pimp. He didn't have girls working for him. He just figured that any woman he was with was going to have sex with other men. If she got paid for this sex, called turning tricks, but gave the money to him, he didn't lose his dignity as a man.

I wasn't that interested any more in having sex with anyone—Dr. Ted or tricks. In a peculiar way, even though I was addicted and living in a degrading, amoral world, I was beginning to learn about power. And I knew I didn't have to give up my power by having sex with any man.

I had also turned twenty-one by now, which opened new doors for me financially.

Shortly before my twenty-first birthday, I had gotten an in. A girl I knew was working as a stripper on Hennepin Avenue in Minneapolis. Nudie bars didn't exist then. Stripping was a funky, borderline glamorous profession. A sweet looking old lady visited all the strip joints. She'd take your measurements, then make you costumes of your choice: flowing, floor-length, belly-dancing skirts with matching veils; little teeny sequined circles called *pasties* to glue over the nipples of the breasts; and G-strings, a little flap of material sewn on a piece of elastic that was used to cover the crotch. I had a black leather G-string and one made from real mink. I had her get me a pair of long white gloves too, the kind that go up to the shoulder. By then, my arms and hands were red and swollen and lined with tracks—rows of needle marks—from shooting drugs. I had to wear gloves when I danced.

A band with a sax player, a bass player, and a drummer pounded out songs like "St. Louis Blues" while you stood on stage and took off your clothes. You'd slowly remove each item until all you had on was your G-string and pasties. Then you'd smile and demurely leave the stage. When I was twenty, I had to accept a lesser salary and have sex with the bar owner to work there. Now that I was twenty-one and could work legitimately in a bar, I could make $500 a week dancing. I didn't have to let anyone touch me. And I didn't have to give my paychecks from dancing to Dr. Ted. The money was mine.

When I turned twenty-one, I was also able to go on the dance circuit. That meant that from Thursday to Sunday, I'd take an engagement dancing—either stripping or go-go dancing, which was popular then—in another town. Some weeks I'd go to St. Louis, sometimes to Fargo, sometimes to Duluth, and once, I think, to Iowa. It was a break in the routine. It gave the men who frequented those joints new faces to look forward to. And the money was even better when you agreed to leave town.

I didn't like dancing, but the money was good. When I'd stand on stage dancing, I'd feel contempt and disgust for all the men who stared, reached out, pawed at me. But most of all, I felt contempt for myself.

Now, even my dancing job was becoming threatened. My arms were so full of tracks, bruises, and scabs from shooting drugs, so swollen from missing—from pushing substances into my hands and arms when I wasn't in a vein but thought I was—and from injecting substances into my veins that weren't meant to be injected, like barbiturates, that I couldn't take off my gloves when I danced.

And recently, I had met another man. He was different than any of the men I had met so far. He was close to my age, but he still lived at home with his mom and dad. Even though I was still living in an apartment in Minneapolis with Dr. Ted, I had stopped having sex with Ted a while back and had begun having occasional sex with this other man.

Ted had found out. He didn't have to hire an investigator to discover it either.

One evening we had gone to a restaurant. I had just sat and looked at Dr. Ted with contempt and disgust while I waited for dinner. Then I had excused myself to go to the ladies room. Instead of going to the bathroom, I made a phone call to the other man, then spirited myself out the back door of the restaurant without saying a word, including good-bye, to Dr. Ted. When I returned to Ted's house three days later, he asked me where I had been.

So I told him.

He punched me in the mouth, breaking one of my teeth.

Mother had always impressed upon me how important it was to take care of your teeth, so I went immediately to the dentist and had it fixed. But things between Ted and me were becoming tense. It just wasn't the same anymore.

Now I was driving his Cadillac up to Duluth. I was supposed to start a four-day dancing job there the next night. Usually Ted didn't accompany me on these dancing jobs. I would either take the bus or the train. But he didn't trust me anymore. He wanted to watch me, make sure I behaved. He knew he was losing control.

He used that same speed-freak, methodical, detail-oriented voice—now tinged with anger and revenge—to nag and natter at me every moment he was awake. That's why although I was getting tired, hypnotized by the monotony of the dark, unlit drive, I didn't want to turn on the radio. I didn't want to wake him up.

I must have closed my eyes for just a second. Maybe it was longer than that. Maybe I nodded. But suddenly, the car was upside down, then rolling over, crashing down into the ditch. Ted screamed. The car landed upside down. I couldn't move. My arm was pinned. I lay underneath that Cadillac, pinned to the ditch.

I screamed at Ted.

He didn't answer. I wondered if he was dead.

I couldn't move or feel my left arm. I wondered if it had been severed, if it was gone. I started to pass out, then forced myself into consciousness. I moved my right hand around, until I could feel, could touch Ted's body. I shook him.

"What happened?" he said.

"It was an accident," I said. "What are we going to do?"

He started to say something. Then he passed out.

With my right hand, I groped around and found the flashlight I knew Ted had in the car. I switched it on. I had deliberately chosen this infrequently traveled stretch of road to avoid any run-ins with the police. By now I had several arrests for possession of narcotics and drugs and I didn't want to get stopped by the police again. It seemed that every time they drove by me, they'd stop me for something minor, like having a burned-out taillight or not coming to a full stop. When I'd get out of the car to talk to them, they'd either see how high I was or drugs would fall out of my pocket onto the ground, and I'd wind up in jail.

Although it was the wee hours of the morning, I hoped that if I shined that flashlight up onto the highway eventually someone would drive by, see us, and send help. All I remember before the police came at daybreak was shining that light as long as I could before I finally passed out.

The good news was that the police and help had finally arrived. Both Dr. Ted and I were seriously injured but alive. The bad news was that the trunk, Ted's pockets, and my purse were full of illegal narcotics and drugs. As soon as the tow truck pulled the car off me, I realized my arm was still attached. It hurt, but that didn't stop me. I made a dash for the wrecked car and dug out my purse.

The car was in Ted's name. What was in the trunk and his pockets didn't concern me. I just had to get rid of the drugs in my purse. I had about twenty-five pills of all kinds—amphetamines, tranquilizers, and barbiturates—in a jar in my purse. I took off the cap, held the jar to my mouth, and swallowed every pill in about three or four gagging gulps.

Then I passed out.

When I awoke, I was in the oldest, crustiest, creakiest jail cell I had ever seen—in real life, in the movies, or on TV. I was the only person in this county jail, and an elderly matron who looked like a grandmother, with the assistance of a deputy sheriff was watching me. The door to my cell was so rusty they couldn't get it closed to lock me in.

The matron told me they were charging me with possession of narcotics. They didn't care that the car wasn't in my name. I was driving. I would take the rap for all the drugs in the car. Ted was being charged too.

If I confessed and told them that all the drugs belonged to Ted and turned state's evidence, they'd drop the charges against me. I'd go free, but Ted, who they'd been trying to arrest for a long time, would go to jail. Maybe for the rest of his life.

If I didn't confess, didn't tell them that the drugs were his, maybe they'd drop the charges on Ted and throw the book at me.

They wanted to know what I was going to do.

I was lying there on a steel frame in this creaky jail cell trying to figure out what came next when something unusual, something out of the ordinary not to most junkies but to me, happened. I started to throw up. I was getting sick. I figured it was from lack of drugs. I convinced the matron I needed to go to the hospital. If I was in a hospital, there was a chance I could talk the doctors out of some drugs.

They transported me to the hospital, took some blood, and ran some tests. I was getting sicker by the moment. I didn't understand this. Every bone and muscle in my body hurt. I was way too sober for my liking. And I couldn't stop throwing up.

I couldn't see the future. I couldn't even see the present clearly. I didn't know, lying in that small town hospital, that Dr. Ted would eventually get clean and sober and would go on to be the man who would bring Narcotics Anonymous, a Twelve Step group that helped drug addicts get clean and sober, to a major metropolitan city in another state. I couldn't image that someday I would get straight too.

And I didn't know, lying in that hospital bed, that I was pregnant with a child who would someday grow up and become a man with a life, a wife, and two children of his own.

All I knew was when the test results came back and confirmed that I was pregnant, I couldn't abort another child. I had had another abortion since the one in California when I was a teen, a back alley one this time. Even though I knew I wasn't a fit mother, I was determined to give this child a chance to live. And I couldn't break the street code. I couldn't and wouldn't turn state's evidence and snitch on Dr. Ted.

That was the end of my relationship with Dr. Ted. I kept waiting and hoping Ted would take his own rap on this drug bust. He didn't. I went to court. The judge must have known in his heart those drugs weren't mine. I was put on probation again, one more time. Probation didn't bother me. I was used to that. Whenever I was arrested for possession, and I was arrested frequently, the charges against me would either be dismissed, reduced to a misdemeanor, or I'd be given probation. Luck was with me, on my side. I kept skating through. Nope, probation didn't bother me. I'd just ignore it, like I always had. I wouldn't even bother to check in.

The difference was, this time I was pregnant.

The difference was, this other man I'd been seeing, the father of this child, was different, different from any man I'd been with so far.

He turned me into the probation officer for using drugs when I was pregnant with his child. The probation officer sentenced me to go to Mora, Minnesota—a quiet little town north of the Twin Cities, and live there with Mother until I delivered this child.

Mother sewed maternity dresses for me. I did volunteer work at the local group home for mentally retarded adults. Occasionally, when I could get it, I smoked a little pot. Overall, my hands were tied. I had to stay straight until this child was born.

The week after the child was born—I named him John—I was visiting at the home where his father lived. It was an impressive two-story home—a fireplace covered one entire wall. I was given a small bedroom on the second floor with the child. The problem was, I was already using drugs again.

I lay on the bed next to that child. I didn't know how to be a mother. I didn't know what any of this meant. In a rush, a roar, I knew then what the future held. This baby wasn't going to be mine. He would be taken away from me.

John's father and I made an effort.

We got married. Got our own place. I tried to be a wife and mother, tried to control my drug usage. I went back to work as a legal secretary—it was the only respectable trade I knew. I could type, take shorthand, and complete all the legal business forms. The one thing I couldn't do, didn't know how to do, couldn't imagine doing, was not use drugs.

I tried to just use on the weekends. It didn't work. Monday would come around. It would be time to go to my job at the law firm, and I couldn't figure out why I shouldn't be using drugs on Monday. I didn't know how to stop. I had to get high.

I had landed a good job. The attorney I was working for was well known, had been on President Nixon's staff. The work was interesting. I was leaving the baby with his grandparents—either his father's parents or my mother—all of the time, trying to give the child a good, respectable home. And I showed up for work every day, with one, two, or three syringes of drugs in my purse, to shoot into my veins on my coffee and lunch breaks.

The war on drugs was just beginning. The problem was, I was on the wrong side.

By then, I had stopped shooting heroin. More and more people were using it. More and more people were selling it. But the quality being sold by most people, now that it was becoming so popular, was inferior. They'd cut it—meaning they'd take out some of the heroin and replace it with another substance, a phony substance, to fill up the bag. You'd pay the same amount of money, but the quality of the dope was no good. Sometimes, you'd barely—if at all—get high. Sometimes the dope was cut with an innocuous substance. Sometimes not. If the dealer cut it with Ajax, you could shoot it and get sick, even die.

I had found another way to get high. There was a pharmaceutical drug called Dilaudid that was very similar to heroin. It was a synthetic opiate. The rush wasn't as good, but then the rush had never been the same anyway, not since that first hit, back at Sammy's house. But because Dilaudid was a pharmaceutical drug, there was quality control. The drugs were clean, pure, and you got high. It was expensive but it got the job done.

I wasn't happy. The child's father wasn't happy. And John's grandparents—on either side—weren't happy. They loved taking care of John, but everyone knew there was a problem with me.

That's when I got my plan.

The law firm I worked for had a major Minneapolis hospital as one of their accounts. I had heard on the streets that this hospital held the key to heaven for drug addicts. It was called the methadone program.

A lot of the junkies I had known on the streets—well, the ones who weren't dead or in jail—were getting on this program. If the program accepted you, all you had to do was show up twice a week, and they gave you a dose of methadone for each day of the week. Methadone was a synthetic substitute for heroin, much more potent than any pill you could buy. It kept you from going through withdrawal. Even though you ingested it by swallowing—either in pill or liquid form—you got really high. And unlike the high from most of the drugs I used, which normally lasted four to six hours, methadone kept you stoned for twenty-four hours, a full day. It was also supposed to block you from getting high from any other drug. If you consumed any other mind-altering substance while you were taking methadone, you wouldn't feel the effects of that drug.

The idea was that if they gave junkies methadone, it would satisfy their need to get high—because they would be high but without the rush from injection. If junkies didn't have to go through withdrawal, they wouldn't be breaking the law and doing all the unruly things that junkies do. They would take their prescription once a day and live respectable lives. The idea was to treat the physiological side of abuse by prescribing methadone and letting it substitute for street drugs.

I saw a few people's lives improve with methadone. On the outside, at least, their lives looked normal. They had clean homes and a family life. They'd cook, eat, sit around, and watch television.

When the methadone program first appeared on the scene, they were administering extremely high daily doses of this synthetic narcotic to program participants—over three times the dosage they give now. Methadone was popular. The number of participants on the program was limited. Most of the junkies I knew were waiting in line.

One day at work, after typing all morning then going into the bathroom on my coffee break and shooting Dilaudid, I walked into the office of the attorney I worked for. I sat down at the desk in front of him and told him we needed to talk. He was a dedicated, brilliant young lawyer with a tousled head of hair.

"I've got a problem," I said. "I shoot dope. And I need the help of you and this firm to get on the methadone program so I can straighten out my life."

The lawyer's eyes widened. "You're kidding," he said.

"No, I'm not," I said. I rolled up my sleeve and showed him my arms.

He made a phone call, then fired me. I started on the methadone program within days. The program worked well for many people. It did not work as an effective rehabilitation program for me.

Getting high on anything made me want to get higher on something else.

I couldn't help myself.

I'd bring home my methadone dose for the next three days. By the end of the second day, it would be all gone.

Methadone was so thick, so heavy, so stupefying, and the dosage administered then was so high, that I was more out of control, if that's possible, than I had been on street drugs.

By now, the baby was living full time with his grandparents. I didn't work. I didn't have anything to occupy my time except being stupefied.

One night, I tried to bake a chocolate cake. I thought I did a good job. When I awoke the next morning, there was chocolate all over the furniture and the walls. Days, weeks, and months began to pass in a blur. I was as close as possible to being dead while still being alive. I don't remember what happened, or what happened next. My entire system was clogged with methadone. I would go to the program, drink my dose, then stay in bed and wait for it to be time to take my next dose.

My mother tried to help me lead a normal life. She took me to a garage sale one day and bought me a used organ to put in the living room of the apartment where I lived. Maybe my mother just wanted her little girl back, the one who would sit at the piano, play those old religious songs, and sing her heart out.

One night, all saturated with methadone, I sat down at the organ and started to play. I banged out one song after another—singing, playing the keys for the melody, and pumping those pedals for the base. I played for hours. When I finished, I yelled into the bedroom, asking my husband how he liked listening to me play.

He didn't answer. I walked into the bedroom, where he had been lying on the bed.

He was gone. The window was open. While I was performing my concert, he had absconded—crawled out the window and ran away. That was the last time we were together under the same roof as man and wife.

He filed for divorce and the custody battle began.

A month later, that apartment burned down.

I was out on the street.

The Red Cross helped a little. Mother helped a lot. She helped me find a nice apartment close to the methadone program, so I could get to the hospital easily by bus. It was only a studio but it was the sweetest place I had ever known. It had a fireplace. It was an older building that had been restored. I got on a financial assistance program. I enrolled in college. I lived close to a bookstore. I loved to read. And I was determined to take my methadone properly. I was determined to make this thing work. My relationship with the child's father was over. He was taking the child. I didn't blame him.

I had given John the only gift I was capable of giving him then—the gift of life.

The problem was, I didn't know how to give that gift to myself.

I met Billy Butler about this time. Billy wasn't my boyfriend. He was just a friend. He was about six feet tall, with strawberry-blonde hair. He was full of life. He didn't use heroin. He didn't use narcotics.

Billy was a speed-freak. He shot drugs into his veins. He liked crystal—methamphetamine—best.

We hung out together a lot. I learned a secret back then. Billy taught me that even if you took a double dose of methadone, if you shot enough methamphetamine, you could counter the dopey effect of methadone and almost get a rush. So I'd take my methadone in the morning and go down. Then I'd shoot some speed and go up. Then Billy and I would run around town, visiting people, just hanging out.

He didn't charge me any money for the speed. He didn't want me to have sex with him or anyone else. Some people said Billy was a pimp, he had a lot of girls working, turning tricks, then bringing the money to him. I didn't know about any of that. It was probably true. But Billy was good to me. He just wanted to hang out.

I was trying with my studies at the junior college, really trying. I even saved a little money from my assistance check and bought some new clothes. One day I took a blanket, walked to the Minneapolis Institute of Arts, and stretched out in the sun. I was trying to do what I thought a normal person would do.

One day, at his apartment, Billy became confused. He said something to me. I said something back. He methodically went to each window in his apartment, closed the windows, and pulled down the shades. Then he walked over to the closet, reached in, and pulled out a wire coat hanger. He bent it, so it was compressed together in an oval, like a wire whip. Then he walked over to where I was sitting on the floor on a big pillow. Until now, I had just watched him. I didn't know what was going on.

Suddenly he jammed his foot across my neck, pinning me to the floor. He started saying something about how his girls minded him and he'd teach me about talking back. He raised the whip into the air, ready to strike me across the face.

"Have you lost your mind?" I asked. "I'm not one of your girls."

"Let's go for a ride," Billy said later. Soon he pulled into a gas station, said he was going inside. I figured he needed to buy some cigarettes.

"Get on the driver's side. When I come out and get in, just drive away," he said.

I did what he asked. I didn't think anything of it.

About four blocks later, he put his hands in his pockets and pulled out fistfuls of cash. "Here," he said, throwing some money at me. "I just robbed that gas station, and you just drove your first getaway car."

I learned something else later that day. Billy wasn't just a speed-freak. He also used the counterpart to boy. It was called *girl*. It was cocaine.

"It's time for you to meet someone," Billy said a few days later. "I've been thinking about putting you together with this guy for some time."

"Who?" I asked.

"You'll see," he said.

Billy had tried that before. He had taken me to an apartment one night to meet a man called John-John. John was an old dope fiend. He'd dress up as a priest and then go to doctors and get prescriptions. Sometimes he'd dress up as a doctor and walk right into hospitals and get drugs. Everybody on the streets knew or had heard of John. Billy had taken me over there and tried to trade me to John for some cocaine. John had looked at me, then shook his head.

"Nope," he said. "Don't want her. She's trouble."

Later, years later, John and I would work in the same treatment center helping other drug addicts rehabilitate. Even more years later, I would stand by his bed with his daughter, holding his hand as he slipped out of this world and into the next. I was curious about who Billy planned on trading me to now.

We drove to a quiet residential section of Minneapolis. I followed Billy up a flight of stairs to the second floor.

"His name is Paul," Billy said, pointing to a man with strawberry-blonde hair, almost the same color as Billy's. This man was even thinner and taller than Billy, at least 6 feet, 5 inches. Billy looked like a boy. This one looked like a man. He had a moustache, a big rimmed moustache that curled over his lip. "Paul Rutledge. But they call him Animal for short. He's going to be your new old man."

Billy walked out the door, leaving me alone with this man, Animal, in this new place.

I stood there, unsure about what to do next.

Paul disappeared down the hall. I waited. I waited some more. Then I heard cursing, loud cursing, coming from the hallway he had disappeared into. I walked down the corridor to the bathroom. The door was open. Paul was down on the floor, on all fours. He had a syringe without the needle on it, trying to suck something up off the bathroom floor.

"What's the matter?" I said.

"Damn it," he said. He looked at me, threw the syringe into the wastebasket, then looked at me again. "I just spilled my last hit of coke."

He stood up and grabbed my hand. "Come on," he said. "We're going out."

We drove around the city for a while. We stopped and visited a friend of his. I didn't say much. I just watched and listened. Paul intrigued me. I liked him. Then we both got in the car.

I didn't know where we were going. I didn't ask. Paul just kept driving around the city for several hours after the sun went down. Finally he parked the car and told me to get out. He grabbed my hand and we started walking through a yard, over a hedge, and into the back parking lot of a grocery store.

When we reached the side entrance to the store, he gently pushed me up against the door and put his face against mine, like he was going to give me a kiss.

I held my breath. A moment like this hadn't happened in my entire life.

But instead of kissing me, he began fumbling with the door. I realized he was holding a tool, something metal in his hand.

"Stand there and pretend like we're lovers," he said. "I'm trying to pull this lock."

I did what I was told.

He pulled out the lock, opened the door, and pulled me inside. He pulled a bag from inside his shirt and starting loading it with cigarettes and cash.

"Help me," he barked. I did what he said.

"We don't have much time," he screamed. "There's an alarm in here. In seconds, we'll hear the police."

My heart was beating, racing. I hadn't shot drugs for hours, but this was a rush too.

He finished loading the bag just as we heard the sirens. He grabbed my arm and pulled me back out the side door. "Let's go," he yelled.

Holding hands, we ran across the lot, over the hedge, across the yard, then raced to his car. He drove down side streets, quietly winding his way. About ten minutes later, he looked at me and kissed my cheek. "We made it," he said, "we're safe."

He drove back to his friend's house, where we had been before, and parked in the alley behind the house. Paul's friend opened the garage door. The entire garage was filled with merchandise. It looked like a store. Paul gave him the cigarettes. His friend gave Paul cash. Then we were off again.

At the next stop in front of a house, he left me sitting in the car. When he came out, he winked. "Now we've got coke."

We went back to his apartment. He set the bag on the table, then taught me how to mix the flaky white substance with water and inject this into my veins. Before he let me do the first hit, he cautioned me. "This can freeze your respiratory system," he said. "You have to take care of me, and I'll take care of you. Always keep hot coffee on the table in front of you when you're doing coke. If I go into respiratory arrest, pour some down my throat, and slap me on the back until I come to. I'll do the same for you."

We sat there, all night, shooting one hit after another.

I was fickle. I was in love with narcotics, but I also fell in love with coke, girl, cocaine. And in the most strange, peculiar, and dysfunctional way, I fell for Paul too.

Paul protected me. He took care of me. He said not for love, not for money, not for sex, was it okay for me to be with another man. He bought me clothes—beautiful clothes, the likes of which I'd not seen before. He bought me coats. He bathed me in jewelry and perfumes. He bought me a car, my own little Mustang—brand new at the time. He gave me money. I was always running around with at least a thousand dollars falling out of my purse.

He bought me lotions and told me to rub them on my feet, said I had to learn about taking care of myself. He said he loved me, said someday we'd settle down, get married, and we'd have a couple of kids—maybe a little boy and a little girl. He made it all okay.

Paul and I had one thing in common. We both loved to shoot

drugs. And he knew how to get all the drugs and money we needed. Although neither his divorce nor mine was final, he called me his fiancée.

ℭ

In the drug culture, there are subcultures. There are street junkies who don't work, who steal from their friends, snatch purses, and break into houses—do whatever it takes to raise money for drugs. There are junkies who mooch off other people, hang around them, beg their drug-using friends to give them drugs. There are drug addicts like Dr. Ted who pride themselves on only taking pills and gain a sense of false control that way. There are drug addicts who live in a good section of town, work normal jobs, use drugs only on the weekends, and think they're in control by doing that.

And then there was the group I ran with at the end of my drug-using career. There were only about ten members in this group. Today, all of them are dead—except me.

These men were professional thieves. They robbed drug stores, medical offices, department stores, and an occasional jewelry store too. It was easy then, because security systems were not routine equipment for merchants. The thieves were connected to people called *fences,* who took the stolen merchandise and in return gave the thieves a portion of each item's value in cash. The people in this group often spent a substantial amount of their lives in jail. They wouldn't snitch. The code was, if you got busted, you didn't tell who did what with you. You did the time. Doing time was the price these men expected to pay periodically—like a dysfunctional kind of union dues.

Sometimes, Paul would disappear for weeks at a time. I never knew where he went, or what he did. I didn't ask. He'd always leave me with more than enough money, food, and drugs. He took me to beauty shops, taught me about getting my hair done. He took me to get manicures and pedicures. Due to my drug addiction, I weighed about eighty pounds, but other than that I looked the best I had since I was twelve.

Paul didn't *deal* drugs. He *used* drugs. He stole drugs solely for the purpose of personal use. And he sold stolen merchandise to make money. He kept all the drugs he stole, willingly sharing with me a portion of whatever he had. For the first time in my drug-using career, drugs, good quality drugs, were in abundance.

About this time, I got kicked off the methadone program.

Although I had plenty of drugs most of the time, I had continued to participate in the methadone program at Mount Sinai Hospital in Minneapolis. It made sense to do that. That daily supply of methadone was a good backup, a reserve. It was like having an insurance policy for my addiction. Just in case I ran out of drugs, just in case something happened, I'd have that daily dose of methadone to keep me if not *high*, at least *well*.

This was the drill at the methadone program. You showed up, signed in, drank one day's dose in front of the staff, then waited around for half an hour or so while they observed you. If you passed all the tests, you left with your dosage for half a week.

When I went to pick up my methadone one day, the program monitoring staff pulled a surprise urinalysis on me. I knew I was in trouble. I had miscalculated. I had used drugs—a lot of drugs—right before I had left the apartment. I had shot some cocaine, then swallowed a large handful of Valium, an intoxicating tranquilizer, on the way out the door for good measure.

I drank my methadone in front of program staff and was hanging around the lobby for my required half-hour observance period. Soon the drugs I had ingested earlier began to kick in. So did the methadone. By the time the results of the urinalysis came back, showing that I was dirty—I had drugs other than methadone in my system—I had passed out from an overdose, falling onto the lobby floor.

Some time later—I had little ability to measure time other than by when it was time to get high, which was all the time—I woke up, came to. I was in a locked room strapped to a hospital bed with leather restraints.

They wouldn't let me out for two weeks. They told me I had

flunked, failed the methadone program; I was no longer an accept-able candidate, and they were kicking me off. They took me off all drugs except Thorazine, a boring, anti-psychotic medication that makes you sleepy without getting you high. I didn't go to therapy or counseling. I was stuck in bed in the locked room, watching tele-vision and reading books. When they thought I had detoxified from all the drugs in my system, they let me out.

I found Paul and told him I had lost my methadone supply. He said not to worry, he'd make sure I always had enough drugs to keep me well.

ର

Even in my stupefied state, I noticed an interesting phenomenon. For the first time in my junkie career, I had access to substantial quantities—boxes and bags—of drugs. But, no matter how many bottles of pills, no matter how much cocaine, morphine, Dilaudid, barbiturates, and Valium, no matter how vast the supply of this vir-tual pharmacy, we always ran out of drugs. First the good stuff—the Dilaudid and morphine—would disappear. Then we'd be taking the codeine just to keep from going into withdrawal, and we'd be knock-ing at a dope dealer's door, trying to buy some good stuff to get us well enough so that Paul could rob another drug store.

There was never enough—especially when the drug of choice was cocaine.

ର

One night, Paul and I got into the car and drove to a small town in southwestern Minnesota. It was about midnight. Paul kept driv-ing around and around that small town. I knew he was eyeing the drugstore. I was too. Something felt odd to me. Paul felt it too.

"We're not going to do it," he said. "Something about it just doesn't feel right." I could sense what he meant. Even in my drug-induced stupor, I could connect with the power we call intuition. The problem was, we were using it on the dark side.

We drove all night until we were in another part of the state. We rented a small motel room in a larger town toward the southern part of the state. It was Sunday morning, about 4 A.M.

Paul said he had a plan.

"This drugstore is always good for a score," he said. "It's one of my favorites. But this time, I need your help."

We got in the car and drove to the main street of town. Paul parked the car on the street in front of the parking lot next to the drugstore. He tucked three white laundry bags, a lock-puller, a hammer, and a screwdriver inside his shirt. We walked down the street, holding hands.

We stood in front of the door to the drugstore. I leaned back against the door. Paul pressed up to me, the way he had on our first date, as though we were lovers. While his arms were wrapped around me in an embrace, he pulled the lock to the front door. I could hear it pop.

We looked around; the street was quiet. We ducked into the store. He stuck the popped lock back in the door so it wouldn't look suspicious if the police drove by, then he closed the door.

I followed him behind the counter to the cabinets where the class A narcotics were kept. I wasn't high. We had run out of good drugs. But I felt a rush of fear that lasted and lasted and lasted and competed with any cocaine high I had ever experienced as we crept around the inside of that dark store.

This was a rush almost like shooting drugs. It was an adrenaline high.

We scooped up all the narcotics we could find. Then Paul said we were going to take one more minute and pop the safe. "There's always cash inside," he said. "Plus, pharmacists usually keep a little cocaine in the safe too. You've got to be careful," he warned. "They keep a vial of tear gas behind the lock. It'll spill when I pop the lock. We'll have to hold our breath, and we'll only have that much time to get the contents from the safe and the other drugs out of the store."

He stuck the screwdriver into the lock on the safe and hit it with the hammer. "Bingo," he said, opening the door. Tear gas flooded through the room.

I held my breath, squinting. Paul scooped up all the contents of the safe, throwing cash, bottles, and containers indiscriminately into the bag I was holding. He grabbed the other two laundry bags and we ran to the front door.

"Shhh," he said. "Just a minute." He scanned the street for headlights or people. It looked quiet. He opened the door and we walked out. He shut the door carefully, putting the popped lock in place. "I don't want anybody to know this store's been broken into until they show up for work this morning," he said.

By then, the sun was beginning to light the morning sky. We walked down the sidewalk toward the car.

"Give me the keys," Paul said.

"I don't have them," I said. "You do."

For the first time since I'd met this man, right there on that street, I understood why they called him "Animal." He started screaming and carrying on like a crazed beast.

This was our first fight. I tried to remain calm. I would certainly know if I had the keys.

"Check the pockets in your pants," I said.

By this time, the slumbering city was beginning to wake up. Cars were driving by.

"I already checked. They're not there," he said.

"Well, you missed them," I said. "Check again."

He swore, said the "gd" words. Then he apologized to God for taking His name in vain. Paul stood right there on that street, looked up at the sky, and said, "I'm sorry, God."

Then he checked his pockets again—his shirt pockets, his front pants pockets, then his back pants pocket. When he pulled his right hand out of his back pocket, he was holding the car keys.

"I told you," I said.

He unlocked the car. "Get in."

We drove to the room we had rented and brought our score

inside. This was a big one. We sat down at a table, looking at, touching, arranging all the bottles, oohing and ahhing at all the good stuff we had.

"Shit," Paul said. "Shit."

"What's the matter?" I asked.

"We forgot to get needles." he said. "We have to go back."

By now, it was 6 A.M. The city would be awake by now. This was cutting it too close for me. I told him I couldn't do it, said I was too scared, he had to go alone. He said he needed my help to get in. I followed him to the car, got in, we drove back to the drugstore, parked the car, walked back to the door acting like a kissing couple, opened the door, went inside, closed the door, got a box of insulin syringes, ran to the door, peeked out, opened the door, left the door open and the popped lock popped, raced down the sidewalk to the car, and squealed away, around the corner, back to the motel, up to the room, right to the table with all those drugs—almost enough drugs to last the rest of our lives—and started shooting dope.

That was one of our best scores. We drove back to Minneapolis that same morning, then sat around my apartment, the sweet little place Mother had helped me find. I can't remember sleeping, I can't remember eating—all I remember is using drugs, passing out for brief periods of time, then waking up and using some more. We had a bottle of liquid Dilaudid cough syrup in the corner of the room on the floor. It was a gallon jug. Whenever we walked by, we took a swig. It was preventive medicine—prevented us from ever getting sick in case we passed out and fell asleep for too long. The rest of the time we sat shooting needles full of drugs into our arms.

I learned this about drug scores. You organize the contents when you get home. There's the top-of-the-line stuff—the Dilaudid and the morphine, the good dope that gives you a good high. Then there's the pills, the stuff Dr. Ted had. Then there's the grunge stuff, like codeine—that doesn't really get you high, but in an emergency, will keep you from getting sick. The other stuff you throw away—carefully—so the police don't trace the robbery to you.

I watched, over the weeks, as the supply of good stuff went down. Pretty soon, we were down to popping pills. Then, we started shooting the codeine—a painful, unfulfilling high that made your veins burn, your face flush, and barely gave you a rush.

For Paul, codeine wouldn't do. He did another robbery. And another. Sometimes, he brought me along. But he never took me inside again. Occasionally, he'd have me wait in the car, slumped down behind the wheel. Then when he came out carrying the white laundry bags he'd jump in the passenger side, and I'd drive us away. Sometimes, he'd leave me at home—waiting, worrying, and wondering.

ભ

Then we started a new phase.

Paul and I both liked opiates—Dilaudid and morphine—the stuff that made you nod. Besides being addicted to opiates, which we both were, Paul liked cocaine. I did too. When I had first begun using drugs, heroin and cocaine weren't that popular. People on the streets had been using marijuana, LSD, popping speed, popping pills. Then, heroin grow in popularity. And soon, a lot of people on the streets were using cocaine too. That meant, just like with heroin, that the quality of the coke you could buy had gone down. When only a handful of people in the drug culture were using cocaine, it was like a delicacy. A treat. The people who sold and bought it were sometimes concerned with quality. Now that all the junkies were into it, dealers were scamming and scheming, cutting it with additives. The quality of the cocaine on the street was extremely poor; we were used to the best.

Paul said he had a plan. He knew how to get good coke and get plenty of it for us. One evening we drove to a three-story Victorian house in South Minneapolis where we picked up Darrell James, a man I had never met before. He was a quiet guy with bushy hair and a bulbous nose. He didn't look thin enough to be a junkie. He looked like an accountant. He got into the front seat with Paul. They made me sit in the back. Then we drove to one of the largest medical office buildings in the Twin Cities area. Paul and Darrell parked the car a block away and told me to crouch down on the floor and watch out the window. When I saw them walking toward the car, I was supposed to climb into the front seat and drive away the instant they were both safely inside.

I couldn't imagine what they were after in this building. There was no pharmacy inside.

What I learned that evening was that ear, nose and throat doctors were among the few medical professionals who had a legitimate use for cocaine. They carried large supplies of it in their offices—pure, liquid cocaine. Because it was pharmaceutical cocaine, the quality was guaranteed and controlled.

When we returned to Darrell's house, we went inside and divided it up. They insisted I take a one-third share. They even had a doctor's bag for me. I filled it up with bottle, after bottle, after bottle, after bottle, of pure liquid coke.

I looked into *my* doctor's bag. I could not imagine using all this cocaine and running out. I had seen a lot of cocaine before—thousands and thousands of dollars worth—but never this much.

It was all mine.

This was the turning point for me.

It was the beginning of the end.

಄

I remember sitting at a table, day after day, sometimes for weeks, doing one hit of cocaine after another. Even my junkie friends began to worry about me. "You've got to eat, Melody," Paul would hammer at me. "You've got to sleep," he said. "You can't just sit there using drugs."

"Yes, I can," I said. "Watch."

My body was starting to break down from using all this coke. My veins began to collapse and disappear. I'd stick the needle in, draw blood, push on the plunger, then I'd hear a whooshing sound and the vein would be gone. I had scabs and scars running in triplicate the entire length of my arms. Soon, I found myself running out of veins. The only way I could shoot drugs was to blindly stab the needle deep into my arm—sometimes five, ten or twenty times— hoping to accidentally hit a vein.

It was like playing darts. The target was my arm.

By now, I barely got high anymore. I'd feel a buzz from the cocaine, a ringing in my ears, then the feeling would disappear and I'd start preparing the next hit.

The first time I had a cocaine-induced convulsion, it startled me. I was shooting coke, shooting coke, shooting coke—obsessively and compulsively and addictively shooting coke—when everything went black. When I came to consciousness, Paul had a spoon in my mouth. He said I had had a convulsion. I saw fear in his eyes. He said he was taking me to the hospital. I refused, sat up, looked for a syringe, and immediately started shooting coke again.

I also discovered that using this much cocaine neutralized or countered the opiates in my system. To do this much cocaine, I had to regularly inject opiates into my system just to keep from going through opiate withdrawal.

One day, after a two-week no-food, no-sleep run with coke, I passed out on a couch at Tommy's house. He was one of Paul's friends, a quiet, friendly drug addict and thief who lived in a respectable Minneapolis suburb. I don't know how long I slept. Maybe days. Usually, I tried not to fall asleep for too long so I wouldn't go into withdrawal while I slept. This time I erred. I miscalculated. I slept way too long. Went way too many hours without putting drugs into my body. My body needed drugs the way most people need water and air.

When I opened my eyes, I couldn't move. I couldn't move one bone, one muscle, one extremity of my body. I tried to move my eyes to look around the room. I could see I was on a couch. But I was paralyzed from the deepest state of withdrawal from narcotics I had ever known.

So this is what it feels like to be a junkie.

This thought was conscious and clear.

The little girl that got the good grades and went to a private high school and played piano at the recitals had finally and unquestionably achieved her goal.

I had pinched myself hard this time. And for the first time, I knew I was real—a real-life, full-blown, completely addicted dope fiend.

Later, I don't know how much later, Tommy walked into the room. I couldn't open my mouth to talk. He instantly understood what was going on. He filled a syringe with morphine, knelt down beside the couch, tied off my arm, and tried to pop up a vein.

"Jeez, girl, what have you done to yourself?" he said. "You don't have any veins left. I can't get in."

I couldn't speak.

Tommy knew I was in trouble, knew I was really sick. "Sorry, kid. I have to do this," he said. Then he stuck the needle in a vein in my neck and pushed in the plunger.

In an instant, I was well.

℘

It was a fall day—late November, maybe early December—when the end crashed in.

I wore high boots because they were practical. I could sit at home and fill syringes with opiates and cocaine, cap them off, and stick them inside my boots. My next hit of dope was always ready and near. I got in my Mustang, my boots loaded with drugs, and decided to drive over to Darrell's house to see what was going on.

Darrell and Paul had been burglarizing a lot of stores lately. At the moment, we were on top. We had damn near enough coke and opiates to last us until the end of the world. When I got to Darrell's house, I pounded on the door.

"Who is it?" he asked.

"Melody," I said.

I didn't hear any answer. I stood there waiting. "Come on in," he finally yelled.

I walked through the door and into the living room. Darrell sat quietly on the couch. His expression was a little odd, but he always looked odd to me—sullen, almost depressed. I remember noticing his posture and thinking that the way he was sitting was odd too. He was sitting slumped back on the couch with his hands behind his back. Another man, one I hadn't met before, walked into the room. We each nodded and said hi. He was a good-looking guy, another strawberry blonde.

I headed for the stairway leading to the second floor. "Going to use the bathroom," I said. "I'll be right back." I bounded up the steps. I felt happy. I had clothes, money, a car, and drugs. I had a boyfriend who was good to me. Life couldn't get much better than this. I walked into the tiny bathroom, closed the door behind me, and sat down on the floor. I unzipped my right boot, and took out a preprepared syringe of liquid cocaine.

Then I took off my belt, looped it tightly around my upper arm and stabbed where I thought a deep vein might be. I pulled back on the plunger. Blood. I got lucky this time. I was in on the first try.

The door to the bathroom burst open. One man pushed his way in. Another man stood behind him. They each held a gun—aimed at me. The man who had barged in on me held the gun right next to my head.

"Police. Put your hands up. You're under arrest."

Put my hands up? I had just found a vein. If I was going to jail, I was going to have this last fix.

"Put your hands up or we'll blow out your brains," he screamed.

"Just a minute," I said. "I'm almost done."

Darrell went to prison. Darrell wasn't a stand-up guy, a guy with heart. To get his sentence reduced, he turned Paul in. Paul was already on parole, so this time they refused to give him bail. He went to prison too.

They locked me up for a while, until I was detoxified from drugs. Then they put me on probation and sentenced me again to go to the small town of Mora, up north where my mother lived. "If we even hear that you were in the Twin Cities for ten minutes, you'll be arrested and sent to jail," they told me. "If you get a traffic ticket, a parking ticket, you're going to go to jail, and your probation will be revoked. If you even think about using drugs, you're going to go to jail."

"Okay, okay," I said. "I'll be good."

"And we're going to take pictures of your arms. We'll be using the pictures in the Minnesota school system as part of our drug prevention program," they added.

"Agreed," I said.

After spending six months in the town of Mora, I began to wish they had sent me to jail. For a while I lived with my mother, then I got a job as a waitress in a local café and rented a small apartment in the heart of town.

I wasn't dead. And I wasn't alive. Occasionally, I found someone who smoked marijuana, but these people were social users. They liked to drink a beer, smoke a joint, get high, and listen to music. It was like eating a hamburger and calling it a steak dinner, compared to where I had been. The amount of drugs that these people had ingested in their entire lives was the amount I had been used to taking in a week. So I went back to the beginning, the beginning of my addiction career.

I started drinking again.

But it was different this time around. I didn't get high from drinking. Didn't even get a warm buzz. I could drink two beers, not feel anything, and then I'd go directly into a blackout state. Apparently I'd be walking around, talking and functioning, but the next day I couldn't remember what I'd said, what I'd done, or where I'd been.

I woke up one morning in a trailer house in bed next to some man I didn't know. I felt revolted, disgusted, and frightened. My clothes were mussed from sleeping but at least I was fully dressed. As I ran out the door, he asked me if I wanted to see him again. I yelled back no.

I couldn't remember where I met him or how I had gotten there.

ᘔ

One morning, I got up early, took the bus to the Twin Cities, and went to the house of some friends, a married couple I had known from the methadone program. I was violating my probation but I was willing to take that chance. I talked them into selling me a bottle of their methadone. At least if I took that, I could get legitimately loaded for twenty-four hours instead of enduring whatever was happening to me when I drank.

"Don't take it all at once," my friend warned. "It's a big dose. You haven't been using for a while."

"Yeah, right," I said.

I waited until the bus got almost back to Mora, then started drinking the bottle of methadone. I waited a little while. Nothing happened. I drank some more, then waited a little while longer. I still didn't feel anything. Then I finished the entire bottle. Still nothing! I had gotten ripped off. I didn't even feel high.

I had forgotten about the different routes of ingestion. Ingestion through the stomach takes longer. Methadone lasts longer, but it can be slower acting. It creeps up on you. When the effects of the methadone started coming on, after I got back to my apartment, I knew I was in trouble. I couldn't see. I could barely walk. It was all I could do to lie on the floor and hold my head up. I just wanted to pass out, go to sleep. I had drunk too much. I couldn't check in for an overdose. They'd put me in jail. Put me away.

I crawled over to the bathtub and filled it with cold water, enough to cover my body but hopefully not enough to drown in if I passed out. Then I started my routine. I'd drag my body into the bathtub, lie in the cold water long enough to shock my system, then I'd pull myself out and lie on the floor next to the tub. When I'd start to pass out again, I'd crawl back into the tub. At seven o'clock in the morning, while I was lying on the bathroom floor shaking and soaking wet, the door to my apartment opened.

Mother walked in.

She looked at me. "Did you forget? Today's your court date. I'm here to pick you up."

I had forgotten. Well, I hadn't really. Today was the temporary custody hearing for my son John. Mother was pushing me to fight for custody of my son. I knew I couldn't do that. I was doing too much wrong. I couldn't take care of a child. Even if I won, which I wouldn't, I couldn't put a child through living with me.

We went to court. The judge took one look at me, a brief look, and then awarded temporary custody to John's father.

I was allowed to visit my son for a moment. He was only three. We went into the attorney's office. This little boy, this child whom I insisted had a right to live, looked at me. I said I was sorry. I said that in my strange, odd, horrible way, I did love him. I took his hand, walked him across the hall to the room where his father and his father's attorneys were. Then I let go of John's hand and gave him to his dad.

That night, when I got back to Mora, I went out and got drunk.

That's when I came up with my plan. Somehow, some way, for the next week, I was going to stay straight. I was going to stop drinking. Stop using all drugs. Not a sip of beer. Not one pill. Not one joint. I was going to stop getting high. The next morning, I opened my eyes and vowed I wasn't going to use. It was the first time I had ever tried to do this.

My plan lasted two hours. By noon, I was sitting in the town bar drinking whiskey sours. I couldn't help it.

I battled with alcohol and drugs for several days. I'd try to not use, but it didn't work. My resolve to not use would disappear, diminish, the moment someone handed me pills or a joint. Or I'd walk straight to a bar, telling myself I was just going to go in, play a few songs on the jukebox, and drink a Coca-Cola. Before I knew it, I'd have a glass of whiskey in my hand and a bottle in my purse for later at home.

Finally, I gave up trying to stay straight.

I didn't understand why some people could just stop using, or could use differently than I did. I didn't understand how some people could just not use at all. What I really didn't understand is why everybody else didn't want to stay high or drunk all the time like me.

I didn't understand what was the matter with me, what the problem was, why I was so different from the people around me. The difference between other people and me had been obvious to me all my life. For a while, in the drug culture in Minneapolis, those differences became diminished. I was around other people like me. Now, here in Mora, I became acutely aware again of how odd I was.

I didn't belong in this town. I had no friends. I couldn't even find peers among the alcohol and drug users. They didn't drink and use drugs the way I did. I didn't have a place. I couldn't get high. I couldn't stay clean. Nothing worked anymore.

I didn't have the courage to kill myself but I wanted to die. *The easiest way to end my life,* I thought, *is to just keep drinking and using drugs.*

That night, as I walked down the side of the two-lane highway on my way home, I looked up and saw the night sky. I hadn't seen the sky, the moon, or the stars for a long time, for years. For just a moment, it felt like I touched something bigger than me. It was an odd feeling, but not a bad feeling. It was like I was touching the edge of something. I didn't understand what it meant. I shrugged it off. I didn't know it then, but an event horizon had just appeared.

A few days later, I came up with my plan.

I'd go to a doctor's office in a neighboring town. I'd work him for whatever drugs I could get out of him. I knew how to do that. I knew what I wanted—a big handful of Valium and barbiturates. This was still the early seventies. It would be easy. All I needed to do was tell the doctor I had a lot of anxiety during the day and couldn't sleep at night. I knew he'd give me the pills.

That was step one. I executed it masterfully, leaving the doctor's office with a prescription for Valium and Seconal, a strong sleeping pill. The problem with sleeping pills was that they didn't put me to sleep. They intoxicated me, and I stayed awake and kept taking more. That night I went to my apartment and took a handful of both pills. I didn't feel high because pills didn't make me feel high anymore, but I felt a little more screwed up than I usually did.

Now I was ready for the second part of my plan. I carefully gathered all the tools I could find: a screwdriver, a hammer, and a few kitchen utensils for good measure. I had seen Paul break into stores many times. Now, I was going to try it too.

I would climb to the roof of the local drugstore, jimmy open the ventilation cover, and slide in. I'd either break into the pharmacy and get all the drugs I needed to stay high, or they'd arrest me and put me in jail. Either way—high or in jail—I'd be more at home than I felt here. It was time to move on. Whatever happened, I won, because even if I went to jail, I knew I could get them to give me some drugs.

I was obviously more stoned on the tranquilizers and sleeping pills than I thought I was. Junkies are always more screwed up than they think, have less control than they think they do. The world just looks normal through their eyes because they're used to seeing it screwed up.

I got to the main street of town and scoped out the situation. It was about eleven o'clock at night. I couldn't see any cars or people. The little town looked quiet, asleep—except for me. I walked around to the back of the pharmacy, a large brick building. Then I climbed up the metal ladder attached to the back wall and hoisted myself onto the roof. I looked around and spotted what looked like the cover to the ventilation system. I sat down in front of it and began rummaging through my bag, trying to find just the right tool. A screwdriver would be perfect. I pulled it out and started to pry off the vent.

All at once, that town lit up. It seemed like someone was holding a big spotlight on this corner of the block. Dogs began howling. People started screaming.

By now the barbiturates and tranquilizers had kicked in. I had taken so many of them I could hardly walk or think to process the situation. I dropped the screwdriver, stood up, and stumbled over to the side of the roof to see what the fuss was about.

Deputies and policemen surrounded the entire building. Each of them was pointing a gun or a rifle. At me.

"Put your hands up or we'll shoot."

"What?" I said, peering over the edge of the roof.

"Get up there and get her down before she falls," I heard someone say.

They took me to a local hospital. They did this because I told them I was a junkie, and I was sick. When I got to the hospital, the doctors wouldn't give me any drugs. They locked me in a room and told me if I was going to be sick, I could be sick in that room until I went to court.

I was infuriated. My plan hadn't worked. I wasn't high. And I wasn't in Minneapolis, stoned, in jail. I was in Mora, sober, in a hospital. I felt a rage rip through me—an aggression and hostility and hatred such as I had never before felt. That's another thing about barbiturates. When you come down off them, you get mean, crazy, mad. I felt like a caged animal. I tore the mattress off the bed and pulled a spring off the side—a two-foot metal spring with a pointy end. And when the doctors walked into the room, a short time later, I lunged at them.

The doctors backed up. "Put it down and get in bed," one of them said.

I wouldn't put it down. I wouldn't let the doctors touch me. I wouldn't be quiet. I wouldn't go to bed.

That's why they wrapped me in chains, from the neck down, put me in the back of an ambulance, and took me to Hennepin County jail. Although I was no longer addicted to opiates because I hadn't been able to get any while I lived in Mora, I lied to the jail staff. I told them I was addicted and was going to go through withdrawal right there in that jail if they didn't get me some methadone. The jail doctor prescribed a minimal dose. I felt a little something, but not much. I wasn't surprised. Drugs and alcohol didn't work like that for me anymore. Although I had been using some form of alcohol and drugs daily for the last twelve years, I couldn't remember the last time I got *high*.

I hoped this judge would be lenient with me, let me off, but I didn't know what to expect. I didn't know where I could possibly go next. Even if this judge let me off, I couldn't go back to Mora to live.

I didn't have a plan anymore.

That's why that judge was so upset, so furious, so absolutely done with me. That's why, as I stood there in my light blue percale good-girl dress, he scowled and frowned and never once bothered to ask what a nice girl like me was doing in a mess like this.

"So what will it be, Miss Vaillancourt? State prison for five years? Or drug treatment at the state hospital for as long as it takes."

It wasn't that I didn't *want* to get straight. I didn't *know* what straight was. I had tried not using in Mora. It didn't work. There was no one inside me except the junkie I had become. I couldn't remember drawing a sober breath. Drugs, heroin, Dilaudid, cocaine, were as essential to my being as air, water, and blood. I couldn't remember being straight. I couldn't recall life without at least trying to get screwed up and get high. This world, this drug culture I had found, was the only world I knew. And this junkie I had become was all there was left of me.

State prison? Or treatment?

I was being sentenced to death.

"Okay," I said. "I'll go to treatment."

ℭ

Although I had been hospitalized throughout my drug-using career for brief periods of time, I had never been to treatment before. The place the judge was sending me wasn't an ordinary treatment center like the rehabilitation centers that are available today. It was a state hospital that in those days housed mentally and emotionally incapacitated people in the state along with the truly insane. It was set up like a large campus, with a receiving center and small dormitories called cottages scattered throughout the grounds. Most of the cottages were used to house the mentally insane patients. A few of the cottages were reserved for drug addicts and alcoholics.

Anyway, I thought, leaving the courtroom and getting into the deputy's car, surely I'll know some other junkies up at Willmar State Hospital, other junkies who have been sent there too. They'll have drugs. Soon I'll be high.

Rehabilitation consisted of attending a one-hour lecture each morning at 9:00 A.M., attending two meetings of Alcoholics Anonymous each week—people from the community came to the hospital and put the meetings on in the auditorium—attending two therapy groups each week, and meeting for at least one hour each week for individual counseling with a chemical dependency counselor.

I had a strange feeling in that sheriff's car, as we drove the several-hour drive from Minneapolis to Willmar, a small town located in the western Minnesota. I felt like I was going to Bible camp again.

When I arrived at the hospital, I was locked in a hospital room in the receiving center. I had to stay in bed and wear pajamas for a few days. I went three days running without drugs and without alcohol.

I started to have thoughts, think about things. Something else happened to me too. At first it felt like sludge kicking loose. Then it felt tingly. Then it felt like more sludge. I didn't know what it was then, but I know now. I was having emotions. Feelings.

I was beginning to come alive.

There was a long underground tunnel connecting the cottages with the dining area of the hospital. Although the alcoholics and addicts had their own cottages, all the people in the hospital ate together in the main dining room. One way to get to the dining room was to walk through the underground tunnel. The first time I used the tunnel, I saw two hospital attendants carrying a huge basket. Inside laid a grown human being, all gnarled up and deformed with the biggest head I had ever seen. He was moaning and flailing, grabbing at the air.

Oh, I thought. *That's where the phrase basket case comes from.*

At the cafeteria, patients had to stand in line, walk past a buffet, and make selections of hot dish, vegetables, salad, and Jell-O to put on their trays. The first time I had a meal in that cafeteria, I got in line and took my place with all the other patients in the hospital. Some of them were talking to no one or talking to someone I couldn't see. Some of them had heads way too large for their bodies. Some smelled bad. Some of them drooled. Some swiped at the air with their hands, like they were trying to catch an imaginary fly.

I was so hungry, for the first time in a long time, until I got to that line. Then I stood there looking. I just looked at the people in front of me in that line. Then I looked at the people behind me in that line.

This time I had pinched myself too hard.

Being a drug addict wasn't fun anymore. I was one of these people in line.

Something had happened to these people, the mentally retarded and the mentally incompetent patients in this place. Some force outside of them, something they couldn't help had made them this sick, this grossly and hideously ill. They couldn't help it. They were here for life. They didn't have a choice.

But me, I had done this to myself. I had gotten myself here, all on my own.

Ơ

I was right when I figured that I'd probably run into some junkies up here that I knew. There were other junkies here and some were people that knew people I knew. Occasionally I could get something—some pills or a joint. The problem was, I was clean and sober most of the time. And I was clean and sober not because I wanted to be, but because I couldn't get my hands on that many drugs in that hospital. I was becoming frustrated. I was obsessing about getting high all the time. I couldn't stop thinking about it.

I shared a small bedroom in the cottage with a woman named Jennifer. She had short, ash-blonde hair, a pretty face, and a good spirit. She was two years younger than I was, but she had heart. I knew she was thinking about getting high a lot too. Everyone in our cottage was thinking about getting high or drunk. After lunch one day, I pulled Jennifer into the room and sat her down on the bed.

I had a plan and I needed her help.

"I've heard you can get high on nutmeg if you eat a lot of it," I said. "So this is what we're going to do. We'll sneak into the kitchen, steal a can and eat nutmeg until we get high."

We crept into the kitchen. I watched the doorway, then pointed her toward the nutmeg. She snatched the can off the shelf and we ran back to our room. I poured out the contents on a paper towel, dividing the nutmeg in two unequal piles. I told her I needed more because I had used more drugs than she had.

We ate as much nutmeg as we could. It tasted bad. Stuck in our mouths like sawdust. We ate nutmeg, washed it down with water, then ate some more nutmeg until our piles were gone. It did alter my state of mind somewhat, but by the farthest stretch of my imagination, it didn't qualify as getting high. It was like taking Thorazine. I felt sleepy and stupid, but I didn't get a buzz. And we were so groggy we could barely move, talk, or get out of bed.

We slept that afternoon, that evening, and all night long. The next morning when the cottage nurse banged on our door to wake us up, we wanted to sleep some more.

Each weekday, besides attending morning lecture and any sched-uled therapy groups, patients in the chemical dependency treatment program were assigned—and expected to go to—a job in the hospi-tal. It was considered rehabilitation for the patients, and it allowed us to make $5 a week for spending money. Jennifer worked in the kitchen. Because of my typing and shorthand skills, I was assigned to work as a secretary for the hospital priest, Father Garvey. It was time to get up, go to morning lecture, and then go to our jobs.

I lay there. Jennifer lay there. "You have to get up," I said. "If we both miss morning lecture and our jobs, they'll know some-thing's up."

"Why do I have to be the one to go to work?" she asked.

"Because," I said. "I'm older than you."

For most of that week, we burped nutmeg. We decided not to use it anymore.

I had another plan.

I had heard you could get high by inhaling aerosol deodorant. Apparently if you sprayed it into a bag, then inhaled the fumes, you'd get a buzz. Jennifer stole a plastic bag from the kitchen. Then we bought a can of spray deodorant from the canteen and sprayed a long spray of it into the plastic bag. I held the end of the bag to my nose and inhaled deeply. At the moment of inhalation, it felt like someone took a hammer and slammed me on the head.

I had one more plan.

This one involved nasal inhalants that came in little tubes like ChapStick tubes. If you inhaled the fumes, they would clear your nose. But I heard that if you broke open the tube and swal-lowed the core, you could get high. It was supposed to feel like taking speed.

Jennifer and I saved our money that week. We didn't buy any candy or sodas. On Saturday, our group was allowed to go to town on the hospital bus with a counselor and go shopping. I slipped away from the counselor and bought two inhalants. When we got back to our room at the hospital, we broke them open, took out the insides, then chewed and swallowed the cores. It tasted and felt like eating Vicks. I didn't feel high. I felt sick.

Being a drug addict was becoming a lot of hard work.

I was getting tired.

Maybe I could marry a doctor, I thought that night, right before falling asleep. *Then he could write out prescriptions for me all the time. Or maybe I could move to South America and get a job in the fields picking the cocoa plants and eat the leaves all day and all night long.*

℞

I sat on the edge of the bed in the small room I shared with Jennifer. This time, I hadn't horrified the people around me. I had scared myself.

I had just finished meeting with my probation officer. He had scheduled a visit with me at the hospital, one of the only two visits I would have from anybody in the outside world for the eight months I was confined there. Yesterday, the day before his visit—of all days—was the day I made my biggest drug score yet since I had been in treatment. A friend of a drug addict I had known on the streets had come floating through the hospital. He'd come up here to get straight and had a big stash of pills. He had gotten them past the receiving center and past the Nazi Gestapo check-in nurse who worked the cottage front desk.

When I asked him if he *had anything,* he knew what I meant.

"Be right back," he had said.

A few minutes later, he reappeared and placed an envelope containing twelve amphetamines in my hand.

I tried to act nonchalant as I sauntered back to my room, trying to decide what to do with my stash. If I got caught with these, I'd not only get kicked out of this treatment center for violating the rules, I would go to jail.

I scanned my room, looking for the best hiding place. Then I grabbed the radio on the nightstand, removed the batteries, and put the envelope of amphetamines where the batteries had been. I replaced the battery cover and put the radio on the top shelf of the closet, sticking a few sweaters and a pair of jeans in front of it.

I couldn't take any pills now, couldn't get high now. My counselor, Ruth, was in the building. She'd catch on to me. She was sharp, to the point, and didn't pull any punches. And I couldn't take drugs around Gene, one of the attendants on the floor who worked the three-to-eleven shift. Whenever he looked at me, I felt like he saw right through me. There was something different about these people who worked here, something different about the relationships I was forming with them. For the first time in my life, it didn't feel right to be fucked up, high, stoned, around people who cared about me.

I didn't even want Jennifer to know I had these pills, for two reasons. First, I didn't want to share. Second, I was beginning to believe that Jennifer deserved a chance to be rehabilitated. I didn't want to be involved with helping her get high anymore because I believed that was a hurtful thing to do to her. What surprised me, what baffled and amazed me, was that the second reason was stronger than the first. These periodic episodes of sobriety, even though they were involuntary and forced upon me by my inability to get enough drugs to get high, were having an effect on me. Sobriety was affecting the way I thought, believed, and behaved.

I was beginning to feel guilt and fear. And I was regaining the first glimmers of something, a part of me I had lost a long time ago.

My conscience was coming back.

So, I'd have to get high by myself. Later. Another day. After my appointment with my probation officer.

Well, maybe I could take one pill now, I thought, pulling out the radio, opening the battery case, and removing a pill from the envelope. I popped a Dexedrine capsule into my mouth and swallowed it without water. I started to replace the battery cover, then changed my mind. *Better take one more,* I thought, *for good measure. I won't even feel the effects from one.* I swallowed one more pill, and not as carefully this time, put the radio back in the closet.

By 2 A.M., I had swallowed all the amphetamines hidden in the radio. The closet was a mess. The cord was hanging down from the top shelf of the closet. The battery cover and empty envelope were lying on the floor.

And I was wide awake, bug-eyed, watching the clock, watching Jennifer sleep, and waiting for my probation officer.

Something strange happened to me in the middle of the night, something that scared me.

I realized I wasn't choosing to get high. I didn't have any choice at all.

Those pills had called my name, called out to me, all afternoon and evening. Even though my freedom, my life, was at stake, I couldn't refuse their call. What had those people been talking about in those groups, those boring ridiculous meetings the treatment center had forced me to attend?

"We admitted we were powerless over alcohol—that our lives had become unmanageable."

That wasn't entirely correct, I thought, watching the sunrise.

I'm powerless over drugs too.

I made it through my meeting with my probation officer, a friendly man in his mid-thirties. I didn't talk much. I let him do the talking, agreeing with everything he said. I became painfully aware of what it meant to be and feel paranoid. I was fearful and anxiety-ridden that every thought and feeling I had would become obvious to him and everyone around me.

When the meeting ended, I raced for my room.

My counselor, Ruth, a solid tall woman of Minnesota stock stopped me in the hallway. "How'd it go?" she asked.

"Fine," I said, averting her gaze.

I'm letting everyone down, I thought, closing the door to my room and sitting on my bed. My counselor, Ruth. Gene, the attendant on the ward. My probation officer. And probably most of all, myself.

Getting high isn't even that much fun anymore. All this consciousness, all this awareness, ruined any buzz I was getting from drugs, when I could get a buzz. I didn't even like feeling this way, feeling drugs in my system. I didn't understand what was happening. Where was the junkie I used to be? Where did she go? Who was this person inside me? Was there anyone there? Anyone at all?

Even though I wanted to be a junkie, set out to be that, made it my goal, and even deluded myself into thinking that I was choosing to get high, I had long ago crossed the line of being able to choose. My behavior was compulsive, addictive, totally out of control.

The insane thing about being an addict is that each next step I had taken in my life since I had been twelve seemed perfectly natural and logical to me—the next thing to do and be. I hadn't seen or noticed how crazy and out of control I was. All I could see was the next pill, drink, or shot of anything that remotely promised to get me high.

This is crazy, I thought. Getting high on those stupid pills when doing that could put me in jail for five years is insane, totally crazy, unmanageable behavior.

For the first time I saw and understood how insane my behavior was.

And I was scared.

What was even crazier was the realization that I still didn't know how to stop using drugs.

That's when it happened.

I looked up, looked up the exact same way I had looked at the sky twelve years ago on my way to church. The only difference now was that I looked at the ceiling in my bedroom in the cottage at the drug treatment program at Willmar State Hospital, instead of looking up at the sun.

"God," I said. "I don't know if you're there or not. I don't know if you can hear me or even care about me anymore. But if you are there and if you are real and if there's a program here that can help me stop using drugs, please help me get it."

That's all I said.

❧

Sometimes we make a decision and that decision—that impacted concrete string of words that turns into a sentence—alters our destiny. It swoops down into the fields of the universe and cuts us a clear path—for good or for ill.

God created a world with thought and belief.

That's how we help create our world too.

It is so rare that we see how A links to B, the cause and effect between our words, our beliefs, and the reality of physical events in our lives. It's only later, after the fact, in retrospect, that the connection becomes clear.

My life changed for the better, the day I decided to believe in God again. I can't tell you the exact moment and day the changes began to manifest. But I can show you, if you'd like to look, where those changes led.

ᙅ

I was sitting on the lawn at Willmar State Hospital. I had scored again. A joint. One stick of marijuana rolled up and ready for me to smoke. I had fulfilled all my obligations for the day—been to morning lecture, did some typing for Father Garvey, and eaten my lunch. Nobody would miss me the rest of the day. They'd probably think I was out here meditating or praying.

By now, it was fall. The leaves on the massive oak trees had turned yellow, red, and orange. The surface of the lake across the highway was still. Soon it would change to a sheet of ice. I'd been through the intense heat, the mosquitoes, the flies, and the humidity of the summer. I'd probably be here for the three feet of snow and subzero temperatures of winter too.

I pulled out a book of matches, put the joint in my mouth, struck a match, and inhaled deeply on the marijuana stick.

When my lungs were filled, filled to the point of bursting, I lay back on the grass and exhaled. My eyes wandered to the biggest fluff of white cloud I could see in the sky. *I wonder what that cloud can turn into if I stare hard enough,* I thought.

The blue from the sky, the white from the cloud, began to mesh into a purple color, a purple haze. One moment, it was a sky with clouds and I was an addict smoking a joint.

The next moment, the heavens seemed to open up. It was as if God Himself were in the molecules of that purple haze, that blue sky filled with fluffy white clouds. It was as if God reached down through those molecules and touched my heart. It was as if I were one with the power, the force I felt.

At that moment, I knew that I knew that I knew that God was real.

And I knew that I had no right to keep doing this to myself, ingesting chemicals into my body, the way I had done for so many years, the way I was still doing, right now, on the lawn at this chemical dependency treatment center.

I took one more hit off that joint.

Then I stood up, dropped the joint on the ground, crushed it into the lawn with my shoe, and walked into that treatment center with a new resolve.

It's hard to explain a spiritual awakening to someone on the outside, just like it's hard to explain the compulsion to use dope when using makes your whole life painful and everything starts falling apart. But in that moment on the lawn at Willmar State Hospital, I knew that God was real and my time as a junkie was done.

I couldn't tell anybody what had happened on the lawn. I figured it best to keep it to myself that the sky had turned purple and I had seen God. I was already incarcerated by the criminal justice system in a mental institution for an indefinite length of time. If I relayed this experience to anybody, they'd never let me out.

But I began to change, even though I didn't tell anybody what had happened. I didn't know it at the time, didn't understand what was taking place, but I was beginning to learn about power. And the power I was learning about was the power of admitting powerlessness, the power of admitting defeat.

I was experiencing a psychic transformation. For so many years, people had been yammering at me to change and do the right behaviors—get a decent job and don't use drugs. Well, I hadn't been able to change my behavior. But I had experienced a change of heart. And new behaviors began to spring naturally, well, almost naturally, out of that.

A few days later, I was standing outside by the tennis courts. The man who had given me the amphetamines walked up to me and casually offered me a handful of pills. My right hand reached out to take them. With my left hand, I pushed back my right hand.

"No thanks," I said. "I don't do that anymore."

He looked at me strangely, shrugged his shoulders, and then walked away. I was amazed and horrified at what I had just done. This was the first time in my life I had turned down drugs.

The staff in the treatment program had been hammering at me that I needed to talk about my feelings, talk about them instead of acting out, talk about them before I acted out. I went inside the treatment center, grabbed one of the other patients, someone I knew was trying to stay straight, and asked if I could talk for a while. I said I had some feelings going on.

For the next three days, with only a few hours sleep each night, all I did was talk about how hard it was to stay straight and how much I wanted to get high. All I could think about, all I could feel was that I had turned down a chance to use, and how I badly, obsessively, compulsively wanted some drugs.

On the third day, this anxiety, this compulsion, this obsession, stopped. It miraculously disappeared. I had survived the initiation into sobriety. Twenty-seven years later, the obsession and compulsion to use have still been removed. It was taken from me, on day three, by the Grace and Power of God.

Sobriety didn't happen without work and effort, but it did just happen. Just like whatever I needed to be a junkie had come to me— if I put forth the slightest effort and intention—whatever I needed to stay straight and do the right thing began to come to me too.

A new thought began to form in my mind: If I take half the energy, enthusiasm, dedication, and commitment that I've put into getting high and being an addict, if I take a portion of the energy I've used for doing the wrong thing and start using it to do right, there isn't anything in this world I can't do.

I had a lot of work ahead of me before I could move forward. First, I had to work hard to clear away the debris and wreckage from my past.

The battle for permanent custody of my son was still pending. I called the father of my son John. I told him I was sober now. I asked if he would allow me to have custody of my son, and for the first time be his mom.

He said no, that wasn't appropriate, John's home was with him. I could visit him under supervision. But if I wanted to take him, I'd have a fight on my hands.

I thought and thought about this. Then I knew what I had to do.

When I signed those papers giving permanent custody of John to his father—by now he and I were divorced—I learned for the first time in my life what it meant to let go. I'd already put this child through enough. I couldn't put John, his father, and myself through a nasty, prolonged, down-and-dirty custody battle too.

As far as I was concerned, a long time ago I had forfeited my rights.

I sent a letter to Paul, the man who had accompanied me on the last steps of my journey as a drug addict and whose presence helped escort me to the doors of this treatment center. When I looked at the blank piece of paper in front of me, I didn't know what to say. My probation officer had told me it would be a violation of my probation if I ever saw or talked to Paul again. But we had loved each other in our own strange, dysfunctional, and probably karmic way. How could I tell him everything I was learning, all that had happened to me? He wouldn't understand, wouldn't comprehend it, anymore than I would have a year ago if someone had tried to sell sobriety and a new way of life to me.

I struggled with all the volumes of information I wanted to convey. I wanted to explain who I was now, but it was beyond my ability to express in words. Finally I wrote one word on a postcard: Good-bye.

I believed that relationship was now over. As far as Paul was concerned, it wasn't finished yet.

And, as part of my rehabilitation, I had to do a fearless inventory of who I was and the things I had done wrong. Then I had to admit these wrongdoings—had to say who I really was and what I had done instead of running from the truth—to God, myself, and another human being.

My work was cut out for me now.

I wrote and wrote and wrote, looking at myself as fearlessly as I could at the time. I didn't have any problem seeing all I had done wrong. I honestly couldn't see anything at all I had done right.

I went in for a session with the Protestant minister at the treatment center. Reeking of shame and guilt, I told him all the bad things on my list. He listened. Gulped. Then said the things I had done weren't that unusual, at least for an addict.

Then he had the wisdom not to send me away yet. He said he had a feeling there might be something else. There was. There were two things.

The first one was something I had to do. It was hard for me. I had never done this before. "I guess if I'm honest, there's one more thing I have to confess," I finally said. "I don't know if I can or if I want to stay straight."

In that moment, a pressure and a weight that had been pushing me down suddenly lifted off me. I felt a freedom I had never before known. In that moment, I tapped into the power of being absolutely honest about more than just my past. I discovered the power of being honest about who I was and what I honestly thought and felt right now. I touched upon the power of the truth of accepting who and what I am.

The minister said there was one more thing. "You've told me everything bad about yourself. I believe you've told me the truth," he said. "But I don't want you to leave this room, this session, without realizing and knowing that there's something good about you too. Tell me one character attribute that you can see about yourself."

I thought. I thought so hard my brain hurt. Then I thought some more. I couldn't see anything, not one good thing, about who I was and who I had been up to and including that day. I told him I couldn't come up with anything.

He said he could. "You are unquestionably and without a doubt the most determined, relentless, persistent person I've ever known," he said.

I sat there and glowed. Hurray! There was one good thing about me that I could, and would, hang onto for the rest of my life.

I didn't know what lay ahead, but I knew I didn't want anymore of this raging fire that was now becoming my past. One day, when I was slumping around the treatment center, enmeshed in shame and guilt, I asked my counselor if I could talk to her for a minute.

"I'm working hard on myself," I told her. "But look at everything I've done. I've been a thief, a liar, a junkie, a prostitute, and a whore. I don't think God could ever forgive me. I don't think there's any place or purpose in the world for me. And I don't see how I can ever forgive myself."

A hush came over that office, her tiny chemical dependency counseling room. I'll remember her words all my life.

"If Jesus were walking around on this earth today, who do you think he'd hang out with? Who do you think he'd forgive? The person who was doing everything perfectly? Or the junkies, whores, and thieves?"

I thought about what she said. I had studied the Bible when I was a child, so I knew what those Scriptures said. Now, it was time to do more than read them. I had to apply them to my life. "I suppose the person Jesus would be most likely to forgive is the person who needed to be forgiven and loved the most."

I had one slip at that treatment center after I decided—or the decision was made for me—to stay straight. It was Halloween night.

A group of patients had sneaked in a bottle of whiskey. They invited me to a party. They were going to get drunk.

I didn't want to drink. Didn't want to get high. But I wanted to go to that party and celebrate Halloween. These people were my friends.

When I sat down on the lawn with the five other patients, I was determined not to take a swig out of that bottle. But when they passed it to me, when it was my turn, I couldn't help it. I took a big gulp.

I felt the whiskey burning its way down to my stomach, just like it had when I was a child. But instead of feeling a warm glow, all I felt now was guilt.

The guilt followed me back to my room. And it hung over me like a cloud all night while I slept. The next day in group, I confessed what I had done, even though I could have been kicked out of the program and sent to jail for breaking the rule about getting high.

I've got a lot more at stake than getting kicked out of here and going to jail for the next five years, I thought. *What hangs in the balance is the rest of my life. And the thread it's hanging by is whether or not I tell the truth.*

"You haven't lost everything you've worked for," the group decided with compassion, "as long as you can see what you've learned by your mistake."

I thought about what I had done. My counselor and the group helped me realize the lesson: If I didn't want to slip, I shouldn't go recklessly playing on the ice.

Staying straight didn't only mean that I could no longer take drugs or drink. I needed to change, and what needed to change was my whole life. I could no longer associate with anybody who didn't have the same values as I did. If I did, I was putting my life and sobriety at risk, in serious jeopardy.

This was a six-week treatment program. I stayed eight months. The judge had said I'd be there for "as long as it takes," and for a junkie like me, it took a long time. This little cottage in Willmar, Minnesota, had become my home. It was a place of refuge and safety.

I died the day the judge sentenced me to treatment. But as soon as I died, I was reborn.

Mother came to visit me once while I was in treatment. By the time she came, I had already begun my new life. She didn't believe it. She thought I was just conning and manipulating, up to my old tricks again. She stared and stared at me, in absolute disbelief.

Then she asked to talk to my counselor, telling her not to be taken in by this act I was putting on. My counselor listened. She didn't say much.

Mother and I walked back to my room. She started in, about how bad I had been and how much I had hurt her. I felt guilty. I told her I was sorry. She said I should pack my clothes, go to court and fight for my little boy, and I should come back to Mora and live with her.

I said I didn't think that would work, not this time around.

Those old familiar feelings began to come back. It was the way I felt right before I used to get high.

Then Mother started in again. She couldn't seem to help herself. I don't know if it was something she said, the way she said it, or just the way she looked at me. But in the next instant, I exploded in a rage.

Feelings I had held back all my life came bubbling out in one long, loud, psychotic scream. I yelled so loud the walls and doors shook. Everyone there—patients, visitors, and staff—stopped what they were doing and looked around, wondering what was going on. The scream lasted and lasted and lasted. I screamed with rage that had built up since the day I was born. Rage at all those men, rage at the man at the church, rage at Shelby O'Brian, rage at Tony, rage at my mom and dad for not wanting me, leaving me so alone. That scream seemed to last an eternity.

My mother just looked at me. She looked so alone and helpless, then she turned and walked away. Father Garvey came to my room and asked if I wanted to come to his office and help him file some papers for a while. Later, he told me the hospital staff had never heard such a scream as that, not once in their lives.

"Did I do something wrong?" I asked, shaken and confused by what had just taken place.

"No. You didn't," he replied.

As I pulled out the metal file drawers and filed his correspondence in just the right folder, I began to understand. When something hurt or scared me, I didn't have to go numb, then pinch myself to cause myself enough pain to know that I was real. Being real in this life didn't have to mean creating pain.

When life started hurting too much, all I had to do to know that I was real was let my feelings out.

With God's help and by learning new behaviors, I was learning how to jump over the wall.

ɸ

"There are very few nights I would want to go to sleep, then wake up the next day feeling the same way and being the same person," Scotty told me, years and years later. "That's why back in the Garden, a long, long time ago, God put a flaming sword to protect the other tree that God forbade us from getting into. After God saw what Eve had done—disobeyed and eaten fruit from the Good and Evil tree—He didn't want us getting into the fruit from the other one too.

"The angels are immortal. They are always the same—yesterday, today, and tomorrow. We're mortal. That means we die. But it also means we can change.

"The other tree in the Garden, the one God is protecting us from even now, is called the Tree of Life. If we ate from that tree, we'd be immortal like the angels. That means we would never change. We'd always be exactly like we are right now, today. That's how much God loves us," Scotty said. "He's given us the power and the ability to change."

We change from moment to moment from the second we're born. These changes lead from infancy, to childhood, to adolescence, to young adulthood, to middle age, then to Medicare, then finally to death. But the same changes that lead from birth to death can also happen inside in our soul. Sometimes they lead to spiritual and emotional death. Sometimes, we're born again—into a new life. By guarding that Tree of Life, God is protecting us and giving us a chance to change.

When I first got sober. I didn't know, couldn't comprehend, staying sober for ten days, ten weeks, ten months or ten years. The secret of change, at least the way I was taught it, is simple. It's called *one day at a time.*

One day at a time is how we get from wherever we are to where destiny wants us, and we want, to be.

It took me twelve years to learn another secret too. It's something the force called destiny knew all along.

"You look so sweet and innocent, all dressed in white," the Babalawo said. "And you're so quiet around me. But there's another side to you too."

He looked at me in a knowing way. "There's a warrior spirit to you. And there's a side that's not so innocent too. There's a special warning here. I've seen it in many people's records. Stay away from alcohol. And don't smell the flowers. [Don't use drugs.] If you do, you'll go insane."

People like me who have these markings have an imbalance. They can't use alcohol or drugs. If they do, they'll lose their minds. Chemical dependency—alcoholism and drug addiction—is a progressive disease. No matter where we are or how we try to manipulate our environment, if we take that first drink, pill, or fix, we've started a battle that we can't possibly win. The chemicals will gain control.

And we'll lose. We'll go insane.

That's why on that trip to Israel, and many other occasions, I turned down that joint or those pills, that line of cocaine or that delightfully aged glass of Italian red wine. If you've got those markings, got that disease, that first pill or fix is one too many and no matter how many bottles or bags of pharmaceutical drugs you've scored, you can never, never have enough.

I will be powerless over alcohol and drugs until the day I die. And whether or not I ever use again, this disease I have will progress. That means if I were to ever use drugs or alcohol again, my using habits wouldn't be better because of all the time I've gone without using and everything I've learned. Statistics show my using habits would almost immediately become worse.

Whether reincarnation, living more than one lifetime, is a reality or not, lessons will repeat themselves this lifetime until they're learned. This is one lesson I would prefer not to repeat or relive.

The problem with identifying these markings, with learning whether you've got this disease, is a slightly complicated one. I've made the mistake. So have people around me. They compare their experiences with drinking and drug use to mine. They think that if they're not as bad as I was, or if someone they know or love isn't as bad as I was, they don't have these markings, the disease. But people can use less, be more controlled, be more sane than I was and still have the disease. The way to measure the disease is not how much or how often we drink alcohol or use drugs. The barometer is loss of control and whether we continue to use despite negative results.

ᘉ

The first time Scotty and I made love, we were in my house in Minneapolis. This was many years after I had gotten sober. We were going at it when he suddenly got up and put on his pants.

"You're just having sex," he said. "Don't you know how to make love?"

I didn't have a clue as to what he was talking about. He left the room for a minute, then came back holding a book. He curled up next to me in bed, and read me the story of Winnie the Pooh. "Making love is not just about friction, intercourse, and continuing to be a victim of abuse," he said gently. "Making love means you're present for the other person. You know who you're with. You nurture them. And you learn to let them nurture you too. Sex isn't the only way to be close. It's not something you have to do. You can choose with whom and when you want to make love. Then let your sexuality turn into sensuality, a way of expressing, showing, giving and receiving pleasure, energy, and love."

Change is always taking place, for the better or for worse—even if we don't understand clearly what those changes are. Thank God we didn't get into the fruit from the other tree in the Garden, the one called the Tree of Life.

There are two ways to look at this story. We can say after what I've done, and what's been done to me, I'll never amount to anything or be able to make a place for myself in this world. Or we can turn it around by reversing those words a little bit. *After all I've lived through and everything I've survived, I can do anything in this world God wants me to do.*

ॐ

"Do people know you're more than a muffin-nibbling, hand-wringing, anxiety-ridden, control-freak codependent?" Scotty asked me once.

"I don't know," I said. "But they will now."

This Old House

My first encounter with codependents occurred in the early sixties. This was before people, tormented by other people's behavior, were called codependents, and before people addicted to alcohol and other drugs were labeled chemically dependent. Although I didn't know what codependency was, I usually knew who codependents were. As an alcoholic and addict, I stormed through life, helping create codependents.

Codependents were a necessary nuisance. They were hostile, controlling, manipulative, indirect, guilt producing, difficult to communicate with, generally disagreeable, sometimes downright hateful, and a hindrance to my compulsion to get high. They hollered at me, hid my pills, made nasty faces at me, poured my alcohol down the sink, tried to keep me from getting more drugs, wanted to know why I was doing this to them, and asked what was wrong with me. But they were always there, ready to rescue me from self-created disasters. The codependents in my life didn't understand me, and the misunderstanding was mutual. I didn't understand me, and I didn't understand them.

My first professional encounter with codependents occurred

years later in 1976. By then I worked as a counselor in the chemical dependency field. Because I had the least seniority and none of my co-workers wanted to do it, my employer at the Minneapolis treatment center told me to organize support groups for wives of addicts in the program.

I wasn't prepared for this task. I still found codependents hostile, controlling, manipulative, indirect, guilt producing, difficult to communicate with, and more.

It was a formidable group, these codependents. They were aching, complaining, and trying to control everyone and everything but themselves. Most codependents were obsessed with other people. With great precision and detail, they could recite long lists of the addict's deeds and misdeeds: what he or she thought, felt, did, and said; and what he or she didn't think, feel, do, and say.

Yet these codependents who had such great insight into others couldn't see themselves. They didn't know what they were feeling. They weren't sure what they thought. And they didn't know what, if anything, they could do to solve their problems—if, indeed, they had any problems other than the alcoholics.

Soon, I subscribed to two popular beliefs. These crazy codependents are sicker than the alcoholics. And, no wonder the alcoholic drinks; who wouldn't with a crazy spouse like that?

By then, I had been sober for a while. I was beginning to understand myself, but I didn't understand codependency. I tried, but couldn't until years later, when I became so caught up in the chaos of loving an alcoholic that I stopped living my own life. I stopped thinking. I stopped feeling positive emotions, and I was left with rage, bitterness, hatred, fear, depression, helplessness, despair, and guilt.

Sadly, aside from myself, nobody knew how badly I felt. My problems were my secret. Unlike the alcoholic and other troubled people in my life, I wasn't going around making big messes and expecting someone to clean up after me. In fact, next to the alcoholic, I looked good.

After floundering in despair for a while, I began to understand.

Like many people who judge others harshly, I realized I had just taken a long and painful walk in the shoes of those I had judged. I now understood those crazy codependents. I had become one too.

"Talk to me about your control issues," I said to my daughter, Nichole, when she was in her early twenties. "Or do you need some time to think about them?"

"I don't need to think about them," she said. "They're right up there. Basically, I want everything how I want it, when I want it, and if it steers away from that path, the Beast is let loose. Control mechanisms, manipulating people, saying things in a contrived, controlled way to create an emotional response in someone—I'll pull out all the stops to get things to happen to my liking. But when I'm trying to control someone, it never works because I'm saying things I don't really feel. When I'm trying to get someone to say what I want them to say or do what I want them to do, I'm reacting from a place that isn't real—a false sense of feeling. I'm not talking about, or taking responsibility for, who I really am."

"Tell me about your control issues," I said to a friend, a male in his early thirties.

"I don't have control issues," he said. "I just like to tell everyone what to do. It's not an issue. It's just my opinion. And I know I'm right."

"When did you begin working on your codependency issues," I asked a married woman in her late twenties.

"When I got tired of beating my head against the wall trying to control everything and everyone around me," she replied.

"The uncontrollable thing the codependent tries to control, of course, is someone else's drug taking or drinking," Mary Allen wrote in her book, her story called *The Rooms of Heaven*.

I think we want to control more than that.

We nag; lecture; scream; holler; cry; beg; bribe; coerce; hover over; protect; accuse; chase after; run away from; try to talk into; try to talk out of; attempt to induce guilt in; seduce; entrap; check on;

demonstrate how much we've been hurt; hurt people in return so they'll know how it feels; threaten to hurt ourselves; whip power plays on; deliver ultimatums to; do things for; refuse to do things for; stomp out on; get even with; whine; vent fury on; act helpless; suffer in loud silence; try to please; lie; do sneaky little things; do sneaky big things; clutch at our hearts and threaten to die; grab our heads and threaten to go crazy; beat on our chests and threaten to kill; enlist the aid of supporters; gauge our words carefully; sleep with; refuse to sleep with; have children with; bargain with; drag to counseling; drag out of counseling; talk mean about; talk mean to; insult; condemn; pray for miracles; pay for miracles; go to places we don't want to go; stay nearby to supervise; dictate; command; complain; write letters about; write letters to; stay home and wait for; go out and look for; call all over looking for; drive down dark alleys at night hoping to see; chase down dark alleys at night hoping to catch; run down alleys at night to get away from; bring home; keep home; lock out; move away from; move in with; scold; impress upon; advise; teach lessons to; set straight; insist; give in to; placate; provoke; try to make jealous; try to make afraid; remind; inquire; hint; look through pockets; peek in wallets; search dresser drawers; dig through glove boxes; look in the toilet tank; try to look into the future; search through the past; call relatives about; reason with; settle issues once and for all; settle them again; punish; reward; almost give up on; try even harder; and a list of other handy maneuvers I've either forgotten or haven't tried yet.

We aren't the people who "make things happen." Codependents are the people who consistently, and with a great deal of effort and energy, try to force things to happen.

We control in the name of love.

We do it because we're "only trying to help."

We do it because we know best how things should go and how people should behave.

We do it because we're right and they're wrong.

We control because we're afraid not to do it.

We do it because we don't know what else to do.

We do it to stop the pain.

We control because we think we have to.

We control because we don't think.

We control because controlling is all we can think about.

Ultimately we may control because that's the way we've always done things.

Codependents like to play God.

On one of my excursions, this time to New Orleans, I wandered into a boutique in the French Quarter. It had been the home of Marie LeVeaux, reportedly once—and some say still—the voodoo queen, the high priestess of black magic down there. I was and am frightened of it—meaning the store, black magic, voodoo, and all. I turned around and left the store, feeling guilty for having looked around. But it dawned on me as I made my way down the street to another, safer boutique, that black magic is just another degree of, and name for, manipulation and control.

In the next shop I wandered into, I looked around for a while. The shelves were full of stones, candles, and curios. One of the stones caught my eye. It was a big crystal ball. I went over and picked it up. It wasn't crystal, at least not on the outside, after all. Mirrors had been set inside the stone. When I looked at the ball, all I could see was a reflection of me and the environment where I stood.

"We can get accurate glimpses of the future," a psychic said to me once. "But the reason we can't see all the details is because if we knew, it would be too much. Besides, if we knew everything that was going to happen, we'd just try to control that—the future—too."

This is what I need to buy, I thought, looking into the crystal ball with mirrors. *I don't need to see what's coming next. All I need to know is who and where I am now.*

In 1986, I wrote a book entitled *Codependent No More*. In that book, I suggested that codependency issues—worrying about other people, and particularly people who cannot or will not help themselves—had probably been around for a long time. I stand behind everything I said and wrote in that book, except for one correction I'd like to make now.

I now believe that codependency has been around even longer than that.

To tell the true story of codependency, we need to go back to the Garden of Eden again. I now believe that's where codependency began. Eve saw the fruit on that tree—the Knowledge of Good and Evil tree. She didn't want to eat it. She knew better. But that serpent slithered up to her and tormented her until she picked the apple and bit in.

"The only reason God doesn't want you to eat that is because if you do, then you'll be just like him," the serpent said.

The bottom line to Eve's transgression, beyond disobeying a rule, is that she wanted to play God too.

Maybe after all is said and done, codependency is the original sin.

"People need to respect other people and not try to play God," the Babalawo said to me. "But the problem I see with most people is that no one wants to respect anyone else, and everybody wants to play God."

"In 1844, Karl Marx called religion 'the opium of the people.'

"In 1988 we have a new opiate. It's pop psychology," wrote Ena Naunton in a Knight-Ridder newspaper article about codependency ("Tangled in Someone Else's Illness? Let's Talk") released in 1988, the crest of the codependency wave.

The twenty-first century ushers us into a marriage of both ideas: religion and psychology. Instead of being mind numbing, like an opiate, this wedding is meant to heighten our consciousness. Self-care, the antidote, the *remedy* for codependency, is where we meet God in an armchair in our living room, and in the grind of our daily life.

That's what this story is about.

☙

What I remember most about the house on Pleasant Avenue is the summers. Wintertime in Minnesota is gruesome. One year it got so cold, so bone-chillingly machine-chillingly cold we had to take the top off the barbecue grill, fill it with coals, light it, and stick it under the car, just to unthaw the engine enough to even try to get it running. But each year, eventually, after that last tricky blizzard that comes toward the end of March—the one that each year most Minnesotans think won't happen that year—the snow does melt, the sun brings its warmth back to the ground, the barren trees fill with green leaves, and the grass and flowers return.

As much as I savor the constant warm but not too hot climate in the part of California where I now live, as much as I don't want to return to those gruesome, almost ungodly cold winters that Minnesotans pride themselves on enduring, there is something about the seasons, something about the way they speak to your soul.

Seeing that kind of reliable, dramatic, intense, almost miraculous seasonal change occur each year helps you believe in God.

I met David Beattie, the man who became my husband for ten years, and became the father of my two children—Nichole Marie and Shane Anthony Beattie—in July of 1975. He was tall. Six foot, six inches. He had big brown eyes, brown hair, a gentle spirit, a quick sense of wit, and usually a smile on his face. He was an Irishman who once upon a time had drunk too much and now had gone straight. He was a brilliant therapist, a good-hearted man whom many people called "friend," and he was smart—well educated in politics, foreign affairs, and the buzz, or trends, going on in the world.

I had been out of treatment for a year and a half by then. It had been a lonely and confusing time. My old life had ended—my life as a drug addict. My new life had just begun. I wasn't certain what was going on or what, if anything, would be coming next.

I went to work every day. I had found good paying jobs first in the town of Willmar, by the State Hospital, then later in

Minneapolis, working as a legal secretary again. I paid off my bills—past and present—and ate peanut butter sandwiches for lunch. I visited my son on the weekends, helped my ex-husband's mother clean and tidy her house, and wondered what was the right thing to do. Go back to the past? Or go into a future that hadn't yet been written?

I was trying to do the right thing, each step of the way. I made a list of all people whom I had harmed in my alcoholic, addictive years, and set to the task of trying to make things right, the best I could. Slowly, I rebuilt my credit, and the smallest amount of self-esteem. Eventually my probation lapsed and I was given a clean bill of health with the criminal justice system in the state where I lived.

Slowly, my life was beginning to turn around.

That's when I met Scotty and made friends with a woman named Echo, who would be a best friend from the moment I met her.

I made other friends too. Twelve Step programs and recovery were just becoming popular. Society was discovering you didn't have to be a back-alley wino to qualify as an alcoholic or drunk. A lot of young people had this disease, these destiny markings that made them go crazy whenever they used alcohol or drugs.

It was a complicated time in my life, spiritually, emotionally, and romantically. My counselors in treatment had strongly suggested that I not date or become romantically involved for a year. For the most part, except for an occasional accident, I complied.

I was looking with guilt and remorse at the failed marriage I was leaving behind. My son John, his father, and his grandparents were looking at me with open hearts but with a justifiable skepticism too.

Retrospect changes so many things. The insane life I had lived as an addict seemed so logical at the time I was living in and through it. But now, it terrified me—both the things I had done, the chances I had taken with my life and freedom, and the person I was—how I had behaved. From age twelve to the time they caught me on the drugstore roof, my life was characterized by a raging, flaming fire. I wanted to get and stay as far away from it as I could.

I understood from my treatment that I had a disease, one called alcoholism, addiction, chemical dependency. I would have it the rest of my life. If I was one of the lucky ones—if I went to recovery groups and asked God daily to help me stay straight then thanked God every night for doing that—I could have a daily reprieve from this disease, a remission. The one thing I feared that could make me go back to my old ways, my old life, and drugs was seeing Paul Rutledge again, the Paul that I had robbed drugstores and done so many drugs with.

One day, the telephone in my one-room apartment rang. A man's voice on the other end asked if I was Melody. I said yes. He said he was a counselor in a local treatment center. One of his clients, a man named Paul, had been sent from prison to his rehab center and had recently escaped.

"He's looking for you with a vengeance," he said. "He's convinced you're supposed to be his wife."

I thanked him for the tip and concern, then hung up the telephone. I didn't know it then, but the man who had just called me on the phone to warn me about Paul would later meet me, in person, and eventually ask me to be his wife. The counselor's name was David Beattie.

I took my name off my mailbox and got an unlisted phone number. Every night, I stayed up until three o'clock in the morning, watching the crack of light under my door, terrified I'd see a pair of shoes standing there.

It wasn't that I was afraid that Paul would hurt me, abuse me, beat me up. I was somewhat fearful of him, after that brief, terse letter I wrote saying only *good-bye*. But what I feared wasn't him. I was afraid of myself, afraid those old familiar feelings of acting crazy and wanting to get high would come back the moment I laid eyes on him. I was afraid that the temptation of running around getting all the drugs I wanted would be too much. I was afraid I wouldn't be able to turn him down if he asked me to run away with him.

It's odd, how we can feel things, sense things. I could feel the energy of pursuit. I was terrified for at least half a year. Then, one day, it broke. Suddenly, I didn't feel it anymore. A short time later, the counselor from the treatment center called me again. Paul Rutledge, the drugstore robber, had overdosed on cocaine and died.

Now I could put that part of my life to rest. About this time, I put my failed marriage to rest too. I decided that the program I was working wasn't one of penance. It was based on forgiveness. I had made a mistake. Well, a lot of them. If God could forgive me, then maybe it was time I started to forgive myself and put what I had done in my past behind me.

About that time, I met a man named Scotty. He was my age. He had a twinkle in his eye. And he started following me around. He drove me home once or twice, then took me out to lunch.

One evening, he came into my apartment after he had driven me home from a meeting.

We started to fool around. Then I told him I was sorry, but he had to go home.

A short time later, my girlfriend Echo introduced me to a man she thought I'd like to meet. His name was David. He was the counselor who had called to warn me about Paul. I liked what I saw in him. He liked what he saw in me. Both of us were convinced that what we felt for each other was love. He courted me for six months. I held my breath the entire time.

When I had been in treatment, the minister had told me that I had one good quality that he could see. I was persistent. Now I wonder if obsessive isn't a better word.

In December of 1975, David and I said, "I do."

Two months later, immediately after debating whether or not to stay on birth control and deciding no, I became pregnant with Nichole.

I started taking night classes at the University of Minnesota. I wanted to become a chemical dependency counselor and use what I had been through to help other addicts. Then I went on to get a job in the chemical dependency field. That's when I began working with the spouses of the addicts, those codependents that I didn't understand.

One year later, David and I bought our first house, the yellow, turn-of-the-century three-story on Pleasant Avenue in South Minneapolis. It wasn't what I had hoped for, but it was the only house we could afford.

The home we bought had been used as rental property for fifteen years, had been standing vacant for a year, and was three stories of broken windows and broken wood. Some rooms had ten layers of wallpaper on the walls. Some walls had holes straight through to the outdoors. The floors were covered with bright orange carpeting with large stains on it. And we didn't have the money or skills to fix it. We couldn't afford to furnish it. We had three stories of a dilapidated home, with a kitchen table, two chairs, a high chair, a bed, a crib, and two dressers, one of which had broken drawers.

About two weeks after we moved in, a friend stopped by. We stood talking on what would have been the lawn if grass had been growing there. My friend kept repeating how lucky I was and how nice it was to own your own home. But I didn't feel lucky. I didn't know anyone else who owned a home like this.

I didn't talk much about how I felt, but each night while my husband and daughter slept, I tiptoed down to the living room, sat on the floor, and cried. This became a ritual. When everyone was asleep, I sat in the middle of the floor thinking about everything I hated about the house, crying, and feeling hopeless. I did this for months. However legitimate my reaction may have been, it changed nothing.

A few times, in desperation, I tried to fix the house, but nothing worked. The day before Thanksgiving, I attempted to put some paint on the living- and dining-room walls. But layers of wallpaper started to peel off the minute I put paint on them. Another time, I ordered expensive wallpaper, trying to have faith I'd have the money to pay for it when it came. I didn't.

Then one evening, when I was sitting in the middle of the floor going through my wailing ritual, a thought occurred to me: *Why not try gratitude?*

At first I dismissed the idea. Gratitude was absurd. What could I possibly be grateful for? How could I? And why should I? Then, I decided to try anyway. I had nothing to lose. And even I was getting sick of my whining.

I still wasn't certain what to be grateful for, so I decided to be grateful for everything. I didn't feel grateful. I willed it. I forced it. I faked it. I pretended. I made myself think grateful thoughts. When I thought about the layers of peeling wallpaper, I thanked God. I thanked God for each thing I hated about that house. I thanked Him for giving it to me. I thanked Him I was there. I even thanked Him that I hated it. Each time I had a negative thought about the house, I countered it with a grateful one.

Maybe this wasn't as logical a reaction as negativity, but it turned out to be more effective. After I practiced gratitude for about three of four months, things started to change.

I stopped sitting in the middle of the floor and crying and started to accept the house—as it was. I started taking care of the house as though it were a dream home. I acted as if it were my dream home. I kept it clean, orderly, and as nice as could be.

Then, I started thinking. If I took all the old wallpaper off first, maybe the paint would stay on. I pulled up some of the orange carpeting and discovered solid oak floors throughout the house. I went through some boxes I had packed away and found antique lace curtains that fit the windows. I found a community action program that sold decent wallpaper for a dollar a roll. I learned about textured paint, the kind that fills and covers old, cracked walls. I decided if I didn't know how to do the work, I could learn. My mother volunteered to help me with wallpapering. Everything I needed came to me.

Nine months later, I had a beautiful home. Solid oak floors glistened throughout the house. Country-print wallpaper and textured white walls contrasted beautifully with the dark scrolled woodwork that decorated each room.

Whenever I encountered a problem—half the cupboard doors were missing and I didn't have money to hire a carpenter—I willed gratitude. Pretty soon, a solution appeared: tear all the doors off and have an open, country kitchen pantry.

I worked and worked, and I had three floors of beautiful home. It wasn't perfect, but it was mine and I was happy to be there. Proud to be there. Truly grateful to be there.

Soon the house filled up with furniture too. I learned to selectively collect pieces here and there for $5 and $10, cover the flaws with lace doilies, and refinish. I learned how to make something out of almost nothing, instead of making nothing out of something.

I fell in love with my home.

And I discovered the transformative power of gratitude.

During this time, I became pregnant again. This time I gave birth to a little boy whom I named Shane. While I was pregnant with him, I remembered a dream I had had, one from when I was a little girl.

I was painting a room in the house one day when I remembered something I had learned about myself when my teacher told me to write a paper about what I wanted to be when (and in my case "if") I grew up. We were supposed to choose three occupations, research them, and write an essay about these careers. I instantly knew what was number one on my list. I wanted to be a writer, a journalist, a reporter. I wanted to write stories. I wanted to work with words.

I had written stories in grade school that made people laugh and cry. Then I wrote one that made Mother angry. I started writing stories about how I felt about what went on in our house. I guess she felt ashamed and scared. The way I told the story didn't agree with her point of view. I got nervous then, started to lose my writing voice. I was irritating her enough already. I didn't want my stories to piss her off more.

In high school, I had been the youngest person ever to write on the newspaper. I loved journalism, research, writing about things and events and people that were really going on. I loved writing fiction stories too—bizarre little made-up incidents that talked about the feelings I had that I didn't know how to express any other way.

The more I drank and used drugs, the more my dream of writing had faded from my consciousness. By the time I went into treatment at Willmar State Hospital, I couldn't remember it at all anymore. I was so foggy from all my years of chemical use, I didn't know how to construct a sentence. Telling stories, writing stories, was out of reach.

But that day as I was painting the house, I remembered how much I wanted to write.

I put the paintbrush down.

How could I have forgotten? Writing stories was my dream.

I looked up at the ceiling in the house, and turned it over to God.

"If you want me to be a writer," I said, "you're going to have to work it out."

Within twenty-four hours, I had my first job writing stories for a community newspaper in the neighborhood where we lived. I received $5 for each story, and the thrill from seeing my name, my byline, in print. I still worked as a counselor part time, but now I worked as a writer too. And I diligently checked out every book and magazine I could get my hands on in the library so I could learn how to be better at my craft.

My typewriter was an old manual portable. The *n* key was missing.

It worked good enough for me.

I was the happiest I had ever known, or imagined, I could be.

It looked like all my dreams were coming true. What they had told me in treatment was right. If I stayed straight and did the right thing, I could do anything I wanted, anything at all. When I was rebuilding a life shattered by my chemical use, I dreamt of getting some of the things other people had. I wanted normal, whatever that was.

That included a job that was meaningful, a husband, and children, preferably two. I wanted a family to love. And a home where we could live together and love each other.

We lived in the kind of neighborhood in South Minneapolis that anyone, anyone at all would describe as friendly. At Christmastime, one of the families hosted a Christmas block party. We'd all get together and eat turkey and sing Christmas carols. In the summer, we'd block off the streets, and all the kids would play and the parents would sit and eat hot dogs and chips.

Although I worked part time, I stayed home a lot for four reasons. One, was that I loved being with the children. I wanted our home to be a place where all the kids could gather, whether they were sitting at my kitchen table stringing popcorn for Christmas decorations or running under the sprinkler in the backyard to cool down from the one hundred degree with high humidity weather, the kind Minnesotans usually get each July.

I stayed home a lot because I didn't have a car. No matter what happened, if we did happen to acquire an old junker for me to drive, the first car would break, and I'd lose mine. David would need to drive it, and I'd be stuck at home.

I stayed home a lot because there wasn't much money. A trip to Burger King once a year—hamburgers and French Fries but no beverage, water please, was about all we could afford.

And I stayed home a lot because if I left for more than a few hours, David got drunk.

ം

Although with each passing day of sobriety, I was getting further and further away from the raging fire of my addictive past, the hot coals of another fire smoldered in my life, unnoticed.

While many people suggest that at least one person in a relationship that could be labeled codependent needs to be dependent on alcohol and drugs, I have found that's not always true. An untreated addiction can be extremely helpful in creating codependency, but any serious, untreated dysfunction will do. Sexual addiction, gambling, an eating disorder, depression, ongoing financial problems, pathological lying, or an abusive or extremely cold and hard-hearted personality will work just fine. Even chronic illness will do in a pinch.

Sometimes, the sheer act of becoming infatuated with someone, or falling in love, can create at least a pseudo or temporary state of codependent insanity. The boundaries, those invisible borders around the energy field that's us, disintegrate. We blend into the other person's energy field. Their thoughts, hopes, wishes, and desires become intermingled with ours. We become, if not one with someone else, at least a talking, walking, appendage to their personality.

In fact, a highly trained, skilled codependent can become codependent on anyone, anyone at all.

Codependency is characterized by certain tendencies, or trends: low self-esteem that becomes bolstered and maintained by comparing ourselves to the addictive behavior of the people around us, a haunting sense of incompleteness that makes us glob onto other people and things, an irresistible urge to take care of the people around us and neglect ourselves, people-pleasing skills that backfire causing the people we're trying to please to wish only that we'd go away and leave them alone.

We only see what the other person is doing, and we forget to look at ourselves.

When somebody tells us he or she loves us, it doesn't warm our hearts. It makes us tense, nervous, afraid. Our first impulse isn't to hug them and say, "Thank you. I love you too." We want to grab them, shake them, and make them tell us exactly what that—saying I love you—means.

Just as codependency can be characterized by a particular set of behaviors and patterns, codependent relationships often have similar characteristics too. From years of professional experience working as a counselor with codependents, and from even more years of being one, there are three classic symptoms of a relationship we can become codependent in. Or on.

First comes the ugly twist and turn. It looks like one thing one minute. It promises to fulfill our every need, dream, wish, and hope.

The other person, whether it's a man or woman, stumbles into our lives. We tell ourselves a story about how things are going to be. What helps things along—for better or worse—is if we've been praying for God to send the right person into our lives. We then begin the relationship on the underlying premise that we're obediently doing and fulfilling God's will.

The second characteristic of codependent relationships is waiting. The codependent person waits—day after day, month after month, then year after year, for things to change and become better. That story he or she wrote in his or her mind, the day they met that person and fell in love, has to take place.

We wait for things to go back to the way they were, the way they were on that first date.

So we begin to control and manipulate to make them be that way.

If I don't tell the other person how angry I am, if I don't tell myself that I'm upset, if I hold my breath and wait, maybe someday, someday, I'll get what I want. The promise is held out, like a carrot on a stick.

The third characteristic of codependent relationships is one that many people describe as losing yourself. That's partly true. The rest of the story goes like this. In codependent relationships, we— we meaning codependent people—stay committed, no matter what, to the other person. But we've never learned how to commit to ourselves. We think it's our job to take care of everyone else, what they want, need, and expect. But we don't have a clue what it means to take care of, and deeply and lovingly, take responsibility for, ourselves.

Some people say God never gives people more than they can handle. That doesn't include codependents because they're handling stuff for at least four or five other people. Codependents—still waiting, still wondering, still hoping. Still mad.

∾

Nichole was just a baby, the first time I found a bottle in the house.

I knew something was up. I felt a funny feeling whenever David and I had a conversation. It would take me years of working on myself to identify this feeling as being how I felt when somebody was telling me lies. He had been in and out of the house all day, saying he had errands to run. It felt strange, dark, and cold being around him that day. Nichole was only eight months old. I was terrified about my marriage, but I loved her so much.

That night, after I fed her and put her in bed, David had disappeared into the bedroom too. He had gone to bed so early. Now he was snoring. I didn't know he had really passed out. The toilet in the bathroom was running, running, running. It wouldn't stop. I jiggled the handle. It still didn't stop. I thought maybe the chain inside was broken.

I lifted up the porcelain on the toilet tank top. Inside was an almost empty bottle of vodka.

I choked in disbelief.

What was it this man had said to me the week before we got married, that had triggered so much guilt? "I really love you, Melody," he had said. "But I'm scared I'm going to come home from work and find you lying in the bathtub, high from shooting dope."

I was a chemical dependency counselor. So was this man I had married, my husband of over a year. We were married, had a baby. This was my new life. Something was terribly, terribly wrong. This was a scene out of a B movie, not something that happened in real life.

I grabbed my daughter, still a baby then, put her in the infant seat, and drove away, heading somewhere, anywhere, with her next to me in the car. I was crying. Shaken. I felt so betrayed. I didn't know where to go or what to do next. My world was falling apart. If David was using, that jeopardized my sobriety. I couldn't stay with him!

Suddenly, Nichole started choking. She had picked up a piece of paper off the seat, chewed on it, then swallowed a corner. It was stuck in her throat. I pulled the car off the road, performed the Heimlich maneuver on her, pushing under her little chest.

She coughed up the piece of paper and started breathing again.

She was fine.

I went to a telephone and called a friend. I told her what was happening.

"Oh, don't worry," she said, when I told her how horrified I was. "Nobody's perfect. Just give David a little time."

I drove Nichole and I back home that night. I had made a decision about what to do next. I'd look the other way and simply pretend that none of this was taking place.

The propensity to believe other people's lies is strong.

The propensity to believe our own is even more powerful.

The problem with chemical dependency is that many people who have the disease, many people who's lives are being controlled by alcohol and drugs, many people who go insane and lose control if they use drugs or drink alcohol at all, are not nearly as bad as I was in my drug using years.

David was what is called a binge drinker. He had learned a destructive form of controlled abuse.

Every few months, he went out. Got drunk. Got screwed up. Lost money, or the car, or his job. After a few days or weeks, he'd pull it together again.

"What's the problem?" he'd say. "Can't a man have a little drink now and then?"

I could see what was happening to him, kind of. I couldn't see what was happening to me.

I should have known. I should have known. I should have known.

I should have known from the wedding. The plans changed several times. We eloped to South Dakota, but instead of having a honeymoon, we had to drive back to Minnesota the next day because David was acting in a live theater play. He had to rehearse. I sat in the hotel in the town where I lived and waited for my new husband to come home. That was our honeymoon.

A few days later, David got the bad news. We were still off from work. I call it my honeymoon. David called it married life. David's father had died. His mother had been dead for several years.

I didn't know a lot about marriage, or married life, or love. But I thought David would turn to me for comfort, help, and support. He didn't. He left and didn't return until the sun was coming up the next morning. When he found me awake on the couch, crying, he told me I was overreacting. He had just been with a friend, playing poker, playing cards.

It would take years of muddled confusion, believing lies, screaming, raging, feeling guilty before I learned the truth. That's the first time in our married life David had slipped away and gotten drunk.

I quietly went along with what he said. My favorite game was playing stupid, thinking there must be something wrong with me. I was afraid of the implications of owning my power.

My next favorite game was wanting him to change, thinking nothing was wrong with me.

By now, David had been drinking sporadically, or perhaps, more accurately, staying sober sporadically, since the day we had said, "I do." All the credit I had worked so hard to reestablish had gone down the drain.

He kept insisting on writing bad checks. He said it was an act of faith. If we just believed, something would happen and we could cover the check. God would see to it that we had enough money in the bank.

He liked to start businesses too.

There was the pallet business. There was the year he had me selling Amway door to door. It was freezing, almost Christmastime, as I walked around the neighborhood pounding on people's doors, asking them if they'd like to get rich or in the alternative, buy some soap. There were gold mines we invested in. And most recently, volcanic ash. Mount St. Helens had erupted. David had become convinced that if he borrowed enough money to buy commercial time, he could get people to buy that damn ash. "A souvenir, a piece of history," the $5,000 commercial proclaimed. The problem was, the commercial only ran in the middle of the night. Nobody bought the ash. It had sat for a long time in garbage bags in our cellar. Now, it had become like in a horror movie, spreading out of the bags and seeping out all over the house.

I couldn't stand it, couldn't take it, much longer. But still, I held my breath. This marriage had to, had to, had to work.

David disappeared from the hospital within minutes after Shane was born. We had one of those special rooms, decorated like a regular bedroom. David would have been able to be in the delivery room with me. He could have spent that night. But he disappeared out of sight.

The next day, I was scheduled to have surgery to get my fallopian tubes tied. I had made a decision that after Shane, I was done having children. Two babies were plenty for me. I watched in the hallway that evening as other husbands and wives held hands and welcomed their babies into the world. I finally fell asleep wondering where David had gone.

When I came out of surgery the next day, my mother called. She had come to help David with Nichole while I was in the hospital.

"He's drunk," she said. "What are you going to do about it?"

"I'll be home tomorrow," I said. Then I hung up the phone. I was too numb to cry.

I had my typewriter. I made five bucks a story, then ten. While I wrote at the big table in the dining room, the kids played with their toys at my feet.

David and I barely touched each other, from that time on.

The years passed. I stayed busy taking care of the kids. I loved them. I loved my writing too. By then, I had written my first book. It sold one thousand copies and won a small award. It was what I needed to keep going on.

David loved his children. David loved me. David just didn't know how to stay straight.

So I decided to devote my life to controlling and changing things—mostly him.

℘

Control is an illusion. It doesn't work. We cannot control alcoholism. We cannot control anyone's compulsive behaviors—overeating, sexual, gambling—or any of their behaviors. We cannot (and have no business trying to) control anyone's emotions, mind, or choices. We cannot control the outcome of events. We cannot control life. Some of us can barely control ourselves.

People ultimately do what they want to do. They feel how they want to feel (or how they are feeling); they think what they want to think; they do the things they believe they need to do; and they will change only when they are ready to change. It doesn't matter if they're wrong and we're right. It doesn't matter if they're hurting themselves. It doesn't matter that we could help them if they'd only listen to, and cooperate with, us. It doesn't matter, doesn't matter, doesn't matter, doesn't matter.

The problem was, I didn't know that then. I thought controlling and taking care of other people was my duty, my God-given job. My motto from then on became "Do for others what they refuse to, but should, be doing for themselves." If other people don't want to be responsible, I'll pick up that slack.

I turned myself inside out to show David how much he was hurting me and to make him stay sober and clean. I should have known from my own battle with drugs not to get in the middle of another person's war with alcohol.

David couldn't control himself. I couldn't control him either. And I couldn't see, couldn't fathom, how out of control I had become.

℘

We knew our neighbors, some better than others. The Sampsons lived a few houses down. They had lived there all their married life.

Laura and George had four children. Their youngest, Katie, was about Nichole's age.

Across the alley lived Laverne. She had a tough lot. She had married her husband when she was young. They had tried year after year to have children, but couldn't. Finally she adopted a little girl and a little boy. Well, as soon as she brought these children home, her husband turned her world upside down.

He left her, walked out the door to be with another woman.

Laverne was sad. She was sad a lot. By the time I met her, her children were ages ten and twelve. She worked, spent a lot of time with her mother, liked to make little ceramic angels and coffee cups and paint them with pretty colors. And she worried about her kids.

Down the street Joey lived with his dad. Joey's mom had been killed in a motorcycle accident—she was riding the bike with Joey's dad when it crashed. He was just a baby at the time. So most of us helped out with Joey, as best we could. We fed him cookies, washed his face, and let him hang out.

Across the alley, directly across from our backyard, lived the Kings, Matt and Marilyn. They had a houseful of kids too. Two were girls from Matt's previous marriage. The boy was Marilyn's son from her first marriage. Her first husband had committed suicide years ago. Then she married Matt. So they had his kids, her kids, and one of their own, a little tyke named Mattie Jr.

We all knew each other, everyone on the block. But the families with children seemed to know each other best. Most of the time, the children played at our home, or at the Sampsons, a few doors down.

Laura and I got close, real close. For the two years I went without a phone, I'd walk down to her house for emergencies and use hers. We ate dinner a lot at each other's house. And Laura understood what I was going through. She had troubles of her own. I'd rant and rave and obsess about David, worrying about the bills that weren't being paid, or when he was going to get drunk next. She'd listen for a while. But she kept telling me I needed to go to meetings of a group called Al-Anon.

I had heard about Al-Anon. It was the counterpart to Alcoholics Anonymous. Although I kept these thoughts to myself, I thought that AA was for the chemically dependent person, the person with the real problem. And Al-Anon was a little auxiliary meeting, someplace the women went so they could commiserate about how awful it was that their husbands always got drunk.

I didn't want to go.

I thought I had been through enough. I couldn't understand why I should have to go to these meetings. I wasn't the one getting drunk.

Summers were good on Pleasant Avenue. I had a little garden out back. I grew watermelons, pumpkins, tomatoes, and corn. The children liked to congregate and play either in the Sampsons' or our backyard. I was busy writing my stories, playing with the kids, and trying to ignore whatever had gone wrong in my marriage. I just pretended to myself most days that everything would be fine and went along with the flow. *And,* I thought, *maybe the problem is with me. Maybe I don't know how to be happy. Maybe this is what married life is supposed to feel like.*

That last summer was a wild one. One day, a tornado cut right through our neighborhood. It was strange, that day. It happened on a Sunday. For some reason, I had decided to take all these neighborhood children roller skating, at a rink way out in the suburbs. To do this, I had to borrow Laura's car, pack all the kids in, and drive to a suburb south of the city.

The weather was odd that day, hot, but with an almost cold pressurized feeling in the air. In our backyard, I had built a little fort. I had tried to get the kids a dog, Bernie, the St. Bernard. He was so big and clumsy he had clumped all over the house. So I bought a saw, some pieces of plywood, and built him a house so he could stay outside.

The first day I had it up, he took one look at it, jumped on the roof, and it collapsed onto the ground. I got rid of Bernie, then put the fort back up. It was just three sides of plywood with a roof, but the children loved playing in it. Sometimes when it rained, they liked to stay outside, climb into the fort, and watch it rain.

I know that if we had stayed home that day, they would have been in that fort.

Anyway, I gathered all the children up, loaded them into the car, and took them roller skating for the day. We weren't there fifteen minutes when the sirens came on. They told us we had to sit down at the side of the rink. A tornado was blowing through town.

I became so upset with myself. Tornados always hit in the suburbs. It was a given, a fact. Why hadn't I stayed home where we would have been safe?

The lights went out. We huddled there for hours. Then, they sent us home.

It took me four hours to make the twenty-minute drive. Trees, electric posts, almost everything that had been standing was now lying down. I finally made my way back to the neighborhood where we lived. That ended up being the area of the city that had been hardest hit.

In my backyard, the vortex had felled a tree.

It had fallen and crushed the fort.

"There was no warning," David said, when they interviewed him for the news. "One minute, the sun was shining. The next, I heard a noise like a freight train. The next thing I knew, that tree went down."

That had helped me believe in God, a little. But for the most part, I felt alone.

Damn him, I thought. Why did he have to drink? Why couldn't he have sobered up earlier? Why did he have to lie? Why couldn't he have loved me as much as I had loved him? Why didn't he stop drinking and lying years ago, when I still cared?

I never intended to marry an alcoholic.

I had expected so much of this marriage. I had so many dreams for us. None of them had come true. I had been tricked, betrayed. My home and family—the place and people who should have been warm, nurturing, a comfort, a haven of love—had become a trap. And I couldn't find the way out. Maybe, I kept telling myself, it will get better. After all, the problems are his fault. He's an alcoholic. When he gets better, our marriage will get better too.

Slowly, I began to suspect the truth. Time passed, but the only thing that changed was that I felt worse. My life ground to a halt. I had no hope that things would get better; I didn't even know what was wrong. I had no purpose, except to care for other people, and I wasn't doing a good job of that. I felt guilty all the time and wondered if I was going crazy. Something dreadful, something that I couldn't explain, had happened to me. It had sneaked up on me and ruined my life. Somehow, I had been affected by David's drinking, and the ways I had been affected had become my problems. It no longer mattered whose fault it was.

My problem wasn't David's drinking; that was his problem. My problem had become codependency.

I just didn't see it yet. All I could see, like a good codependent, was what other people were doing to me.

"Don't play with fire," I warned the kids. They loved lighting candles, being the one allowed to strike the match, see the blaze, and set the wick aflame. "Only light a match when I say it's okay, and I'm here to supervise."

Shane, who was four years old by now, loved watching his daddy light the barbecue grill. He liked to collect sticks, add them to the coals, and watch the burst of orange and red heat explode into the air when David added fuel to the smoldering coals.

On this particular December morning, Shane sneaked a packet of matches from the kitchen pantry, then peeked around. No one saw. His daddy was getting ready for work.

On this same December morning, I went out to the car before David left for work to retrieve my notebook. I had done an interview for the paper and I wanted to try to work on my story. When I went to open the passenger side backseat door, I noticed the door was ajar. A snarling, growling German shepherd jumped out at me, and ran down the street.

That's an omen of something, I thought.

While I was out by the car, Shane slipped up the stairs to our bedroom.

He had a plan.

He ripped two matches out of the packet, and struck them against the rough edge of the box.

They didn't light. He hadn't done it right. He tried it again.

This time, his little experiment worked. The first match exploded in a tiny blaze. In a moment, the one next to it lit up too.

"Shane! Where are you! What are you doing?" I called from downstairs.

His little heart beat faster. He'd be in a lot of trouble if he got caught doing this. He lifted up the bedskirt and threw the book of matches and the two lit ones under the bed. Then he ran across the room and turned the television on.

"I'm up here. In your room. Watching *Sesame Street*," he yelled back.

"Okay. Just checking," I said.

"Don't worry," Shane hollered. "I'm being good."

Unbeknownst to Shane, the tiny flames from the matches reached up to the underside of the mattress. Mattress batting is thick. It burns slowly but is highly flammable, a fire waiting to spread. Shane was so young he didn't understand. A fire can smolder for a long, long time before it reaches the point of no return and breaks into raging flames. He sat next to the bed watching television, waiting for me to begin my day. He had thrown the matches under the bed. He couldn't see the flames. Like a child he thought, *If I don't see it, it's not there.*

I dragged myself up to the bathroom, on the second floor, and stared at myself in the mirror. Brushing my teeth, combing my hair, doing anything to fix myself up and begin this day seemed more than I could do.

Shane popped into the bathroom.

"Mom," he said, "come with me."

"In a minute, in a minute, honey," I said. "I'll be right there."

He looked at me.

"Mom," he said, "you'd better come right now."

Flames enveloped the room. The fingers of orange heat had spread across the walls, eaten up the curtains, and were crackling across the ceiling.

I stared for a moment.

"No problem," I said, reaching for the fire extinguisher in the corner. "I've got it under control."

I sprayed the contents of the fire extinguisher at the blaze.

It didn't daunt the flames, didn't make a dent in the raging fire.

I was so numb, so stuck, I couldn't even panic anymore. I grabbed Shane's hand, stopped by the bathroom long enough to grab a robe, then threw it on over my pajamas.

It was time to get out of the house.

I ran down the sidewalk to Laura's house, called the fire department, and walked back to the front of my house, stood there, and watched it burn.

The next hours, the next days, were a blur.

The insurance company put us in a small apartment in a seedy part of town.

I bought a small plastic tree.

We celebrated Christmas there.

"I don't even want to see that house again," David said. "You handle everything. Just surprise me. Bring me back there when it's done."

He left town to investigate another business. He said it could make us rich. Quick.

I finally mustered up the courage to go see that old house. I sat among the wet ashes in the living room, on what used to be our couch, and cried. I was so very, very tired. I worked my way up to the second-floor bedroom, the place where the fire had begun.

The damage was the worst in that room.

The heat had melted everything the flames hadn't burned. Even the hard oak dresser was now just a solid piece of well-formed ash. The television set had melted. Everything that had been on top of the dresser was a piece of loose ash, formed in the shape of what that thing once was. In the middle of all the ashes sat my old black leather Bible.

It was the only thing in the entire room that hadn't burned.

I grabbed it and left the house.

That's when I came up with my plan.

David was off in the Dakotas. He had left me with this mess, on my own. The old blue Pinto I was driving had no heater. It was thirty degrees below zero. The window wouldn't shut. Neither would the door. Every time I got in it, I had to tie it shut with a plastic telephone cord. There was no insurance on the car. Shane's preschool bus wouldn't pick him up in the apartment where we now lived. Neither would the bus that took Nichole to school.

I had no money.

I had no home.

I had no clothes, except for the jeans and shirt I had on.

I hated my husband.

And now my whole life had just gone up in smoke.

If this was the new life I had been promised, God could have it back.

I stopped at the liquor store on my way home. Everyone around me did as they pleased. It was my turn now. I carefully selected two bottles of alcohol. They were fancy liquors, kinds I had never tried. When I was using, drinking fancy drinks wasn't my style. Tonight, I was going to get drunk.

I had lost almost everything I had. I might as well lose my sobriety too. People around me were supposed to be recovering. They got drunk whenever they wanted. Why couldn't I do that too?

I brought the bottles into the apartment, hid them in the top cupboard, then went to pick up both children from school. My children had both been born after I had become sober. If I was going to do this, at least I could wait until they went to bed. They didn't deserve or need to see their mother drunk.

At ten o'clock that evening, after both children had gone to bed, I decided it was time to have a drink. Then I reconsidered. It was late. I was tired. There was no sense drinking tonight. I was ready to go to sleep.

The next day, I took Nichole to school. Shane stayed home with me. I watched the clock, waiting until it was time to put the children to bed. I was still determined that these babies weren't going to see their mother drunk.

That night, after I put Shane and Nichole to bed, I took the bottles out. I stared at them for a while. There wasn't a reason in the world I could see not to get drunk. Nine years I had stayed clean and sober. I had watched people around me do whatever they pleased, while I cleaned up after their messes. It didn't seem fair to me.

I thought, and I thought, and I thought, while I stared at those bottles on the sink. I took the top off the Irish cream, ready to pour myself a drink.

I walked back into the tiny bedroom, and saw the Bible lying on the bedstand.

I thought about the God of my sobriety. I decided to give Him one last chance.

"Okay, God, this is it," I said aloud in that tiny, shoddy room. "You've got one chance. Give me one good reason why I shouldn't take a drink."

I opened up the Bible at random, then read the verse under my thumb.

"You cannot serve two Masters," is what I read aloud.

That was good enough for me.

It didn't matter what anybody else did, or didn't do. When I drank, alcohol and drugs ruled my life. I walked out to the kitchen and poured the contents of both bottles down the sink.

As the weeks passed, life began to require activity from me. Insurance inventories, negotiations, cleanup, and rebuilding plans demanded my attention. I felt anxious and insecure, but I had no choice. I had to think. I had to get busy. I had to do certain things. Once the actual reconstruction began, I had to do even more. I made choices about how to spend thousands of dollars. I worked with the crews, doing everything I was able to do to help cut costs and expedite the project. That included physical activity, a part of my life that had become nonexistent. The busier I got, the better I felt. I began to trust my decisions. I worked off lots of anger and fear. By the time my family and I moved back into our home, my balance had been restored. I had begun living my own life, and I wasn't going to stop.

It felt good!

Maybe God knew what I needed after all. He had lit a fire under me.

At least I was moving again.

"Honey, I've got a chance to go to Vegas for a few days during the week. You don't mind, do you?" David asked one day.

Mind? Of course I minded. We hadn't been on a trip for years. We didn't have money to pay the bills. How dare he even suggest taking a trip?

That's what I thought. But I felt guilty for what I thought. So this is what I said.

"Of course not," I said. "But promise me one thing."

"What's that?" he asked.

"If you go to Vegas, you won't drink."

David promised. I believed him. I asked him for another promise. Laura had put herself through nursing school. I had offered to have her graduation party in my refurbished home. The day after David got back, we were supposed to have the house festively decorated and host a party for eighty people at our house. I asked him to promise to be home in time to help me prepare for the party.

On David's third day in Las Vegas, the day he was supposed to be traveling home to help prepare for the party, that sinking feeling, that gut-wrenching anxiety, flooded my stomach again. I knew something was wrong. I called him on the phone, called the number he had given me.

"Are you drinking again?" I asked, in that whiny, accusatory, codependent, nagging, control-freak voice.

All I heard on the phone was glug, glug, glug, as the whiskey, or vodka, or beer, or whatever it was, ran down his throat.

Then he hung up on me.

I called him back immediately.

"David? David?" I screamed. "You're drinking again."

Click.

I sat at the table and dialed the phone all afternoon and into the evening hours. Obsessively, compulsively, over and over I dialed that number.

David was smart. Or drunk. Or dumb. He didn't pick up the phone.

Undaunted, I continued to dial.

If I can get him to pick up that phone, he'll put down the bottle, get on a plane, and come home, I thought. *If I can get him to answer the phone, everything will be fine.*

At ten o'clock that evening, I stopped dialing. I looked around the room. David was out of control. David was lying. David was getting drunk. David was breaking his promises to me. But what about me? I had eighty people coming to the house tomorrow. It was ten o'clock at night. I hadn't begun cooking yet. I hadn't cleaned.

Instead I had sat by the phone all day, compulsively dialing the same number over and over, trying to get a drunk to pick up the phone.

Maybe, just maybe, I was out of control too.

Even if he did put down that bottle and come home, everything wouldn't be *fine*.

I had my second spiritual awakening, right there at that table between telephone calls.

For the first time in my marriage, I stopped pointing the finger at David.

For the first time, I began to see myself.

It was time to detach, let my husband go, and begin taking care of myself. What taking care of myself meant would change and become enhanced as time went on. That evening, it meant putting down the phone, cleaning the house, preparing the food, and letting David make his own choices about getting sober or getting drunk.

The next day while the party was going on, the telephone rang.

David was at the Minneapolis airport. He was broke and needed a ride home.

It's interesting how behaviors like letting go and detaching transcend time and space. David could feel the change in me even though we were fifteen hundred miles apart. The minute I let go, he put down the bottle and headed for home.

I took a deep breath, then I let it out. I had done everything I knew to get him sober, build us a home, not lose what I wanted so badly—my family dream.

"You got yourself to Vegas. You managed to find your way around out there. Right now, I'm hosting a party," I said. "I have every confidence in the world that if you really want to, you can get yourself home without my help."

Click.

This time I hung up the phone.

I cried when I attended my first Al-Anon meeting. All I could do was sit there and cry. But at least I was legitimately feeling emotions again, instead of pointing the finger and screaming, *look at what you've done to me now.*

In the months ahead, I discovered a new power. It was the power of admitting powerlessness, of admitting defeat, again. This time, my powerlessness wasn't over my use of alcohol. It was over the effects of alcohol on somebody else and the effects of their drinking on me.

I was beginning to learn about the power of detaching from things and people—what I could not control—and instead taking care of myself. I should have known better, from my experience with alcohol and drugs. After all, no one could have controlled me. But I didn't. First, I compared my using to what David was doing. Although I later realized he was an alcoholic, it was deceptive at first because he wasn't as bad or as out of control as I had been.

This was one of the most powerful lessons I would ever learn, and a lesson that would consistently reappear—like a test. It was one of those things that I had to go through, like the Babalawo said.

Another dream came out of the ashes of that fire. I began to obsessively and persistently want to write a book about what I was learning to help other people, like myself, who were codependents too.

David and I got offered a good deal on a house in Stillwater—in the heart of a better neighborhood. We moved away from Pleasant Avenue, and that whole part of our lives after I fixed that old house up twice. I didn't know whether to stay with him or leave him, so I decided to let go for the time, stay with him, and let that issue work itself out.

Soon after we moved, Laverne developed cancer in the area around her heart. She died a few years later, leaving her two young children behind. The Kings divorced. He ran off with his secretary, then got cancer and died too. The Sampsons, George and Laura, are still together, and to this day we remain good friends.

Unlike recovery from my addiction, recovery from codependency soon became fun. It felt good. And once I started, there was no turning back. I didn't want to stop and become codependent again.

And that's the story about how *Codependent No More* was born.

ℭ

Maybe codependency did start back in the Garden of Eden with Adam and Eve. But the solution to codependency has been around for a long time too.

Rav Brandwein was a rabbi who studied and taught about kabbalah, an ancient spiritual path connected to Judaism. "For once a person begins on this path of knowledge," he wrote, "they will only look inward, learning how to fix themselves, instead of trying to fix other people."

Hmmm. Sounds a lot like recovery from codependency to me.

Going to Extremes

Abigail was a sturdy Scandinavian girl, in her early twenties. She was from Minnesota or Wisconsin or Iowa or possibly the Dakotas—one of those Midwestern states. At first when you looked at her, you didn't notice her too much. But after you looked at her a while, she transformed, became pretty. She spoke quietly—the kind of voice that made you move in closer to her and listen more intently so you wouldn't miss whatever she said.

I prayed for Abigail every day. I asked God to bless Abigail. I asked God to bless her finances, her work, her career, her success. I asked God to bless Abigail emotionally. I asked God to take care of Abigail, and take damn good care of her too. Abigail was on my mind and in my heart most of the time, so I prayed and prayed and prayed for Abigail. I deliberately sent out positive thoughts to and about Abigail every time she crossed my mind.

I didn't pray for Abigail because I liked her.

I prayed for Abigail because I envied, resented, and despised her.

Abigal personally hadn't done anything to me. But she had what I thought was and should be mine—a full-time job as a reporter at the daily newspaper in the small town of Stillwater where I lived. Abigail had everything I wanted and thought I couldn't have—the ability to earn at least an adequate living as a writer, a college degree in journalism, and the newspaper job that I was convinced should have been given to me. Mostly, Abigail had the ability to write clearly, confidently, succinctly, honestly, interestingly, and *fast*.

I hated Abigail.

If you have a resentment, pray for the person you resent, my friends said. *Resentments will eat you up inside. Resentments will kill you, send you back to drinking, keep you in a state of spiritual and emotional discontent, fragmentation, and darkness. Resentments are bad. They're bad for your health—your spiritual, emotional, mental and physical health. Don't resent. Love people. Think good thoughts about people, especially those whom you resent.*

That's why I prayed for Abigail daily—sometimes ten times a day. I resented her *that* much. I couldn't help it. Those feelings wouldn't go away.

By then, David and I were living in a small tract home in Stillwater. Living in a tract home was something I vowed I'd never do, but my mother had offered me a good deal on a home she was selling. Although I loved the house on Pleasant Avenue in Minneapolis, David and I had both known we were done in that old house. Besides, Stillwater had an excellent school system and it would be a good place to raise the children. It would be safe.

I spotted the building that housed the *Stillwater Gazette* as soon as we moved to Stillwater, a historical, Victorian picture-book town situated on the banks of the St. Croix River on the Minnesota-Wisconsin border. The *Gazette* was the daily paper serving the area and at that time, it was the oldest family-owned daily in the United States. I knew the first time I saw the building that I was destined to work there as a reporter.

When I went down there in person, my resume in hand, I learned that right now, this moment in time, they had an opening for a reporter. The problem was, I didn't have a college degree in journalism. Abigail did. And the publisher and owner of the paper, John Easton, thought Abigail was the one for the job.

As soon as David, the children, and I moved to Stillwater—the day we were moving our cardboard boxes in and stacking them in the little rooms scattered throughout the chopped-up house—I knew that this was going to be a transformation house. I knew that I knew that I knew that the divorce that I was dreading and fearing, the loss of the first family I had ever felt I had, was on its way.

About once a month, for years now, I had vacillated about whether to stay in or leave this marriage. On a few occasions, David and I had broken up. We'd have an argument, I'd kick him out, or he'd leave. Then a few days or weeks later, when the old fears of abandonment and being alone kicked in, we'd kiss and make up. We'd get along splendidly for a while, then that uncomfortable but familiar undercurrent of resentment, distrust, betrayal, and sometimes downright hatred would kick back in.

Over the last year we had settled into an uncomfortable routine of ignoring each other. We were like strangers sharing the same house. At one time, we had genuinely loved and cared for each other, but his alcoholism and my codependency had eaten away at the relationship. Now we were together for other reasons. We felt guilty about breaking up our marriage. We were fearful of being alone and discovering what was next. We worried about not having enough money to support two households.

And we loved our children.

David adored Nichole and Shane, and they adored him. He would tell them stories, roughhouse with them the way only a father can do—especially a big man like David. The children wanted us to stay together. And we didn't want to break their hearts, have them be products of a broken family.

So we pretended everything was fine. Recovery from codependency, I would affirm to myself, does not mean *leave* the alcoholic. It means, as one Al-Anon member harped at me, *get on with your own life*. I knew many recovering codependents who decided to stay with the alcoholic. I knew many who decided to leave. I wasn't certain which kind I was going to be.

Sometimes I wanted to take things into my own hands, force the issue, to relieve my anxiety about what was going to happen next in this marriage, but it felt like my hands were tied. Each time I would try to figure out what to do or what was going to happen, the answer I got was the same: let go and take care of yourself. Your marriage—or your divorce—will work itself out.

The children acclimated quickly to the new town where we moved. They loved their new school. Shane started kindergarten. He became involved immediately in athletics—he loved sports and had since he was old enough to catch a ball. Nichole made new friends. We had a big back yard.

Finances were still tight. I hadn't yet been able to buy new clothes for the children or myself. Our entire wardrobes came from garage sales and secondhand clothing stores. But Mother had helped me find a car I could afford at a garage sale. So for the first time in married life and my sobriety, I had my own transportation. Now that both children were in school, I had more time to devote to my writing career.

So I started two projects. The first was that I began going to the *Stillwater Gazette* every week, pestering John, the publisher, to hire me as a reporter, even though he had already added Abigail to the staff and I saw her byline in the paper—daily.

The second project was that I sat down and outlined a proposal for the book that was in my heart to write, a book for codependents who, like me, thought they were doing everything right by controlling people, taking care of other people—mostly addicts and alcoholics—and not taking care of themselves.

John Easton at the *Gazette* kept telling me he didn't want to hire me; Abigail was working out just fine.

And all twenty publishers I sent the book proposal to sent me a letter back, politely rejecting my proposal. "Good idea, but doesn't work for us." "Besides," one publisher had added, "we really don't think there's that many codependents out there anyway."

I kept pestering John Easton and praying for Abigail, anyway.

I packed away my boxes of research materials for the book on codependency I wanted so desperately and passionately to write. I couldn't afford to write a book that nobody was interested in publishing.

It was time to let at least that much go.

ᴄ୍ୟ

I stood in the parking lot outside the courthouse in Stillwater, Minnesota. The judge had just granted my divorce from David. David had moved out of the house.

I had already turned in the manuscript for *Codependent No More*. One of the book publishers I had queried, a local company that specializes in recovery materials, and my number one choice, had changed their mind. Out of the blue, they had called one day and said, "We want that book."

"Right away," they added.

The decision to divorce had also come out of the blue while I was writing that book. I had been down in my basement office in the house, a cement room with no windows that was smaller than most bathrooms. I was writing about the ABCs of codependency— Alcoholics, Boundaries, and Controlling—when I found myself writing the words, *You don't have to stay in relationships that make you miserable.* I realized I wasn't just writing to potential readers.

I was writing to myself.

I had a sudden burst of clarity. Getting a divorce was a far better, more loving thing for all of us—David, myself, and the children— than continuing to dwell on my angry fantasies about David, which included but did not amount solely to the one where I counted the years until he would be old and die from his drinking and then I'd finally be free.

I walked upstairs and told David it was time to get a divorce. I spoke not in anger, rage, or spitefulness, as I had so many times in the past. It was a clear, peaceful decision, a knowing feeling that it was time.

David peered at me over the newspaper he was pouring through, nodded, then went back to reading his paper. I repeated myself. He didn't respond. We both knew it was time. The marriage had been dead for years. The act of divorcing—burying this dead relationship—was long overdue, the final step in a grieving process that had begun a long time ago.

I had broken the news to the children soon after. Nichole, by then eight years old, was pained by our decision, but immediately rose to the challenge. "We'll be fine," she said, hugging me tightly, as if to reassure me. "A lot of parents I know get a divorce."

Shane got sad, real sad. We tried to keep the news from him as long as we could. I told him little pieces at a time, as much as I thought he could handle, until he finally understood. We made a pact then, the three of us—Nichole, Shane, and I—that we'd be a real family, no matter what. We made a pact that we'd get closer together, not farther apart. We made a pact then that the children would continue to be children, Shane would not become the man of the house, and I'd do my best to function in the role of both mother and father.

We made a pact that we'd always be together and love each other no matter what.

Also by this time, and also out of the blue, John Easton of the *Stillwater Gazette* had changed his mind. Well, he partially changed his mine. Abigail still had the full-time reporting job. But he had agreed to hire me as a freelancer. Twenty-five dollars a story. While Abigail churned out two and three stories a day, calmly and quietly interviewing people, getting them to speak loudly and excitedly give her the facts with her quiet demeanor, I was chugging away writing one story every two days, then turning it in for my reward—$25 and a byline for a story tucked away on the inside pages of the paper.

God, I hated Abigail.

∽

Months passed since the divorce. At least when I had been married, I had a body in bed next to me at night. I had finally gotten over sleeping with the phone in my hand, with 9-1 punched in, ready to punch in the last 1 if someone broke into the house. I had been terrified by being alone, much more frightened than I thought I would be. It had been one of the worst, most hidden, fears I had to face so far in my life. And I was only beginning to see how that fear drove me, quietly controlled so much of what I did, or didn't do.

David was out of work. He wasn't doing that well without me standing guard, acting as the self-appointed sobriety police. That meant no child support.

I watched Abigail, watched her real closely every time I went to the *Gazette* to turn a story in. She'd focus on her interview, then focus on her notes, then pound the story out—sometimes one, two, and three stories a day.

After watching her, I started playing a game with myself. I'd do my interview then go down into my little office and put an hourglass or an alarm clock next to me. I began timing myself. *Faster, faster, write faster,* I'd tell myself. *If Abigail can do it, you can too.* Although I was still praying for Abigail every day, we had started to talk and become friends. Even though I still resented her, Abigail was giving me strength.

I had come close to giving up my writing career. Although I'd been studying about writing and trying to build my career ever since I'd been pregnant with Shane, I had convinced myself after the divorce that the responsible thing to do was give it up. I had gone on welfare for a few months, while I wrote the book. Now, I needed a full-time job with benefits like insurance and sick leave and guaranteed pay. But I was torn. I had worked so hard to get to where I was, whatever and wherever that place might be. I hated to give up my dream now. And I didn't want to be gone from the house forty hours a week. I liked being there in the morning to see the kids out the door. I liked being there in the afternoon when they came home, even if I was in my office downstairs, hard at work. I liked being there if they were sick and had to stay home from school. I liked knowing it was me watching them during school vacations instead of a baby-sitter or daycare center.

I was walking down Main Street in Stillwater, filled with anxiety about what to do and where to go next. *I really should get a regular, full-time job*, I thought. Then another thought occurred to me: *Just because you're divorced, what makes you think you can't still follow your heart and dreams now. What makes you think you can't trust God's will?* So I went back to freelancing at the *Gazette*.

When David and I divorced, I had to assume thousands and thousands of dollars worth of debt. If I wanted to rebuild my credit, I not only had to pay my monthly bills, I had to pay these old bills too.

I had tackled all the bills, all the debts, in the most responsible way I knew. For a while, I had kept them hidden in a drawer, hoping that if I couldn't see them, it would mean they weren't there. The bill collectors kept calling. And even though I couldn't see them, the bills kept calling my name too. I avoided them for as long as I could, then I couldn't avoid them anymore. I was so enraged, so angry, so furious and overwhelmed by all this debt. But I had gotten myself into this mess, I had married David and divorced him, and I was responsible for myself. And all these bills.

I had taken all the bills out of the drawer and put them in nice, neat little piles. Then I called my creditors and told them I intended to do the best I could, even if that meant sending only $5 a month. Even if I didn't have the funds to pay everyone off, which I didn't, I could still approach it with an attitude of responsibility and faith. I made out a budget sheet, showing when I needed to send payments on each bill, and what I needed coming in to run the house.

I had set my financial goals, written them all out on a sheet. Then I had taken it one step further. I took out another sheet of paper and wrote down my dreams. If anything were possible, if I could have anything I wanted and it wouldn't be bad and wrong, what would I like to have happen in my life? Let's see, I thought, nibbling the end of a pencil. Money in the bank. Some new clothes for the children. And some food.

It was an admirable effort. It turned things around inside my spirit. But the money coming in each month didn't come close to the total that needed to go out. I kept trying, but I was getting tired.

One week, I was completely broke. Some of the stories I was working on took longer than I thought. A check didn't come in when I thought it would. I couldn't ask my mother for any more money. She had already helped David and me way too much. My poverty was beginning to strain that relationship.

Trusting God is good, I thought. *Going for my dream of being a writer is admirable too.* But my relationship with the universe had become a little codependent. It felt like I was giving and giving and I wasn't getting anything back.

Doing God's will is fine, I thought. *But God needs to know it takes money to live here in this world.*

ℂ

I got in the car and headed toward the little building, the one I was so familiar with in the town of Stillwater—the one I crept into and out of regularly over time. I didn't want anyone to see me. I didn't want to get caught. I had to hurry. It was getting late and I was frantic. I had no money, not one dollar in my purse. The children and I were down to one potato and one can of green beans. I had to go to the charity food shelf. We needed to eat.

I pulled into the food shelf building. It was Monday night. The parking lot was empty of cars. The interior of the building was dark. I walked up to the door. "Be back Wednesday," the sign said.

I went out to the car, lay my head on the steering wheel, and cried. I had been as strong as I knew how. The kids were home, hungry and waiting. I was drained, exhausted, and tired.

It was taking a lot of energy to be poor, and I didn't have it in me anymore. I was tired of juggling, hoping, doing without, fighting off the creditors, and telling the children why they had to be the only ones in their class with secondhand clothes and minimal food.

I was tired of being strong. I didn't know what to do next.

"Soon, you're not going to have to worry about money again—unless you want to," a quiet voice said. I got goose bumps all up and down my arms and on the back of my neck. I knew that I wasn't really hearing a voice. I was hearing these thoughts in my head. But the thoughts were not my own.

I had heard that voice before. The other time was when I was still in Willmar hospital, and the staff refused to let me out until I had a job. I had searched the want ads and the entire town, and I couldn't conjure up any work. I had applied for every possible job, from clerk to waitress. After two months of being rejected each time I applied for work, I had run out of hope. I had been waiting on a corner in the city of Willmar for the hospital bus to pick me up, when that same voice had spoken to me. It had clearly told me to look behind me, which I did, then walk up the stairway, which I did too. It was the stairway to the most prestigious, prominent law firm in town. "Go up and tell the head of the firm you're living at the state hospital and you want a job." I hesitated. If I did that, I'd never get work. But I did what the voice said, anyway.

I walked into that law firm, asked to talk to the head attorney. He was there and agreed to speak to me. I told him I had been an addict and now I was sober and clean. I told him I was living at the state hospital. And I told him I needed work.

He cleared his throat, said that was a coincidence, he had just been thinking about adding another secretary to his staff. Then he said he understood about alcoholism. Someone he cared about had that disease too. Two weeks later, he called me back and hired me for the job.

That's why I recognized the voice in front of the food shelf that gloomy night.

It was my angel. And he, or she, was talking to me again.

I turned on the ignition and drove back home. The children and I split the bounty—the potato and can of beans—remembering to be grateful for what we had. A million dollars didn't come flying through the door. There was no check in the mail. But something changed inside me that night.

I became filled with hope and peace.

I remembered something my fear and deprivation had almost caused me to forget. If I'm following my heart and trudging the road of destiny on my way to the Promised Land, all my needs will be taken care of. The catch is this: On some days, I might have a little more than I need. But sometimes those needs will only be provided one day at a time.

༉

I walked into John Easton's office at the *Stillwater Gazette* filled with embarrassment. He had finally, finally—after months and years of me relentlessly badgering him—agreed to put me full time on the staff. Abigail and I were getting along. I wasn't praying for her anymore. Well, hardly ever.

And now I had to quit. Something had to go. I needed to take some pressure off, maybe be a freelancer again.

I was getting calls all the time to do speaking engagements, make appearances at little gatherings, and talk about what I had learned about being a codependent. I wasn't making any money to speak of. By the time I paid travel expenses and paid the baby-sitter, there was hardly any money left. It amounted to about the same as what I'd had coming in before. But I couldn't stay at the paper full time. There was too much going on in my life. I had recently come down with pneumonia, trying to do the speaking engagements, raise the children, and talk to the media people who were calling me on the phone, interviewing me about *Codependent No More*.

I had loved my work as a reporter. I had gotten to live homeless on the streets and write a story about that. I had flown to Central America and reported on the Air National Guard controversy in Honduras. I had written stories on murders, city council meetings, and chemical dependency too. I had an editorial column that I loved writing each week.

I barely paid the bills each week, but somehow we were getting by. Ever since the angel had talked to me that day, I had been filled with serenity and peace—at least much of the time, and at least about the money part of my life.

I had started dating. I had naively gone out in the world thinking everyone was recovering, just like me. Men are going to be honest, I thought. I can finally have a meaningful relationship with a man who knows what it means to commit.

It would be years before I would realize some simple and apparent truths. I had written about the ABCs of codependency, but the learning and healing process had just begun. What I was learning now were three more Cs about codependency—compassion, completion, and commitment.

I was learning that taking care of yourself requires compassion. Extricating yourself from undesirable situations can be a difficult and entangled process. Sometimes it hurts a lot to let go and move on. It's one thing to say, "You're not a victim. Just take care of yourself." It's another to say those words gently and with compassion, whether we're speaking them to a neighbor, a stranger, or ourselves. I was learning that sometimes living life is more complicated and complex than following a recipe to bake a cake, and sometimes we have to make some hard calls. That's when we only have two options and we don't like either one of those, but one choice is definitely unacceptable and the other is one we don't prefer.

I was learning about completion too. Completion doesn't mean finishing our business with people, although that definition would fit too. Whenever I talked to people about meeting someone, a man with whom I could have a relationship and build my life, a soul mate, a lover, the missing piece that would make my life complete, they all said the same thing: "You're not ready for a relationship, and you're not going to have one until you know that you're complete just as you are."

I found the idea of completion irritating, annoying, frustrating, and sometimes mean. For one thing, the people who told me this were women who had been in the same unsatisfying, unfulfilling, and dysfunctional relationship all their adult lives, and it eluded me when, if ever, they had learned this lesson themselves. The second reason this completion thing irritated me was because I didn't understand what they meant.

Whole? Of course I am, I'd think. *I know I'm complete. But isn't it reasonable to want what most other people have, or at least think they've got—a committed partner, a relationship, a romantic love?*

It would be years before I understood this significant piece. What people were talking about when they mentioned the importance of knowing you're complete is absolutely true. But what they were really talking about is detaching and letting go.

It's admirable and healthy to go after our dreams, know what we want to accomplish, what we want to achieve, get, and gain. But whether it's a person, place, attribute, value, or thing, after we identify what it is we want and are seeking, then we need to let it go and know, not in our minds although that's a good place to start, but in our hearts and souls that we're okay—whole, complete, and at peace—whether we ever get what we're after or not.

A friend described it another way. "You know, it's the old Zen-Buddhist thing," he said. "When you're one with yourself, it becomes magical. You can get whatever you want."

Commitment was also an important concept for me to grasp. When I was a little girl, it looked and felt like no one was committed to me. It looked like the people around me weren't even that committed to themselves. When I grew up and got sober, I made a commitment to my sobriety. Then I had made a marital commitment to my husband David—one that I chose later to end. I had made a commitment to Nichole and Shane. I had committed to my writing too. I was about to learn what it meant to be unconditionally loyal to and committed to myself.

ॐ

"You have several guardian angels," the Babalawo said. "They're guarding and protecting you all the time. Everyone has at least one. You've just got to have faith in God."

"I do have faith," I said. "But it's also an issue of whether or not any particular thing or person is what God wants us to have."

"In some cases that's true," he replied. Some things and people don't belong to you. They belong to someone else. They're not yours. But faith is something you participate in. When you have faith, it means that even before an event comes to pass, you know and believe it's already yours."

"You have the potential for great ups and downs," the Babalawo said. "You can go to the most meager extremes of poverty. You can also go to the heights of great wealth. But don't forget the antidote for your personality: be grateful for what you have and for who and where you are, exactly as you are, today."

ฺ

I parked my car in the long-term parking lot at the Minneapolis–St. Paul International Airport, scanned for a luggage cart rack, didn't see one, picked up my overstuffed suitcase, and ran.

For some reason, probably because we always long for what we don't have, travel had seemed so glamorous. All those years I had been locked in the house with no money, no phone, no car, and a minimal life, I had envied people who got to go to the airport and take off in a jet. Now that I was traveling much of the time, travel had become frustrating, annoying, tiring, lonely, and a lot of hard work.

But this was a trip I had been waiting for a long time. I was on my way to the ABA—the American Booksellers Association convention. It's an important, annual publishing convention, one that most writers dream of attending. And I wouldn't be traveling alone. The people at the publishing company would be attending with me.

This weekend trip would be a treat.

I reached the ticket counter, produced my identification, and asked for my ticket that was to be prepaid and waiting for me. The clerk checked the records. There was no ticket there, no flight arrangements had been made in my name, and no one had paid for my fare. I ran to the gate where the group from the publishing company was supposed to meet. I didn't recognize a face in the milling crowd waiting for the Northwest flight to Los Angeles.

I ran back to the ticketing area, still dragging my luggage, and found a phone. I called the publisher and learned that the group had already left on an earlier flight. They were sorry they had forgotten my ticket and me. They wanted me to attend, but I'd have to purchase a ticket and fly alone.

I made my arrangements for the flight leaving in an hour and went to the gate. In half an hour, the airline made an announcement. Due to mechanical problems that flight was now cancelled. If I still wanted to go, I had another four-hour wait. For a few minutes, I thought about turning around and going home, canceling the entire trip. I was hurt, angry, frustrated, and I felt like I had been ditched.

I finally boarded the airplane and headed for Los Angeles. I was tired, frustrated, and crabby by the time I got off the plane. I didn't have time to check into my hotel. I wasn't sure where I was supposed to go. The other people had left with my itinerary. I decided to take my scraggly self straight to the convention hall.

The taxi dropped me off at a huge convention hall, the largest, most spread-out affair I'd ever seen. I dragged my suitcase across the lobby and reached the registration desk. What I didn't know about the ABA was that it was guarded like Fort Knox.

"You can't get in without your badge," they said.

I started to tell them the story—being ditched at the airport, waiting for my plane, lugging this suitcase halfway across the country, and I was too tired to dig through my suitcase looking for the name badge—then I realized I should save my breath. The guard didn't care.

"Badge please," he said. "Or you don't get in."

I started to cry, then bit my lip.

I laid my suitcase down on the floor. I opened it and started digging through all my clothes. I was crouching there in the lobby of the biggest publishing convention of the year with my personal belongings, clothes, including bras and underpants, spread out on the convention floor, digging for that damn badge, when I heard a familiar voice. It was one of my editors and friends from the publishing company.

"Hurry up," he said. "Show them your badge and come in."

I finally found the piece of paper I needed, repacked my suitcase, and started dragging it across the convention floor as I followed my friend to the publisher's booth. He seemed excited and happy. "Sorry we left without you," he said.

"That's okay," I said.

"Sorry we forgot your ticket," he said.

"I took care of it," I said.

He looked at me in a strange way. "Haven't you heard the news?"

"No," I said, still pouting. "What news?"

"Your book just hit *The New York Times* best-seller list."

Maybe Abigail didn't have my job after all.

৩

Other people don't have what's ours. Sometimes people we resent and consider enemies are displaying qualities we don't like in ourselves. Sometimes people we resent and consider enemies are teaching us attributes we can have too. They aren't enemies after all. They're really our friends.

Months after the book became a best-seller and I started making some money, I drove to a friend's house to have lunch. I was driving a new car. Well, it was a used one, but it was new to me. She looked at my car, my smile, and me.

"Girl, you've got it made," she said. "Now you get to have whatever you want."

Her words made me nervous. I knew that success and money didn't equal that much power.

There are many powers in this world—fame, money, love, sex, death, and the power to change are but a few. This is a story about the tremendous power that's available to each of us—the power of belief. We each have certain limitations, things we can't have, things we may want that aren't available to us. Part of becoming comfortable with our power means understanding what our limitations are at any particular time and working within that set of rules. Some of our limitations are real but some are unnecessary and self-imposed. Part of becoming comfortable with our power also means transcending the limits we've placed on ourselves and realizing what it is we can really accomplish and do.

Although we've each got an angel helping us—at least that's what many people believe—and we have surrendered to God's will, we still need to do our part too. After we surrender to powerlessness, it's time to learn about our power to co-create our lives. We do that by clearly stating our intentions to ourselves, God, and the universe about exactly what it is we want.

Don't be afraid to go for the impossible. Find out what you love, what you hate, what you like, and what you despise. Try something new, something wild. Get out on that edge. Go for it. Go for broke if you must.

Sometimes it's fun to go to extremes.

What I didn't know was that the days of poverty and writing stories for the paper, struggling as a single parent, worrying about the next meal, would in retrospect be some of the best days of my life.

Breathe

"You've got three hours, Mrs. Beattie. We'll give you three hours. That's it. If you haven't made the decision to pull the plug by then, we're going to make it for you."

The two neurosurgeons—a tall, thin man with dark hair and a sturdy woman with short, curly, ashen-colored hair—turned and walked out of the hospital room. I looked at Echo, my best friend. Usually smiling and ready to bubble forth words of hope, Echo averted my eyes and silently looked down at the floor. I walked over and stood by Shane, all tied and strapped to the hospital bed.

The respirator whooshed as it pushed air into his lungs. He was hooked to needles, monitors, tubes. I held his needle-taped hand, gently squeezing his fingers. Then I moved the bottom of the white bedcover a little, just enough to bare his feet. I had always loved touching his little feet, ever since he'd been a baby.

I put the covers back on Shane, then I walked to the corner of the room and sunk down into the blue vinyl armchair. This wasn't happening, couldn't be happening. We were just sitting at Perkins, eating strawberry pancakes and joking around with each other, after his basketball game.

Only a few weeks ago, he walked up to me. It was late in the evening, about nine o'clock. "Let's go sledding," he said.

"I'm too old," I said.

"No, you're not," he said.

"It's too cold," I said.

"Put on snow pants," he said. "Let's go." So we did. We took his sled to a hill across the street.

After ten runs down the hill I was tired. "You go alone for a while," I said. "I'll watch."

He climbed to the top of the hill, then slid to the bottom. But instead of slowing to a stop in the open area, he veered to the right, slamming into a tree and rolling off the sled. Then he lay there on his back in the snow, motionless, like he was now.

"Shane, are you all right?" I yelled. He didn't answer. I knew he was teasing. I ran over to him. "Stop it," I scolded. "You're not funny."

"Psych!" he said, sitting up and smiling.

"Don't tease like that," I said. "If anything happened to you, I don't know what I'd do. I don't think I could go on. Do you understand that?" I asked.

"Yes," he said. "I know that."

Now I kept wishing he'd sit up, smile, and say psych. He didn't. Echo stood there, looking down at the floor. I rested my head in my hands. The ticking of the clock on the wall and the whooshing noise from the respirator were the only sounds in the room.

༚

In the introduction to *Codependent No More*, I told an anecdote about stopping the pain. A friend who is a professional in the mental health field told me this story a long time ago. He heard it from someone, who heard it from someone else. It's one of my favorite stories. Here it is, again.

Once upon a time, a woman moved to a cave in the mountains to study with a guru. She wanted, she said, to learn everything there was to know. The guru supplied her with stacks of books and left her alone so she could study. Every morning, the guru returned to the cave to monitor the woman's progress. In his hand, he carried a heavy wooden cane. Every morning he asked her the same question: "Have you learned everything there is to know yet?" Every morning, her answer was the same. "No," she said, "I haven't." Whereupon the guru would strike her over the head with his cane.

This scenario repeated itself for months. One day the guru entered the cave, asked the same question, heard the same answer, and raised his cane to hit the woman in the same way, but this day the woman grabbed the cane from the guru, stopping his assault in midair.

Relieved to end the daily battering but fearing reprisal, the woman looked up at the guru. To her surprise, the guru smiled. "Congratulations," he said, "you have graduated. You now know everything you *need* to know."

"How's that?" the woman asked.

"You have learned you will never learn everything there is to know," he replied. "And you have learned how to stop the pain."

For most of my life, I've held my breath—sometimes in dread and fear, sometimes in excited anticipation. Sometimes I held my breath because I was waiting to see what would happen next. "Breathe," people would tell me, after I began working on my issues and myself. "Just relax and breathe," my aikido sensei regularly reminded me, when I began studying martial arts.

I learned that breathing, deep breathing, is a key to life.

In the late eighties and early nineties, I began getting body work done. When the chiropractors and masseuses who worked on me would find a sore spot, a spot that really hurt, my inclination was to flinch. "Don't touch that," I'd say. "It hurts." My doctor or masseuse would then tell me those were the spots we needed to work on most. One doctor in particular would press on the sorest, most sensitive spot, and he'd push hard. When I'd jerk away, he'd touch it again. "Just relax and breathe," he'd say. "Breathe into the pain. That's how we'll get it to dissipate, then ultimately disappear."

This is a story about breathing into the pain. It's about what we can do when the pain won't stop.

∽

My writing career had skyrocketed. *Codependent No More* was still on the best-seller list. *Beyond Codependency* hit the list too. For a while, both books were on the nonfiction list at the same time.

I didn't have to go groveling after editors and publishers, pulling on their pants legs, begging them to look at my work. Editors, publishers, agents, television, radio, and newspaper people were coming after me. I was able to use my past and what I had learned from it, to help others and myself too. And I was finally making a living doing the work I loved—writing articles, stories, and books.

It was my moment in the sun. Well, not really my moment, it was codependency's moment in the sun. Being popular was fun for a while. But sometimes being the spokesperson for the caretakers, control freaks, martyrs, and victims of the world overwhelmed me.

At the beginning of 1990, I was sitting at the kitchen table with my head in my hands. I had a contract to write a meditation book, *The Language of Letting Go.* The manuscript was past due, and I couldn't figure out how to begin. I didn't even know how I had gotten here, to this place in my life.

Shane was eleven years old at the time. He watched me with an amused air of concern and confidence.

"Why am I even doing this?" I asked.

He got up from his chair. "Because it's what you do best," he said, gently patting my head.

Shane was always able to bring out the best in me. Even while I was pregnant with him, his presence had changed my life. I had stopped feeling sorry for myself in that old house. Instead, I had become grateful for what I had. I started writing for the newspaper a month before he was born. I was still pregnant when I wrote my first story, turned it in, then had the thrill of seeing my byline in print.

Something about Shane gave me the courage to move forward, go on, connect with my life in a way I hadn't before.

I felt strong, full of chutzpah. Spunk.

I had been so worried before he was born about whether I could love him as much as I loved Nichole. Those fears vanished the moment he was born. He came out upside down, breech. That should have been my first clue. I wasn't going to breastfeed, but Shane nestled right up to me and began nursing before they cut the cord.

Sometimes when people come into our lives, they're more than a mother, a brother, a friend, or a child. Those people ignite our spirit. Those people are kindred souls.

I wrote *The Language of Letting Go*, then immediately followed it by writing another book. I had a stack of book contracts sitting by my computer in my writing office at the home on Northland in Stillwater. Where I was in my career and my life was every writer's dream. For the first time in our lives, the financial struggle was gone. The bills were paid. I had paid off all my debts. I had paid back the welfare department the money they had given us while I wrote *Codependent No More*. We had money in the bank. We were living in a nicer house.

But a still small voice spoke to me again. It was time to stop. Take a break. Spend some time with my kids.

Shane came to me one day. He had a magazine opened to a particular ad. It was a beautiful, two-page spread featuring the aquamarine waters of the Caribbean. "Can we go there, Mom?" he asked. "Please . . . Please . . ."

Sometimes, when your children ask you for something, you know it's not the usual demand or request. You know a message is coming through them to you and that what they're asking for is right. That's how I felt that day.

"Sure we can, honey."

"When?" he asked.

I looked at the ad. "I'll put it together this month. We'll go soon," I promised.

The children and I laughed and played in the sunshine all summer. We went to the Caribbean and rented a house on the beach for two weeks. We went to movies. We fished. We watched television. We made candy apples. We went out to eat.

In September, the children returned to school. We were a happy family but busy with life. Shane loved his teacher. Nichole was finishing junior high. I was so busy with the children, I didn't have much time to date. I didn't know what to do with my needs and desires as a woman. I told myself that maybe later I would meet someone who was right. *Maybe you could have it all in life,* I thought, *but maybe you don't get to have it all at once.*

One day, a reporter from the *St. Paul Pioneer Press* came to the house to interview me. We spent most of the afternoon sitting at my kitchen table talking about my history, codependency, and my life now. At three o'clock, the front door burst open and Shane bounded into the kitchen. He stopped long enough to kiss my cheek, then raced down the steps. "How was school today?" I hollered after him.

"I got suspended," he hollered back.

The reporter's eyes widened. I excused myself and started walking rapidly after him.

"Just kidding!" he hollered back.

Early one evening I walked in the door. I had been out attending to some business. The Jeep was parked in front; I had driven our other car.

Shane met me at the door. He said Nichole was hiding in bed. She had been driving the Jeep and had had an accident. Driving the Jeep? She was only fourteen.

I went outside. The right front of the Jeep was smashed. I went down to Nichole's bedroom. Nichole was cowering under the covers. She had taken the Jeep for a joy ride and crashed into a neighbor's mailbox. She confessed that occasionally she and Shane would wait until I fell asleep at night, then they'd sneak upstairs, get the keys, and go for a little ride on the dirt road that ran behind the house.

"I don't understand why you would do this," I said to Nichole. Then I turned to Shane. "And you," I said. "Why would you go along with this. What'd you do? Just go along for the ride?"

He looked at me thoughtfully. "I fastened my seat belt first," he said.

I learned many lessons from and through my children.

There was the day Shane and I went out on the St. Croix River on a Waverunner. A Waverunner is a small boating vehicle that you straddle like a motorcycle. We donned life jackets and took off. I was nervous; Shane was exhilarated. Midway through our ride, my worst fear came true. We took a spill. We were floundering in thirty feet of water. The Waverunner was bobbing on the waves in front of me like a motorized turtle on its back.

"Don't panic," Shane said.

"What if we drown?" I said.

"We can't," he said. "We're wearing life jackets. See! We're floating."

"The machine is upside down," I said. "How are we going to turn it over?"

"Just like the rental guy told us to," he said. With an easy gesture, we turned the machine right-side up.

"What if we can't climb back on?" I asked.

"We can," Shane said. "That's what Waverunners were made for—climbing on in the water."

One day the children and I were down at the St. Croix River, walking on the dock. I turned to Shane. "Teach me what it's like to be a kid," I said.

Without missing a beat, Shane pushed me into the water. "That's what it's like to be a kid," he said.

I had told him when his dad left, that he wasn't the man of the house. His job—his only job—was to enjoy being a child.

He did his job well.

One day, Nichole came home from school and set down her books.

"Do you know what we learned in class today?" she said. "It's a statistic." Nichole loved history, trivia, and statistics.

"Before the next year is up, one child we know will die."

୬

I found the magical Christmas tree that year too. Echo was with me when we found it, all set up at the store. Iridescent needles, the color of pearls, were illuminated with tiny pink lights. It was decorated with beads, crystals, hearts, and life-size birds with feathers on their tails. A train chugged and whistled around the base. It was so pretty I just stood there and stared.

At first, I didn't think I should spend the money. But finally I bought it. I knew I had to have that tree. I brought it home and assembled it. It took my breath away, as it had in the store.

"Not bad for a fake tree," Shane said.

"It's pretty. Real pretty, Mom," Nichole said.

Magic was in the air that Christmas. We all felt it. I didn't know where it came from or what it meant. But it was there. It felt the way you think every Christmas should feel when you're a kid.

For New Year's, the children and I were invited to attend a private gathering at Hilton Head Island. People from all walks of life got together to talk on panels about what they believed were important ideas that helped change our world.

I was surprised I was invited. I was intimidated when we were told to bring clothes to *dress for dinner.* Dressing for dinner until now had meant putting on your winter jacket so we could drive to McDonald's.

We rose masterfully to that occasion. I participated on panels. The children played with the dolphins. We even got to meet the man who was at that time considering running for president—Bill Clinton.

It hit me hard one night. Shane and I were at the movie theater. We went to the movies a lot. I was sitting there watching the show, acutely aware of his presence. He was resting his feet on the back of the seat in front of him. I thought about scolding him then decided not to bother. No one was sitting there. And some things weren't worth fussing over.

I tried to watch the movie, but a thought interrupted my concentration. This isn't going to last forever. Time is racing by. My children have been such a big part of my life for so long, but someday they'll be gone, moving on with their lives. And this night, sitting here at this movie, will be a memory.

Make every moment count.

For Shane's birthday dinner at the end of January, the children and I and a few of their friends went out to eat.

We toasted Shane's birthday, each of us holding up our soda or our glass of water. The waiters sang "Happy Birthday." Shane looked embarrassed, but we could tell he really liked it. We talked about his goals and dreams for the next year. Then we promised each other that no matter how old we were or where we lived, we'd always get together on our birthdays.

When I asked Shane where he'd like to go this year, whether he had any new suggestions for trips, he thought about it for a while, then shrugged his shoulders.

"I think you've taken me everywhere I've wanted to go, Mom," he said.

That's when Nichole came up with her idea for her birthday present to Shane. She apologized that she didn't have a gift. "But how about this?" she said. "You can come skiing with Joey and me this Saturday."

Shane's eyes lit up. He'd like that a lot, he said.

At home later that evening, Shane sidled up to me while I sat at my dressing table brushing my hair. He opened my jewelry drawer and took out a small gold cross, one his father had given me at the time of our divorce. "Can I have this?" he asked.

"Don't be silly," I said. I thought he was teasing. He repeated his question and I knew he was serious. It was that tone again, that tone in his voice. "Sure, honey," I said. "You can have that."

The following day, Shane stopped me in the kitchen on his way out the door to school. He pulled down his sweater neck and pointed to the cross. It was hanging on a gold chain around his neck.

"God is with me now," he said.

Friday night was busy. My son John, the one I had given birth to when I was an addict, was now grown, a married man. His wife, Jeanette, had recently given birth to their first child, a boy. The children and I were baby-sitting Brandon that night. It was fun to have a baby in our lives again. And it gave John and Jeanette a night off.

Brandon fussed all night. I let him sleep next to me for a while, then put him into his crib. About three in the morning, I finally fell asleep. At six thirty, Shane nudged me. He kept at me until I finally woke up.

"I've got a basketball game this morning," he said. "Please come with me. You haven't watched me play sports for a while."

I was tired. But I pulled myself out of bed, fed and changed the baby, and the three of us—Shane, Brandon, and I—went to Shane's basketball game. I remember sitting at the sidelines holding the baby, watching Shane play ball. Some people say you don't know how much someone means to you until it's too late. Well, I watched Shane out there on the basketball court and all I could think of was how much I loved him and what a blessing he was in my life.

When we left the game, Shane suggested we go out to eat. When we got home, he started getting ready. Today was the day he was going skiing. Chrissy, the baby-sitter who watched the children when I had to leave town, was driving the children to Afton Alps, a nearby ski resort where the children frequently skied. Another mother would be driving them home. Shane and Nichole bundled up. They asked me for some money. Then when they were almost out the door, Shane turned back to me.

"I love you, Mom," he said.

"I love you too," I said. "Be home by six."

At six o'clock the children weren't home.

At eight o'clock, the telephone rang.

It was the ski patrol from Afton Alps. A man's voice informed me my son had been hurt in a skiing accident. I was frightened but not too badly. Shane had been injured before playing sports. Shane was young, strong, healthy. He was always fine.

"He's unconscious," the man said. "But don't worry. This happens to skiers all the time. We'll call you back in ten minutes." The baby started crying. I picked him up and sat by the phone.

A few minutes later, the telephone rang again. "Your son's still not conscious," a man told me. "We're sending him to St. Paul Ramsey Hospital in an ambulance. Meet us there." He paused. "But don't worry," he added. "Everything will be fine."

When I burst through the doors to the emergency room, a nurse was standing there waiting for me. I thought she would take me to my son. Instead, she put her arm around my shoulder and guided me to a small room with a cross on the wall. "Do you have someone you can call?" she asked.

She said something about Shane slipping, hitting his head on a mogul, an icy patch on the ski slopes. She said something about brain tests and no brain waves. She said something about his brain stem being knocked loose. But what I heard most clearly were these two words: *no hope*.

They had him hooked up to IVs and monitors and the machine that made the whooshing sound, the one that was doing his breathing for him. I had called in every doctor, every specialist, every neurosurgeon I could find. I had called in ministers and healers. I was surrounded by friends and family. I was doing everything I knew to save my son's life. But he just lay there.

Then they told me Shane's liver and kidneys had shut down. It was too late. They were going to unplug the equipment at one o'clock this morning.

I exploded in a rage. I started screaming at the doctor. "Damn it," I told her. "This is my baby you're talking about!" I slammed my foot into a metal door as hard as I could. Echo calmed me down.

I looked up from the blue vinyl chair in the corner of the room where I sat.

Time was almost up.

Now I understood what was happening this past year. We were saying good-bye.

I left the room while Shane's friends and relatives came into the room and said their good-byes. Then I cut off a lock of Shane's hair. I touched his foot, one more time. Then I held him while they shut off the respirator. "I love you," I said. "Always have. Always will."

The week of Shane's funeral, many people called to offer comfort and inquire about funeral arrangements. Friends called. Family members called. Even Bill and Hillary Clinton called.

And a friend who had gone back to using drugs called.

I just wanted three or four hours of relief. I figured God would understand.

My friend picked me up. We drove around for a while. He asked if I really wanted to get high, and I said yes, I did. He asked me what I wanted, he said he could get whatever I desired. I said I wanted to shoot dope, I said I really needed a fix. For a moment I thought about all the people I had been writing to and trying to serve with my work. I felt like I was letting them down. But I figured that they'd understand and forgive me too.

My friend asked me exactly what did I want—he couldn't get something for me unless he knew exactly what it was I wanted. I said we had to start with the syringes first. By then, HIV was rampant. I said I had to have a clean needle, and nothing less would do. I didn't want to kill myself. I had Nichole to think about too. So we drove around the Twin Cities, looking for an all-night pharmacy. After about an hour, we found one. I had my syringe. Now I needed something to put in it.

"What do you want to use?" he asked again.

I thought seriously about cocaine. The euphoria, the pain-relief from that would be good. But I didn't want to get energized and stimulated. There was nothing I wanted to stay awake and do.

Besides, I knew that coke was an extremely dangerous drug. A dosage used one time might be fine. The next time that same dosage could produce a heart attack. It was like playing Russian roulette with your respiratory system and heart. I couldn't do that to Nichole and myself. No, cocaine wasn't a safe bet.

Heroin would give the pain relief I sought. But I knew about that too. The people who sold it mixed it with all kinds of substances to increase the volume of their sales. There was no quality control over what I'd be injecting in my veins. I had worked so hard to clean up my body. Eighteen years earlier, the police department had taken pictures of my arms to use as drug prevention in schools throughout the state, to help educate children. Now, I didn't even have tracks on my arms anymore. No, I didn't want to put something toxic and dirty into my arms.

"I'm waiting," my friend said. "If you don't tell me what you want, I can't get it for you. It's getting late. Could you hurry up?"

Well, there was Dilaudid and morphine. But that was for pain relief, a medical prescription. If I really needed that, it was up to a doctor to decide and prescribe.

I turned to my friend. "I'm sorry," I said. "I changed my mind. I guess if I legitimately need any medication, I should call my doctor tomorrow and see what he says. Please take me home. I feel sick. . . ."

I didn't hear any angels that night. I didn't feel any rush of spiritual enlightenment. I didn't feel anything except that God-awful pain. But I still call what happened to me that night, *experiencing the grace of God.*

Shane's schoolmates and friends, relatives from all sides of our family, people we barely knew, packed the chapel at Lakewood Cemetery for Shane's funeral. My friend Louie hired a hot-air balloon. It hovered in the background, ready to float into the air. After the ceremony, we each received a balloon. Then all together, we let them go.

I reluctantly released my balloon last. It hovered, lingering in the air as the other balloons disappeared.

When the children were little and I'd buy them a balloon, some-times their balloons would break free into the air. The kids would cry and fuss because they lost their precious balloons. Then I'd tell them a story about how God saves all our balloons and when we get to heaven, everything we lost will be waiting there.

Now, I had to tell myself that story too.

"Do you cry a lot?" the Babalawo asked me, sincerely and thought-fully. "Not so much, anymore," I said. "But for a few years I couldn't stop."

"Get out into the sunshine. Enjoy life. Laugh. Dance. Play," he said. "Sometimes we need to cry, and that's good. But when you cry and you're sad and depressed too much and too long, you open the door to letting more negativity in."

"This is what I believe about destiny," he said. "I believe destiny brings the people into our life that we're supposed to be with. And when it's time, destiny takes them out again."

For the first time in our visit, I wanted to argue, but I didn't. It just seemed to me that sometimes this power called destiny and fate let certain people linger around way too long, and it took others away too soon.

What many people don't understand is that it's not just living through the tragedy that hurts. The problem, the challenge, and what really hurts is trying to find the will and passion to get up and live in the aftermath.

Years later, when I was doing a book signing in Minnesota, a young girl stood in line. She had the sweetest face and great big glasses that kept falling down her nose. She cleared her throat, looked at me, and started to speak in the softest voice. "I didn't want to bother you at the funeral, Mrs. Beattie, but I thought maybe I could come to talk to you here. Shane was in my class. For two years in my family, everything went wrong. My dad went to fight in the war in the Gulf. My grandfather had just died. My mother was sad. I was lonely and sad too. Every day at school, Shane would spend time with me. No matter what was going on in my life, he always made me feel better. He always made me laugh. I just wanted to come here today and tell you this," she said. " I really, really miss Shane."

"I know," I said. "I miss him too."

I didn't work for a long time. My job was to write, and I didn't have anything to say.

My friends got tired of calling me and asking me how I was. The first year wasn't the worst, although that was difficult. The pain went on day and night, and I barely had a break. The second year was harder. I can't remember a moment when my heart didn't ache. And the thing about losing somebody you love deeply is that time alone doesn't heal that wound. The more time that passes, the worse your heart hurts. Every day you miss that person more.

Nichole was going through her struggles too. She grieved as much as I did. We went to therapy, got help, but it didn't stop the pain.

"Everybody thinks you're doing okay, Mom," Nichole said one day. "I'm the only person who knows you're not doing that well."

She was right. I had given up.

That's when Scotty came along, wandered right back into my life. Scotty had come to Minnesota to tend to some medical problems. My friend Echo directed him back into my life. Destiny crossed our paths again.

The first time Scotty saw me, all those years since we'd seen each other slipped away. He cupped my face in his hands. "I don't know what it feels like to lose a child," he said looking into my eyes. "But I know what it feels like to live knowing you can never have what you want in life. I know what it feels like to lose something valuable to you. And I know what it feels like to lose hope."

That's when he showed me his legs. They had been paralyzed since he was eighteen.

"I have a lot of compassion for what you're going through," he said. "But it's time for you to get up."

Scotty took me to the ocean, to the park, to the lakes, and to the mountains. He made me listen to old people—passersby on the street—really listen when they talked. "Isn't that great?" he'd say. It didn't matter what the people said. He thought just listening to people chatter away and figure out their lives was fun. Sometimes he took me to the grocery store and we spent time looking at all the foods.

"Isn't this beautiful," he'd say, holding up a mango or an orange. "Taste it. Mmmm. Good, isn't it? God really does beautiful work."

Sometimes Scotty would read me stories, like *Winnie the Pooh* or the writings by Kahlil Gibran. Sometimes he'd read to me out of the Bible or another holy book. He talked to me about Merlin and the knights of long ago. He talked to me about Avalon and wondered when it was coming back. He made me watch *Star Wars* and lectured me about the force.

"Teach me more about magic," I said one day.

"I don't have to," Scotty said. "Just remember what you already know."

Then, our relationship became complicated. Scotty had problems. He had to leave. I was back on my feet, dedicated to fulfilling my commitment to Nichole. With the help of God, Nichole's persistence, and much screaming, bribing, threatening, begging, and pleading from me, Nichole finished her senior year of high school. The day of her graduation party, the movers loaded our belongings. That night we left Minnesota and moved to California, the West Coast.

I was slowly learning to breathe again, learning to breathe into the pain.

Obsession

What I remember most about writing *Codependent No More* was wanting to write a book that helped people understand codependency. I wanted to help them get it.

I didn't want people to have to stumble around in the dark for years, waiting for the answers to why they were doubled over in pain when all they were trying to do was help another person who was wrong, sick, and obviously out of control. I didn't want therapists and helping professionals to have to spend the first twenty or one hundred sessions waiting for their clients to finish obsessing about the other person before beginning to talk about themselves.

I wanted that light to go on in one moment.

"My husband was in treatment for his alcoholism when he called and told me he had arranged for me to go stay at a place that would help me understand and heal from what had happened to me because of his drinking," Anna, a dark-haired women with feisty raven eyes, told me. "I agreed instantly, packing my finest clothes, some divine chocolates, my favorite romance novels, and a bottle of Valium. What had happened to me because he drank was simple. I sat in a darkened house staring out the window, night after night, waiting for him to come home after pulling his drunken disappearing acts and plotting ways I could kill him when he did. When he finally would come home, I'd scream, rage at him, then give him the silent treatment and take his credit card and go shopping. I'd sleep alone on the couch wishing he were dead and feeling overcome with grief because the man I had married, or thought I had married, was gone. Healing from his drinking would be easy. I'd rest and watch television while he changed.

"When I walked in the door, a nurse met me in the lobby. She took away my chocolates and my Valium, then handed me a copy of *Codependent No More*. I sat in that lobby and read that book cover to cover in one sitting. Then I started crying and couldn't stop.

"That was years ago," Anna said. "My husband didn't stay sober then. But I began healing from my codependency issues. We're still together. He's sober today. But now, if he wants to get crazy, I know I don't have to go there with him anymore. I just look at him and say, 'Honey, you can go there if you want, but you're going to go there alone, without me.'

"That's how it is with codependency," Anna said. "You either get it, you understand it, or you don't."

ॐ

I went to a party in Los Angeles one evening and approached an attractive woman in her mid-thirties. "Will you talk to me about your codependency issues and your recovery from them?" I asked her, after a few moments of informal chatting.

This woman reared up, stiffened up. I could see her eyes widen and feel the hairs on the back of her neck bristle. "Excuse me," she said. "But you must have me mixed up with someone else. I'm not codependent. I'm perfectly fine."

I said I was sorry; I had gotten confused. What I didn't tell her—what I wanted to tell her but didn't—was that although she didn't think she was codependent, all her friends did. They had pointed her out and told me to interview her.

"I understand codependency," my daughter Nichole said to me one day. "But I'm not in a relationship with alcoholics or addicts, trying to make them stop drinking and feeling victimized because they don't. I don't get what codependency has to do with me."

I explained a few ideas to her.

"Isn't everyone codependent?" she asked after a while.

"No," I said. "Everyone's not." *Well, maybe almost everyone is,* is actually what I thought. And it's not so much that everyone's codependent. It's that codependent behaviors consist of crossing a lot of thin lines. Many of the things that good codependents do—most things in fact—are normal behaviors that most people do. But we take them over the edge.

Being sensitive to other people's feelings, caring about what others think, is a good and decent behavior. But caring too much about other people's feelings and worrying too much about what they think while at the same time ignoring what we feel and think—devaluing our emotions and instincts and feeling guilty, ashamed, or unconscious of what we think—is a codependent kind of thing.

Helping others do things can be a friendly act, a good neighbor doing good deeds. It's fun and it's important to serve people we love, strangers, and people in our community. But becoming entangled in a relationship or many relationships where we take on another person's responsibilities out of guilt, an undue sense of obligation, or because we've been manipulated to do that is a codependent kind of thing.

Codependency can help other people stay sick and trapped in diseases, such as drug addiction, alcoholism, gambling, or their own fears. And it can really wear us out and make us mad. Most people are involved with people who have problems because most people have some issues or troubles they're trying either to escape or resolve. When we're sinking in quicksand because everyone we're trying to help is sinking too and pulling us under and we're waiting for someone to come and rescue us, that's untreated codependency.

Being charming, speaking and behaving in a diplomatic, friendly way can be a necessary, helpful ingredient to getting along in the world. But if we cross the codependency line, we find ourselves being only who other people want us to be and forgetting who we are.

Caring about people we love, nurturing and helping them through rough times, being there when they need us without expecting them to do something to pay us back, is exemplary behavior. But always giving all we have, being manipulated, lied to, deceived, and hurt reflects a lack of love for ourselves. We deserve better than that. Pampering ourselves excessively can be a sickening kind of thing. But giving all our love and nurturing to others and not giving any to ourselves is another, well, codependent kind of thing.

Forgiving people for things they do is essential if we want forgiveness ourselves. But too much repeated forgiveness for the same behavior done to us repeatedly by the same person might mean we've crossed the line to denial. This kind of forgiveness can be a trick that keeps both people trapped. This doesn't mean we don't forgive. It means we need to first acknowledge and accept the truth.

There are a lot of thin lines we can cross that take us from the green range of normal into the red zone of stark raving codependency.

Passion is a necessary ingredient for many of us. Going through the motions, living like robots, making all our decisions—from work to where we live—only from our heads leads to sterile, colorless lives. But living life and making decisions based solely on emotions can take us across another line. Obsession is on the other side of passion, right across the bridge.

That's what this story is about—crossing that particular thin line. I didn't write it, but it could easily have been written by me. My daughter handed the following story to me, right before she told me she had made a decision that was going to twist the course of my destiny once again.

ॐ

I'd been sitting by the phone for three hours. I tried to rationalize that the reason I wasn't going out on a Friday night was because

I was tired. Well, I was tired but I was also expecting a call. Well, I wasn't actually expecting the phone call but I was hoping for it. Really hoping for it. It had been a week since our first and last date and he hadn't called. I checked the ringer. It was turned on but you never know. Just as I was about to call Pac Bell to complain, the phone rang.

"Hello," I answered in my sexiest voice—after the first ring.

"Hey! It's Arnold. Sounds like I interrupted something."

It was my gay friend, Arnold.

"I have to call you back," I responded quickly, terrified that HE would call at the same moment Arnold had called and I wouldn't hear the call waiting and then it would go to voice mail and he wouldn't leave a message and . . .

"So you do have company? Who is it? Oh my God, it's . . ."

Click. I had to hang up. I threw myself on the bed. Should I call him? No, I couldn't. I had already hung up on him three times this week. But he didn't know it was me. Maybe I will call him. One more time couldn't hurt. I dialed the number. He answered after three rings.

"Hello."

Click. I had to hang up. Now I'll have to wait at least an hour before I can call him back. What was I doing? Our date hadn't gone well enough to even mention another date and forget about an unsolicited phone call. This guy lived on the opposite coast. What was I going to say? "Oh, I wanted to see what you're doing tonight?" or "I'm in your neighborhood. Thought I'd stop over."

I called him again.

"Hello."

I just sat there not saying anything.

"Whoever this is, you're pathetic," he said.

Click. I had to hang up.

Sylvia Plath once wrote, "Dying is an art, like everything else. I do it exceptionally well." And I understood her words. Well I didn't understand literally, but I understood what drove her to declare suicide as an art form. I knew.

Obsession is an art. I do it exceptionally well. And better and better each year, each passing moment. It may be the only thing I will ever be an expert at. Obsessing is deeply embedded in my DNA. Sometimes I think it's a gift I was born with and other times a curse. Regardless I obsess, therefore I am.

I am currently obsessed with Charles Bukowski. There is no other writer. I tried last night to read Hemingway, who by all accounts is an amazing writer, but I could not do it. I must read more Bukowski until there is nothing left to read and then and only then can I move on to another. The downside to an obsession of this nature, for me, is that I cannot read or enjoy another writer's work until I am finished with my current object of obsession. When I try to read someone else, I only compare and of course there is no comparison at all. The upside to this obsession is that there is an end in sight. There are only so many Bukowski books to read and I have damn near read them all. Once I am finished I will be forced to find another object of my obsession. I know this because this is not the first or second or third time I have been through this. You might ask, Why not read a little of everything? And to that I tell you, there is no gray area. I hate or love. One or the other.

My other recent obsessions include Aveda. I own everything from the store, even shampoo for red hair and I'm a brunette. Then there are my more embarrassing and shameful obsessions, like *The Jerry Springer Show,* which I do not watch in front of just anyone. In fact, if we are not that close I will flick past the show and make some judgmental comment about all the pathetic people who watch that trash. We must be extremely close for me to watch this in front of you and once you have won my trust I will watch and shout along with the guests secretly feeling superior because I have never resorted to being a guest on a talk show. Yet.

Fill in the blank: I am currently obsessed with _____ (insert his/her name, a store, an article, his/her name, an entertainer, a writer, a city, his/her name, a TV show, his/her name, a food, his/her name). I have been obsessed with many writers, foods,

TV shows, astrology programs, stores, entertainers, and cities. But nothing, nothing at all, has driven me more than my obsession with a man. This is my forte. My darkest, most obsessive moments have come at that dreadful time when the one man I want more than anything—the one who would complete me, take me places I've never gone before, fill my mind with ideas unknown to the rest of the world—when that knight in shining armor doesn't have the faintest clue that I exist. Actually he does. He just doesn't seem to care all that much.

My obsession with the man of the moment has brought me to one of the most desperate, pathetic places I have ever been in my life. My realm of normalcy has been stretched so far at times that I've had to write the following note to myself and post it on my bathroom mirror to bring me back to earth.

Dear self:

Call for help when you've already done or are about to do the following:

Call him and tell him I'm pregnant when we haven't yet had sex;

Show up at his door, unannounced, with my bags in hand;

Call the phone company to file a complaint that there is no way in hell my ringer is working properly;

Surprise him by appearing on a talk show to talk about my relationship with him;

Get his name tattooed anywhere on my body;

Call and hang up more than once a day;

Drive by his house more than once a day;

Plan it so I just happen to be in the same place, at the same time, as him.

I'll admit it. I've gone to most of those places. The biggest lesson I learned from partaking in the preceding activities is don't, under any circumstances, perform these tricks under the influence of any mood-altering substance. I do not care how badly you want to.

Throw the phone out of the window, break it, do anything, but do not call him if you are drunk. Go to treatment. Get help for you alcoholism/addiction. Get sober.

Then call.

I have a friend who has scars on his back and chest because of one woman's obsession with him. When he fled to my house for safety and told me the story of how this woman had showed up at his apartment at 4 A.M. (prime obsessing hour) and forced her way in only to start screaming at him how much she loved him and showing him by biting and scratching him until the police were called, I tried to comfort him. But it really was her whom I wanted to comfort and take in my arms and tell her I understood and would do anything to help her get him back. I knew what she was going through. Instead I told him, "Wow. This girl sounds crazy. I would never do anything like that." Then he told me that was the reason he liked me so much.

I once dated (and was obsessed with) someone who had a restraining order against him from his ex-girlfriend for "stalking" her. I must say that forty phone calls a day and banging on her window sounds more like, well, love to me. She didn't think so and neither did the judge. Remember the good old days when there were no stalking laws, no caller ID and no *69? Those were the simple days. Now there are laws and we must obey them, or figure out ways around them.

I mentioned earlier that I have been obsessed with certain cities in my life. I am currently, and probably will be for life, obsessed and completely in love with New York City. I love everything about it and naturally hate anything about any other city. I started visiting New York on weekends when I was seventeen and fell in love instantly. I started coming back a year ago and pretty soon I was blowing my entire paycheck on plane tickets to New York every other weekend. I had made plenty of friends in New York and planned extravagant weekend plans with them before coming and no one could understand why, when I so carefully and thoroughly planned out my weekends, I was nowhere to be found for the entire time I was there. I'll tell you why. I was obsessed with this certain man who didn't particularly care if I existed and I was coming here to win him, to capture his heart, and take him hostage. When I ultimately and inevitably moved to New York, I told everyone it was for career reasons and had this elaborate story of how I could only really succeed in New York . . . blah blah blah. I lied. I moved there because I was obsessed with the one man who didn't want me and I knew if he could only see how wonderful I was on an everyday basis he would love me, fall for me, and we would live happily ever after.

Well, we dated and it was fine but the second he was interested, I wasn't. Those are the rules of the game. Of course I never let him know how actively I pursued him—you cannot let them know. I cannot imagine his reaction if I told him the countless times I called and hung up on him or walked by his apartment or just happened to be taking another business trip to New York and that he was the only reason I moved to New York. He would, no doubt, commit me.

This person is now a good friend of mine and of course I spend countless hours wondering what about him I was so obsessed with and I still have no idea.

Recently, while he was away on a business trip, he let me stay at his apartment and house-sit. One night at 3 A.M. the phone rang.

"Is Troy there?" this woman asked me in that fake, sexy raspy voice that I knew all too well.

"No. He's not. Can I take a message?"

"Yeah. Just tell him Sarah called."

I lay back down to go to bed wondering who Sarah was.

The phone rang again.

"Hi. It's Sarah again. Can you give Troy this number for me?" She proceeded to give me a New York number.

"You do know that it's 3 A.M.?" I asked in an irritated voice.

"Yeah, but I saw Troy today and he told me to call him at 3 A.M."

"You saw Troy today?" I asked her.

"No. I talked to him and he told me to call him at 3 A.M."

"He told you to call him here, in New York?"

"Yes, he did and now I am calling him. Why are you questioning me?" she asked in another tone I knew all too well.

"Troy isn't in New York and he hasn't been for a month."

"Whatever. I know him so much better than you do." Click.

I lay in bed for a few minutes replaying the conversation in my head. I picked up the phone.

"Troy, it's me. This girl Sarah just called for you." Then I told him the entire conversation while he tried to figure out who this girl was.

"Whoever she is, she's crazy," he said.

"Yeah," I agreed. "I would never do anything like that."

"I know," he said. "That's the reason I like you so much."

And we hung up the phone. Before I could go to sleep, I couldn't resist calling Sarah just one time and hanging up.

ᘐ

"It's fiction," Nichole said, when I finished reading her story.

"Of course," I said.

"You know how for years you've been telling me I'm probably going to be a writer, and I said no, I wasn't going to be a writer, I didn't want to be like you?"

"Yes," I said.

"Well, you're right," she said. "I am a writer. Well, at least I want to be one, but not like you. I don't want to be the self-help kind. You know how I've been thinking about my career and what I have to do to take it to the next step?"

"Yes?" I said, waiting for the sacred duty of any writer, which is getting to the point.

"The point is this," she finally said. "I'm leaving California and moving to New York."

Now that the pieces of our lives had finally been pasted, glued, and taped back together, Nichole had grown up. And she wasn't just leaving home. She was moving to the other coast.

I started to argue with Nichole. She just looked at me.

"You've always taught me to follow my heart. You can't tell me not to do it now," she said.

I had sacrificed much of my life for my children, willingly and with—most times—great joy. After Shane's death, my commitment to Nichole was what kept me alive. Now my baby was leaving.

It was time to make a new commitment. It was time to start living for myself.

"Love and respect yourself," the Babalawo said. Then he repeated these words again to me. "If you don't love and respect yourself, neither will anybody else."

"Is your mother still living?" asked the Babalawo. I said yes.

℺

My mother's a writer, too. She started writing when she was in her seventies. She wrote her memoir.

I called her right before my birthday in May 1998, after I had read her self-published book. It covered her life from birth to age twenty-one. "I read your book," I said. "I liked it too."

"What part did you like best?" she asked.

I thought about the question. I liked reading about her industriousness and imagination, the way she thought up the best carnival booth at her school fair when she was a child. She held a guessing game contest for people. The one who could guess what the initials I.P.T.A. stood for would win. Nobody guessed right. The initials stood for "it pays to advertise."

I found it enlightening, compelling, and horrifying to read about the abuse she had endured. Her father had viciously killed the family cat before her eyes. Her mother and her father then began sneaking in her room in the middle of the night, lifting up the bedcovers, shining a flashlight, and examining her breasts and genitals, then counting her pubic hairs. But the part I liked best was when she grabbed the knife she slept with as a child and cut her father on the penis the night her mother was gone and he climbed into bed with her and tried to commit incest. He had run into town and told his wife, my grandmother, that the reason he was hurt and scarred was because he had suddenly decided to get circumcised.

Yes, that was my favorite part—the part where she stood up for herself.

I vaguely remembered my grandfather. When he was old and sick, Mother had let him come and live with us for a while before he died. What I remembered most was that she was kind to him. After reading her book, I was surprised that she hadn't tied him to a chair, and each time she passed by him, hit him with a stick.

I also found it interesting that she had vowed that suffering abuse was something that her children would never experience. And if I am honest, I would have to say that I did many things my parents had done and experienced that I vowed I would never do.

I know my years as a drug addict hurt me. I know they hurt my mother too. I was her baby, her last child. Her life had been hard enough when she got pregnant with me. I made her world even tougher to bear. She made it *clear* that she was stuck with me.

"You know that you weren't wanted as a child," my mother said on the phone, as though she could read my thoughts.

"Yes," I agreed.

"Well," she said. "I need you to know this. I need to say it to you now. You've turned into a good person, and you've helped many people, a lot of them too. I'm proud I'm your mom. I'm really, really glad you were born."

Like Mom always said, if it's worth doing, it's worth doing well. She also said that sometimes you have to work and wait for what you want.

Those words were worth all the hard work and waiting it took to hear.

Finally I could sing "Happy Birthday" to me.

◌

"I was talking to a friend the other day," my daughter Nichole said one month later, when she called me on the phone from New York.

"I told him that there was a thin line between his irresponsible behavior and my irrational responses. Do you know what he called me?" she asked.

"He called me a daughter after her mother's own heart."

Peace and War

I was researching a juicy story on the trip I took to the Middle East in 1997, but nothing was going as I hoped or planned. It was a jagged, confusing energy that constantly twisted and turned. I was having serious doubts about whether I was being guided at all in my life or on this trip when I found myself standing in front of the Tomb of David in Jerusalem, Israel.

Many people have heard the story of David and Goliath; they're familiar with at least that part of David's tale. But there's more to David's story than that. It's a story about obsession, passion, revenge, hatred, control, and love. It's a story about living life from the heart.

It's a historical biography mentioned in Biblical text, and in the Torah and the Koran too. It's about the man called the greatest king that Israel ever had.

David was a handsome youth, the youngest child in his family. His duties included tending the sheep. He also enjoyed playing the harp. He took his job as a shepherd seriously. Often, he needed to protect the sheep in his care from bears and lions.

That's when he became adept with a weapon then called the

sling, or slingshot. To fend off animals attacking the sheep, David learned to put a stone in his sling, aim accurately, and use that stone to help him and the sheep survive.

Chances are, he only had one chance, one shot.

In his years as a shepherd, he used that one shot, that single stone, to kill a bear and at least one lion. He became highly skilled at what he did.

About that time in Israel, King Samuel had passed on the throne to a man named Saul. But Saul made some mistakes. Samuel warned Saul that God had found someone different to do the job. God was replacing Saul. The new king had already been selected, Samuel said. And he was *a man after God's own heart.*

This made Saul edgy. Saul knew that his will had run rampant at times. He knew he had abused his power.

According to the Bible, the Spirit of God had departed from Saul and sometimes a depressed spirit came upon him instead. To relieve this feeling of sadness, Saul put out a request for a harpist, someone whose music would help him feel comforted. That's when Saul met David, the young shepherd who was also a skilled musician. When David put down his sling and plucked at the harp, his music brought comfort and healing to King Saul's heart.

During this time, Israel had been in a long-standing dispute with a group of neighboring people called the Philistines. The leader of the Philistines was a giant called Goliath. He wore brass armor and was six and a half feet tall.

One day the giant Goliath went to the middle of the battlefield and drew a line. Goliath said that instead of killing masses of people in a traditional war, he thought only two people needed to fight. Then he put out a challenge to Israel: Send in the best man that you have. If I kill him, Israel must surrender to the Philistines. If the man you send in kills me, the Philistines will serve Israel.

Goliath said the Israelites could try to beat him, but he didn't think they would. "I'll cut off the man's head, the man you send in to kill me, and I'll feed it to the birds," Goliath said.

The battle line had been drawn.

The challenge went out to all of Israel. For forty days the challenge went unmet.

One day David went down to the battlefield where many of Israel's warriors and citizens had gathered and were milling about. David had been sent there by his father to deliver food and a message of love to his brothers, who were in the military. David began asking a few questions about what was going on and what would happen to the man who killed Goliath.

One of David's brothers scoffed at David. "What are you doing here?" he said in an accusatory way. "You're just here to enjoy the battle and watch all the drama. Why aren't you tending the sheep?"

David kept looking around and asking what would happen to the man who killed Goliath. Finally David spoke up, and said that he was the man who could do it.

King Saul called him in. When Saul recognized David as the handsome young boy who played the harp, Saul shook his head. "You can't do it. You're not a warrior. Israel will lose and you'll get killed."

But David stood steadfast in what he believed. "I've killed a lion and a bear. I know I can kill Goliath too. And I know it's what God wants me to do."

He convinced Saul, who then dressed David in regal battle armor and armed him with a special sword. David put the armor on, but felt uncomfortable in these new clothes. He couldn't move freely as he needed to do. He took off the armor King Saul had given him. He told the king all he needed to wear was his usual clothes and the only weapon he needed was his sling and a couple of stones.

The next part of the story is the one that most people know best. David took his sling and went to the battle line that Goliath had drawn. Goliath laughed when he saw the handsome lad dressed in shepherd's clothes and carrying a sling. Goliath drew his sword. David slung a stone. The stone landed in the middle of Goliath's forehead and knocked Goliath down.

David walked over to check the felled giant. Goliath was dead. David cut off his head and fed it to the birds and the animals in the field.

From that moment on, David bonded like a brother with King Saul's son, Jonathan. This was also the beginning of one of the most famous love-hate relationships in all history between David and King Saul. Saul realized that David was going to replace him and become the next king.

"Man looks at people and sees their appearance," Samuel had warned Saul. "But God looks at the heart."

David had gained a reputation from his battle with Goliath. He became known as the greatest warrior in the land, even greater and more proficient in battle than Saul. Saul became jealous and vengeful. Sometimes he'd pull David in close to him and his family; other times he'd try to have David killed.

Because of David's relationship with Saul's son, Jonathan, Jonathan would warn David when Saul was ready to strike. Then David would run for the hills, living and hiding in the caves.

On two occasions, when Saul was trying to find and kill David, David had a chance to kill Saul. Both times David refused; he let Saul live. David said he had no right to kill King Saul even if the king was trying to kill him because Saul had been appointed by God.

Then a seer, a prophet in the land, warned Saul that his time as ruler was at an end. Shortly after that, both Saul and his son, Jonathan, were killed in a battle.

At age thirty, David was appointed king. From that day forward, David honored a promise he had made to Jonathan. He took care of Jonathan's descendants, treating them like royalty in the land.

The battles went on in the land for a long, long time. Because David was a skilled warrior, his men usually won. He also took many beautiful wives and concubines, a common practice at the time. He retrieved the Ark, a powerful holy item that had been lost from the land. He acted as a judge, making decisions about people's lives and arguments with one another. Whenever David had doubt about any significant decision, he would consult God first then wait for an answer, a clear sign from God and from his own heart.

One day David looked across his courtyard. He saw a beautiful woman bathing herself in oils.

The woman's name was Bathsheba. She was married to Uriah, one of David's loyal warriors. That didn't stop David.

He had fallen in love.

He wanted this woman, Bathsheba. Wanted her at any cost. They got together. They made love. Bathsheba immediately became pregnant—on their first date.

David left orders for the military officers to take Uriah, a faithful servant and warrior of the King, to the front lines in a battle currently taking place. Then David ordered the officers and warriors surrounding Uriah to withdraw, leaving him alone and unprotected on the front lines. David knew by giving this command Uriah would be killed. Then he could take the widow Bathsheba to be his own wife.

Things went exactly as King David had planned. Uriah was killed. Bathsheba became David's number one wife. But now, he had blood-guilt on his hands. Not only had he committed adultery, he'd committed murder too. This time David had forgotten to consult God.

One of David's advisors, a man he trusted, approached David. He told the king a parable, using the story to offer a lesson and send a message from God. The parable concerned a wealthy man in the land who had everything a man could want and a neighbor who had only one little lamb, a ewe. The man who had everything took the poor neighbor's only ewe, the advisor said. What did David think should be done? Because King David also acted as a judge, David thought his advisor was talking about a situation that David needed to adjudicate. David didn't realize his advisor was really talking about him and what he had done to Uriah.

David said the man who stole the poor man's only ewe should be killed.

The advisor said that the rich man who took the poor man's

only ewe was him—the King. And that the parable was a message from God.

David repented on the spot. He sought atonement and forgiveness for what he'd done. But David's life took a turn from that moment on. Bathsheba's baby died, breaking David's heart. Later, another one of David's children, a young man born to David from another wife, committed murder and had to be banished from David's court. This son turned against him and began competing to be the greatest judge and ruler in the land. He even publicly took his father's concubines, an act that had been foretold. Later on, this son was killed as well.

"You'll be forgiven," God had told David, "but from this time on, your family will live by the sword."

Order was eventually restored to David's court. Another son he had with Bathsheba, a boy named Solomon, went on to succeed David as king and gained a reputation for being the wisest man ever known.

With all his faults and successes, David is still remembered as Israel's greatest king and *a man after God's own heart*.

ᔓ

Power. You know when you have it. And you know when you don't. You know when you have it in relationships—in love, in the family, or on the job. Whether you're an employee making $6 an hour or a high-tech negotiator doing deals for $30 million, you know when the power ball is in your court. When you're in a relationship you know who has the power. You instinctively know who loves and needs the other person the most. So does the other person. You know when you're in a position to make a power play—a nasty move that slams the other guy into the wall.

And you know when the timing isn't right.

When I first began studying aikido, a martial art that's both spiritual and physical in practice, my sensei (teacher) would walk up to me and suddenly hit me for no reason, at least none I could see. He'd walk over and just punch me in the stomach or the arm.

The first few times he did this, I felt confused.

Later, as he continued to intermittently and unpredictably hit me for no apparent reason, I began questioning him. "Why did you do that?" I'd ask.

He wouldn't answer me.

After passing my first two tests or levels, I finally asked him again. I thought I deserved to know.

"The answer is simple," he said. "I hit you because I can."

Sociologists suggest that people spend their lives trying to meet a hierarchy of needs, beginning with food, shelter, then love, meaningful work, and so on. We start at the bottom of the needs pile, according to Maslow, and work our way up. That's probably true. But I think there's another undercurrent happening too—simultaneously.

Some people say it's all about communication. Some say it's all about money. Some say it's all about sex.

I think it's all about power.

When I began recovering, I thought we had to stiffen up, rear back, beat our chests, and scream. I thought owning our power was something we had to do independently, on our own, all by ourselves.

Now I believe something different. We don't really own our power. We align with it. The power is already there.

That's what this story is about.

∾

I was sitting in the bookstore one day, a small independent bookstore I ran for about one year. Business was slow that fall day. The store was on the second floor of the building. The air wasn't moving much. It felt unbearably hot.

A tall, muscular dark-haired man walked into the store.

The man didn't miss a beat. He walked over to me in a confident stride, asked if I was Melody Beattie, and when I said yes, immediately slapped some papers into my hand.

"There," he said. "You've just been served."

I dug out my glasses and read the papers in my lap. The words *Superior Court for the County of Los Angeles* jumped out at me first.

I stared at the papers, horrified.

A past business associate had filed a lawsuit against me.

War had just been declared.

The man who was filing a lawsuit against me had come into my life at a vulnerable point, soon after my son had died. I had been floundering, unable to write and unable to get clear enough to guide my own career or negotiate any deals. I had voluntarily given him an enormous amount of power in my life. My favorite phrase was, "I don't care. You decide." He had stepped up to the plate.

As time went by, I became stronger, though in barely visible and minuscule increments. And, as inevitably happens, I became infuriated at the people to whom I had voluntarily forfeited my power. This man was one of them.

Then, a business transaction took place, one I didn't understand.

I had blown up, fired him on the spot.

He had tried to talk to me a few times after that; he had tried to work things out. I was filled with too much fear. I wasn't afraid of him. I was afraid of going back to the way I was—helpless, not knowing my own mind, not knowing what I thought. I was afraid of myself. By the time I had taken my power back, I was so angry I couldn't think. All I could do was feel and by now the only feeling I had was mad. We disagreed on what our original deal had been.

"If he doesn't like what I'm doing," I told my attorney, "tell him to take me to court."

Now, years later, that's what he had done. He was taking me to court. These papers in my lap declared an official war. But it was me who had fired the first shot.

I called my attorney on the telephone, then faxed him the papers.

"What do you want to do?" my attorney asked.

"I don't have a ton of money," I said. "But I'll use every penny I have to fight him in court. Let's take it all the way."

The months passed. At first, all I had to do was gather old paperwork, but that was a chore. Most of my business papers were stored in boxes in the garage. Many of them had been misplaced. Since my dealings with this man had begun, I had moved several times, once to a different state. Still I was doggedly determined to fight this battle—whether I won or not.

"Are you sure you want to go through with this?" my attorney asked, more than once.

"It's the principle of the thing," I said. "That's why I want to fight."

"Good," my attorney said. "I think you can win." What I wasn't considering was that my opponent's attorneys had told him the same thing. He believed he could win too.

In the past, the mere thought of going to court had terrified me. It was a carryover from appearing in court in my drug addict days. Now I had my power back. And by God, I was going to fight.

In California, lawsuits run rampant. For some people they're a way of life. So judges often call the parties in before the actual trial to try to get the parties to work things out.

I went in for a preliminary meeting with my opponent and the judge. My attorneys and I sat on one side of the courtroom. My opponent and his attorneys sat on the other.

They made a settlement offer. I told my attorney to tell his attorneys *no*. Everyone left poised, dignified, but mad.

The battle went on. And on.

The next step was preparation for depositions. But that wasn't the only next step. The next steps were regularly paying my attorney's bills.

The cost of war can be high.

I went into my attorney's office to prepare for a deposition. He asked me all the questions he thought the other attorneys would ask. The problem was, most of the questions that I was asked centered around the time of, and the first few years after, my son's death.

I had a dream once, it was a strange one and I didn't understand it at the time. In the dream, I was walking into a quaint little white French café. The sign on the front of the café said, "Hier, Adjourd'hui et Demain." In English, those words mean, "Yesterday, Today, and Tomorrow."

I began to understand what that dream meant. The café was a place where the past, the present, and the future are the same. When it comes to great pain, a loss, something that hurt horribly at the time, it doesn't matter how long ago it happened. When you remember the pain of that loss, it's as though it happened today.

Going through the preparation for the deposition took me right back to the time of Shane's accident.

The price of war had gone up. Now, it wasn't only financial. The price I was paying had an emotional toll. I cried for three days in a row. It was all I could do to go to the grocery store, but I was still determined to go on. After all, a fight was a fight, a principle was a principle. But I was determined. I wasn't going to back down or get weak. I would fight this thing to the end.

On the way out of court the day we unsuccessfully tried to settle, my attorney had turned to me. "I hate to do this," he said timidly, "but I have to ask. Were you two ever lovers?"

I laughed out loud. And I laughed because I was beginning to see that's how incensed and enraged my ex-associate and I were. This was as ugly and heated as a divorce. There were that many emotions involved. "It's okay for you to ask," I said. "The answer is simple. No, we weren't. We worked together, and we were close friends."

The first round of depositions lasted almost all day. The court stenographer was there. My attorney and I were there. So were two attorneys from the other side. Ex-associate was absent. The questioning went on for hours.

They asked questions. I tried to answer. My attorney kept objecting. So did the other side. We weren't in court yet, but the battle was going on. It was heated and *intense*.

My ex-associate had his side of the story. I had mine. And there was no way that we saw things the same. We each had our own point of view. We each felt legitimately injured, damaged, and hurt.

Between the time I had walked away from this associate and had first consulted an attorney, something else had transpired. My attorney too had lived through a tragedy. A close family member had been killed, throwing his entire family's life into turmoil and pain. Now he understood what it meant to be overpowered by grief. Tragedy had hit way too close to home.

Toward the end of the day at the deposition, I started crying and couldn't stop. My attorney got protective, said questioning was over for the day. The other attorneys objected; they wanted to push on.

I couldn't stop crying.

Then my attorney became enraged. He started hollering. He stood up, slammed his fist on the table. The more he objected, the harder I cried.

Finally, the court reporter couldn't take it any longer. She looked at me. "Just leave," she said. "Go. Just get out."

The first part of the deposition was finished. It had been grueling. I didn't feel like I had won. But I was still determined to go on.

The next deposition got postponed several times. Finally, the day arrived. It was time to do battle again.

I got in the car, drove to Los Angeles, prepared to continue the fight. Traffic was heavy. The drive took longer than I had planned. I parked my car in the underground garage in the middle of Beverly Hills and hurried to the elevator. I was nervous. I didn't want to be late. I hoped the deposition wouldn't be as tumultuous today.

The elevator seemed slower than usual. It went up one floor, then another. *Let's go all the way up,* I thought. Then the elevator stopped and the doors opened. The man who walked in was my ex-business associate and friend. But we were now enemies, opponents. We stood staring at each other face to face.

My heart raced as the elevator doors quietly closed. "Hi," I said, trying to break the ice.

"Hi," the enemy said back.

"How's your family?" I asked.

"Fine," he said. "How's Nichole?"

We exchanged small talk, then the doors opened, and together we walked into the deposition room to continue our fight. For the first time, I realized I wasn't fighting an enemy. I was fighting someone I had once cared about. I was battling someone I once considered a friend.

The questioning began. I was sworn in. I answered each question as clearly, forcefully, and truthfully as I could. I could hardly wait to testify. I had wanted for a long time to speak out and be heard.

At lunchtime, my attorney and I walked outside to a courtyard café. My eyes began watering uncontrollably. The sun was burning, stinging my eyes. It wasn't just uncomfortable; it was overwhelming. I couldn't walk. I couldn't see anything. I was literally blinded by the light. This went on for an hour.

I was so angry, so furious, so livid. Everything I was feeling seemed focused in my eyes. Yes, I had my side of the story; I thought what I had done was correct and appropriate. But my associate had a point of view too. He thought he had done the right thing. He did what he felt was best for me at a vulnerable time in my life. He felt wronged by what I had done. Well, I felt wronged too.

But beyond our differences, there was the overview, how things had worked out in the overall scheme of things to consider too. In all my stubborn positioning I had forgotten the power of gratitude.

Despite our disagreements, the work he had done for me had forced me to begin writing again after my son's death. Even though I didn't like how certain business deals had worked out, what he had done for me had forced me back to work. Some of what I was feeling was legitimate rage because I had given up my power. I had felt overwhelmed, struck down by grief, confused. Even though I had been limited by my grief and need, I had let someone do my thinking for me.

Getting enraged was a predictable consequence when it came time to take back my power. But, I wondered, as I stumbled across the courtyard on the way back into the tall, shimmering office building, was some of what I was feeling the rage of a person forcefully brought back to life? Was I this enraged because I was still alive after all I had been through? Maybe that's what all this anger is really about, I thought, as the elevator slowly rose from floor to floor.

The last deal he had negotiated for me was what had pushed me over the edge. On the other hand, this deal had pushed me through my numbness and had helped bring me back to life. I was beginning to think and feel again, beginning to believe in myself. With all its betrayals, pain, disappointments, and loss, maybe life was worthwhile too.

I followed my attorney off the elevator, and back into the conference room, our battleground. I sat down and finished answering, as firmly and powerfully and as honestly as I could, every question that was asked of me that day. I still had a case. Still thought I could win. My ex-associate felt the same way. When the clock struck four and the questioning was complete, I stood up and walked over to the chair where my ex-associate sat. I put my hand on his shoulder. "Aren't you going to say good-bye?" I asked. I looked at him. No response. I started to walk away.

"After all those things you just said?" he asked.

I didn't respond with any malice. I didn't have to. Testifying had dissipated my rage.

When my ex-associate wouldn't acknowledge me, wouldn't say good-bye, I hesitated a moment, then quietly turned on my heels and began to walk out of that room. I had spoken my truth to an adversary, then tried to open my heart to a friend. When he didn't respond, the only thing left for me to do was to walk out of the room.

I had reached the door when he finally spoke. "Wait up," he said. "I'll walk out with you."

We rode down the elevator without speaking too much. "Want to get a cup of coffee?" I asked as the elevator doors started to open.

He said, "That would be nice."

∾

Did you ever hear the one about the Buddhist monk who walked up to the hot dog stand? The hot dog vendor asked the monk what he wanted. "Can you make me one with everything?" the monk asked.

There is a mystical spiritual concept of being one with all that is. Some mystics, monks, and sages believe this oneness is the basis for spirituality, the foundation for how this world works, and the ultimate theory of enlightenment.

The problem with codependents is that they not only don't feel one with everything, they don't even feel at peace with, or one with, themselves.

I was sitting back in a chair in a hotel room in Redondo Beach, California. I looked like I wasn't doing anything, but I was. I was praying and praying hard. Scotty and I had been arguing all day. Several times, I had started to storm away, but then something held me back. I was determined to sit still and figure out what the lesson was that kept drawing me to him. I was begging God to help me get it, help me to understand why this particular relationship had been in my life, and what I was supposed to learn from it.

Scotty and I stopped arguing. The mood between us changed. Instead of looking at each other as the object of unfulfilled romantic fantasies and unrequited love, we began talking like two human beings. I had just returned from my trip to the Middle East. I started to tell him about what I had seen, and what I had learned, and the pieces I had gathered there when a strange thing began to take place.

I had eaten a well-balanced breakfast and lunch that day. I wasn't suffering from malnutrition. I had two cups of coffee earlier in the day, a minimal dose of caffeine for me. I had no alcohol or drugs in my system—none whatsoever. But a peculiar state of altered consciousness suddenly began to occur. It happened so quickly I didn't have time to feel frightened, stop it, or react. It was a phenomenon I had read and heard about. Now I experienced it for myself.

What once appeared as solid curtain fabric, solid chairs, solid tables, a solid bed headboard—all began to weave together into one vibrating energy field. This vibrating energy from each object in the room—every single thing I could see—blended into the energy field of the next object in the room. Everything was made of this same vibrating, nonsolid energy—even those things that appeared to be solid. For the next two hours, I saw the energy grid that makes up all that is. Energy permeated the chair, the headboard of the bed, and even the space between objects that looked like thin air. A living, vibrating energy permeated even the stuffed animal on the floor. The same life force made up everything I saw. The only difference between objects was their color and shape. They appeared like dream forms, nonsolid arrangements of colored energy.

This same energy also permeated both Scotty and me. I saw our souls.

We were vibrating masses of that same energy too. Being one with everything was more than a joke or a concept that some people believed. It wasn't just New Age jargon or a mystical concept understood only by monks. It was real, whether or not I believed it.

When David declared war on Goliath, he didn't act from a place of rage, fear, or past pent-up emotions. When he went to war with the giant Philistine, he acted from a place of peace—of oneness with himself, the people around him, and God.

There is a time and place to declare war, to go to battle, and to stand up for what we believe. But when we act from injury, insult, vindictiveness, hurt, wrath, anger, or rage, what we're really doing is getting revenge. And ultimately when we do that, although we may hurt others we're hurting ourselves too. When anger or hatred or deliberate meanness is the basis for any action we take, that action will sooner or later blow up in our face.

Sometimes the anger, rage, resentment, or hatred is buried so deeply we can't see that's really the place we're acting from. We think that by getting even, lashing out, striking out, we'll stop our pain. We won't.

An alternative to revenge is to feel whatever it is that has so deeply wounded us then release those emotions. Just let them go.

I had proven to my ex-associate and myself that I could stand up, own my power, take action, go to battle, get into the front lines and fight. But the price I had paid was high. Positioning myself for battle had cost more than money or emotional strain. By owning my power in the way that I had, I had lost my spiritual and mental peace.

I wasn't just at war with someone else. I was at war with myself too.

My ex-associate sat across the table from me, clinking the ice in his tea. I opened and poured a container of cream into my coffee, stirred it, then looked at him. "What do you say?" I said. "Why don't we try to work things out ourselves?"

He agreed.

"Now don't think you're going to get everything you want," I said.

"Don't you think that either," he replied.

Over the next few weeks, we met day after day. I said all my feelings. He listened without responding. Then it was his turn, and he said what he felt too. Now it was my turn to listen and respect his point of view.

Then we each said what we wanted from the other person. What we each wanted to give and receive didn't match—except for one thing, the most important thing. We both wanted peace. He gave a little. Then it was my turn to give. When things got too heated, we'd break for a day or two, then we'd meet again. We each knew we could go back to court any time we wanted. War was always an option. But we were both serious about wanting peace.

After days and days, we arrived at a middle ground. We struck up an agreement, after having hashed out our emotions and each detail of every term.

I had proven I had the power to take a stand, be stubborn, fight, be persistent, and even begin a ferocious battle by firing the first shot. But I had also learned about an even more valuable and productive way to use and focus my energy in this world. I had acquired the power to negotiate.

ॐ

Statistics say that most lawsuits are settled before they ever get to court. Statistics say most people don't even get to, or through, the deposition stage. I can understand why. The process of war, of going to battle, is expensive financially and emotionally too.

Most people are battling about more than money. There's usually another battle going on. It's really a war about power. It may be injustice, being unwilling to be victimized anymore or standing up for our rights. Or maybe going to war with someone is a way we have of taking back our power, power that for many reasons, we may have given away a long time ago.

We want more than our money. We want to take our power back too.

The problem is that each warring party feels the same way. Each person feels hurt, used, like they need to take their power back and fight for the principle of the thing.

Each person in the battle feels some stake in the thing, although sometimes we're just responding emotionally to the person who fired the first shot. We're coming from a place of hurt, rage, victimization, and pain. When we've given up our power, when we haven't expressed what we felt, wanted, and needed, when we finally feel indignant, and when we're not willing to take it—whatever it is—anymore is when the battle begins.

Sometimes the battle is in business. Sometimes, it's with a lover or friend. We can go to war anytime, any place where we feel injustice is at hand or where we may have given up our power. But the place we're coming from, although it may feel vindicated and strong, isn't always clear. And it may not be clear until all the pent-up feelings and emotions are released. The situation is too emotionally charged. And the battle will continue until the charge is gone.

Sometimes, after feeling so powerless for so long, we may not understand how much power our behaviors, thoughts, feelings, words, and beliefs really have.

We may look at others codependently, perceiving them as having all the power. They may be looking at us, perceiving us in the same way. The words we speak, the feelings we express, the things we do may impact others more than we believe. We have the power to incite, hurt, gain revenge, and even declare war on enemies who are really, or were once, friends.

If we don't acknowledge and use our emotional power properly, all the thoughts and feelings we've repressed eventually catch up with us. The universe always and ultimately balances itself out. One day all the feelings and thoughts we've repressed and denied finally come into the light of consciousness. They come out—often in a most unmanageable, untimely, and sometimes inappropriate way.

We finally own our power. We tell ourselves we're right. After all, we've repressed ourselves for so long we can't hold back anymore. But the teeniest event can trigger this reaction. And it's not a slight response or reaction. Often it's a messy explosion of all that's gone on for a long time before.

The person we're dealing with looks at us like we're crazy. All they can see is that we're overreacting because we've been so quiet, so agreeable, so timid, and so passive with everything that happened before. They don't understand, or at least won't admit, that there's any validity to us feeling this way, why it's suddenly a big deal now.

It's not just *what* we do it's how we do it that counts as much or more. Intention and delivery are important things. We can storm about in anger and rage, and have our behavior be interpreted as contentious and a bid for power. Or we can calm down, start from a place of peace, communicate the same message without challenging the other person with showy displays of power.

We can choose whether to use our powers to think, feel, act, and speak to instigate peace or war. Sometimes we don't mind a battle. There are times when many people enjoy the drama of a good fight. There's a time and place to clear the air. And sometimes we seek out battles just to test our powers.

We aren't as separate from others as we think, nor are we as bound in chains, cords, and unhealthy ties of any kind, as many of us used to believe in our more codependent days. We are truly one with everything, but in a healthy, quantum physics kind of way. And then remember, there's that mystical karma thing happening too. Which means that when we attack others, when we declare war on anyone else, when we stand back, rear up arms, and fire that first shot, we're really declaring war not just on the other person. We're going to war with ourselves too.

In the beginning, we may have had to shout to set limits, to say no, or to get our point across, to tell others what we really mean. Sometimes we needed to shout to convince ourselves and gain confidence that we finally meant business.

It's true that sometimes we do need to speak up, but as we progress in aligning with our power, we can let go of our need to carry on in showy displays of control. We learn to deal with others calmly and from a place of inner peace—especially when the things we have to say are uncomfortable or are in opposition to what the other person wants. The more peacefully we conduct ourselves in all our affairs, the more we demonstrate how powerful we are and how much we believe in ourselves.

We're no longer coming from a place of fear—fear that we'll back down or somehow won't take care of ourselves. We're coming from a calm clear place of peace. The louder we speak, the more others will resist, become afraid, feel attacked, and refuse to listen. The more softly and calmly we speak, the more they'll lean into us to hear and take in what it is we are saying.

Be certain when you attack that you really want to go to war, even if you feel confident that you will win. Even then, come from a place of peace with yourself and your own heart. We can be diplomatic, tactful, and use our abundant supply of people-pleasing skills to avoid unnecessary wars.

To be a man or woman after God's own heart, you've got to know your own.

"People do a lot of things to other people," the Babalawo said. "They can send a lot of negative behaviors and energy their way. It's important to learn to defend yourself. But most people fight too much. The test, the mark, of a person that's on a true spiritual path is whether they can live in harmony."

ℬ

"The most important technique to increase your power and your ability to live in harmony with yourself and the world is to meditate," Virginia, one of my martial arts instructors, a sixty-nine-year-old woman, reminded me. "To grow in balance and harmony, to become effective and strong in this world in a physical or spiritual sense takes only five or ten minutes a day. It doesn't matter how old you are, or the circumstances you're living in. To gain awareness of yourself and the world, to improve your ability to deal with others, to improve your intuitive sense so you always know what to do next, spend a few minutes a day, at least five, meditating.

"It doesn't matter which technique you use. It could be reading from a meditation book, taking a long hot bath, or sitting cross-legged on the floor smelling incense burn. Each of us will discover the form of meditation that works best for us."

"And when you've finished with your meditation time," she added. "Don't forget to pray."

ℬ

One day, when I convinced myself I couldn't stand it anymore, I headed for the mountains. I had business troubles. I was trying to decide whether to continue to battle to keep the bookstore open. I had a war going on in my relationship. I didn't know what to do next. I loaded my journal, a Bible, and a few changes of clothes into a suitcase. I would go to a favorite cabin, lock myself in, feverishly meditate, and pray. And I wasn't coming out until I had figured out what to do next.

After forty-eight hours writing about my problems, praying about my problems, and meditating about my problems, I remembered what Scotty had said to me a while back. "What are you doing?" he asked. "I'm trying to surrender to God's will," I said. "No you're not," he said. "You're trying to figure it out."

The immediate solution to each problem was the same: surrender and relax. I had done everything I could. Now it was time to stop using force. Sometimes it's time to try harder. Sometimes, it's time to let go.

Over the next six months, the specific solution to each problem I was struggling with appeared in its own time.

If you don't like the word *surrender,* try calling it *making peace.*

Bang

"Do you have issues with drama addiction," I asked my daughter, in a serious, interviewer kind of voice.

"Of course I do," she said. "I'm the original drama queen."

"Can I interview you about them?" I asked. "Will you talk to me about what that means to you?"

There was a long, long, expensive pause on the telephone. I was talking to her long distance. I was in California. She was in New York.

"I've got a better suggestion," she finally said. "Why don't you interview yourself?"

I've been addicted to many *things* this lifetime—alcohol, heroin, morphine, Dilaudid, cocaine, barbiturates, Valium, and any other substance that physically or psychologically promised to change the way I feel. I've been addicted to caffeine, tobacco and nicotine—cigarettes and Cuban cigars—and opium and hashish too.

I've been addicted to other people's addictions to many of those substances as well. I've been caught up in the intense emotional roller coaster rides, the ups and downs, the lows and highs, of their addictive process, their ride on the Jellinek chart, that old but timely

graph that explains the predictable loss of spiritual, mental, emotional, and physical freedom when the disease of chemical dependency rules our life—and the predictable gains we can expect to
make when we begin recovering too. I was enmeshed and entangled
in their battles to have power over what they could not—to control
the uncontrollable, the effects of the addictive process in their lives.

Some people might say I have an addictive personality. I would
probably agree, depending on my mood, my desire to argue seman-
tics, and the time of day. Very early in the morning or extremely late
at night I would probably but not necessarily be too tired to debate.

I don't know if I agree with the concept that we can become
addicted to people, but if the folks that say you can are right, I've
probably been addicted to certain of those too.

People become caught up in, entangled in, enmeshed in, compulsively drawn to, and sometimes addicted to a lot of things in this
world. They can become addicted to the chemical substances I've
been addicted to—alcohol and most categories of mood-altering
drugs. People can become addicted, some experts suggest, to food,
gambling, work, money, and sex. Although I've known people who
have struggled with those problems, and at times I've found a
salmon steak grilled to perfection and physical intimacy with a
person I cared deeply about almost intoxicating, thank God these
were a few things I haven't had to struggle with addiction to—at
least not yet.

But of all the addictions possible on this planet, I've found my
addiction to drama absolutely the hardest to recognize, accept, deal
with, and overcome. The rush of emotional energy I feel from drama
at the theater, on television (small or big screen), in a book, and most
preferably acted out in real life (mine) is the last legal, legitimate
jones that society allows.

It's another one of those tricky thin lines we talked about before.

Action. Adventure. Tear jerkers. Thrillers. Romance. Science
Fiction. Comedy. Drama. Horror. Making a fool, hero, or heroine of
ourselves is the stuff that life is about. Expecting the unexpected,

twists and turns that give us whiplash without ever getting into the car, taking the e-ride—the emotional roller coaster ride—in our lives can help us learn our lessons, teach us invaluable wisdom and timeless truths about life, and can mean that finally we have a life to live and that's exactly what we're doing. Hurray! We're living stories out. We're really and truly alive. That's what we came here for, came here to do. We're spiritual beings stumbling around living fallible human lives.

But taken over that edge, wandering across that thin line from being fully alive to being full-blown drama junkies can also take us off our spiritual path.

It was a nightmare has become one of the most popular phrases used—by people I know and, against my better recovery judgment, also by myself. It can be used to describe traffic jams, an argument with a lover or boss, or in rare occasions, a truly bad night's dreams and sleep. But the interesting thing about so many people using this phrase, sociologically, is what it says about this world.

It's not politically correct to smoke, act out sexually, be a nonrecovering alcoholic, or shoot drugs. But despite all the evolution in consciousness that's unfolded, taken place, and gotten us to this point, drama addiction is more than politically correct.

Drama addiction is in.

Right now, for many people, it's one of the only things that gives meaning to life.

Potential guests line up, volunteering to have their court battles and what once were guarded secrets broadcast via cable TV and satellite to the world. We sit home and watch. Some people don't volunteer. Our society decides to peek and snoop into their lives. Broadcasting real-life soap operas guarantees the ratings will soar.

And if we're not watching drama on TV, we're creating it in our lives.

It can be a little incident, one that creates just the teeniest rush of rage, excitement, or fear. It can be a major blowout, an up-all-nighter pulling out our hair. The key to drama addiction is creating, generating, and feeling that breathtaking, monotony-relieving, boredom-distracting, and hopefully stomach-churning and heart-catching emotionally and glandular driven adrenaline rush.

It's a temporary, translucent hit of energy, excitement, and power. And you don't need to use a syringe to get it into your blood.

"I was young, about nine or ten, the first time I acted out with this drug," reported a close male friend of mine. "My brother and I had been fighting. He hit me in the head. He won the fight—and ran. I wanted to get even, torture him, get back. I went into the kitchen, poured ketchup on my head, then wrapped it with a white rag, using it like a red-stained bandage around my head. Then I stumbled out to the front yard, to where my brother had run. I cried and moaned and told him I had just called Mom home from work and an ambulance was on the way. My brother freaked out. He was frantic, terrified, spun. What a rush! I had the power. Then my mother came home, saw what I had done, spanked me—really hard—yelled at me, and sent me to bed. I've been addicted to drama ever since," he said quietly, like he was confessing and somewhat ashamed.

But I detected a hint of pride.

"Addicted to drama? That's me," another friend, a male too, said to me. "Let me tell you about one night in my life, an event that happened a while back. I had been dating one woman for a long time. We were having some arguments, but we were still committed and in a monogamous relationship. I was hurt and angry. She was punishing me, or something, by not being intimate. Actually, she turned frigid on me. Didn't want me to touch her at all, for a long, long time. And she didn't want to talk about it, deal with it with me either. I loved her. But I felt hurt, angry, and rejected too. So I was fooling around on the side. The deal is," my friend said, "I knew it would get back to her, what I had done, that I was carrying on. The town where I live isn't that big. I had created a real mess. I talked to one of my friends. He told me to do the right thing, and by that he meant I should tell Julie first, before she heard from somebody else. I made my decision to tell her while I was talking to my friend at his house. I knew if I was going to do it, tonight would have to be the night. I felt bad. I didn't want to hurt her. I don't like hurting people or being mean. That's not my game. It's not who I am, although I confess I do like to stir things up. Anyway, while I was driving home that night, a feeling was going through me like I had never before felt in my life. Even with all the chemicals I had used in my past, I had never felt a rush like this before. It was fear, terror, anticipation—a complete adrenaline high. I'm doing differently in my life now, trying to deal with things differently and not make such a mess, especially one that hurts people I love and ultimately hurts me. But I still like to stir things up in other people's lives, get them going, or at least get in on the buzz of what's happening to everyone else. My drama addiction is the hardest thing I've attempted to give up."

Emotions—emotional energy—and proper use of them are powers available to all of us in this life. We can use that power appropriately, to feel and release our feelings, to stay clear when emotions come up, to guide us about what to do next. We can use our power to feel in harmony with our other powers—the power of will, thought, desire, and guided action, or we can use it to create an unnecessary, time-consuming, and dramatic fuss.

Sometimes we like to stir things up, stir the emotional pot. We like to get others going. We enjoy getting ourselves worked up too. It's one of our powers. We all have the power to create problems that aren't real and say things in the hope of getting someone else worked up. Then we sit and watch them explode, react, or carry on. Sometimes we jump in the stew pot with them too.

Sometimes our emotions are legitimate. They're blocks of resentments, hurt, or fear triggered by a present circumstance, and sometimes buried within us from our past, from a time when it wasn't safe and we didn't have the support to feel whatever it is we feel. Other times all this emoting is a misuse or misdirection of our power. We've created the turmoil within ourselves. It's a distraction for taking spiritual responsibility for ourselves, and it distracts and diverts us from the power of being clear.

That's what this short story about an incident that happened to me in Charles DeGalle Airport in Paris, France, is about.

ᑲ

"Passez! Passez!"

A tall, brusque young man wearing a beret and a uniform waved his hand at me, speaking these French words in an unemotional monotone voice as I stood in line to check my luggage at Charles DeGalle International Airport in Paris, France. I didn't understand what he was saying or why he was saying it to me. And I found his brusqueness annoying.

It's not that all French people are arrogant. But this man was. He was haughtily waving his hand, like he was brushing me off as insignificant.

I deliberately scrunched my face, trying to show him how confused I was. "What?" I asked.

"Passez," he said, waving his hand again.

I didn't have a clue what he was talking about. I turned my attention from him to the line I was standing in. I had half an hour to change planes in this airport. I was flying from Istanbul and changing airlines, so not only did I have to change planes, I had to recheck my luggage, get my boarding pass and seat assignment, get to the gate, and get on the plane that would take me home.

The line I was standing in was barely moving.

There was some activity going on behind me but I was ignoring it. Right now everything was irritating me.

I'll admit it. I'm a drama addict. I've said that my trips overseas—especially to war zones and troubled countries that most people wouldn't consider touring, much less touring alone if they were a woman—weren't solely daredevil trips. And for the most part, they weren't. On the other hand, a little drama, a little action to jump start the muse, even an explosive adventure would have helped.

The last time I had been to Algiers two years past, a fear and trauma were noticeably present in the air. You could feel what was going on. The terrorists were hiding out in the hills. People were cowering in their tenements in this beautiful, seaside town. The military had taken over the land.

But this trip had been different. There was still some evidence of the trouble brewing. Occasionally when traveling by car, my Algerian friends and I had run into the military blockades that used to be present every few blocks. Sometimes, the military even performed a half-hearted search.

But the charge, the electricity, the drama was gone. The people had even gotten used to living in the midst of their civil war. Before, they were hiding in their homes in fear. Now, they shrugged their shoulders and went on with their lives. Many of the younger Muslim women had even stopped wearing their veils as they went about their day.

"Can't you see and feel the difference?" one of my Algerian friends had asked. "Don't you know what's changed our country?" he said. "Now we've got cable TV. . . ."

I had walked to my hotel window, as I had done on the trip before. On the trip past, gunfire had filled the air outside at night. This trip, things looked fairly calm, even though it was election week, a trigger to hostilities and eruption in many countries.

The next day a demonstration parade was going to march through the main part of town. I rode in the back seat of the car with my two Algerian friends, past the chanting voices of the leaders of the parade. One of them looked straight into my eyes. I didn't feel any fear. I just felt compassion for these people who were trying so desperately to restore peace and abundant living to their country and to their lives.

We drove around the parade route. My friends pointed out several locations where in years past, terrorists had planted bombs that had exploded during the parade. This year, couples walked, holding hands, turning to watch as the demonstrators marched by.

The biggest drama scene had occurred at the airport on my way out of the country. When I was going through customs, the agent kept asking me what my occupation was. I kept saying I was a writer, and he kept scrunching his face at me. I scrambled in my mind for the right words in French, but I couldn't remember. I couldn't think in French.

Finally the agent lifted his arms in frustrated rage and screamed at me.

"Speak French!" he said.

"J'écrite les livres [I write books]," I said clearly, suddenly able to speak perfect French. It was a miracle, one of those tiny ones.

"Go ahead," he said, giving me the okay.

I had gone on to Istanbul, Turkey. I pounded around in the outskirts of the country for a while, impressed by the land, mostly the hills. The entire country exuded a particular energy. It took me a while to recognize it. It was sheer, raw power. As I followed my guide through the streets of Istanbul on one of my last nights there, a rumbling noise started filling the air; a herd of footsteps shook the cobblestone street. My guide grabbed my hand.

"Come on," he said, pulling me around a corner, down an alley, and away from the noise. "That's a demonstration, a protest against the government. Let's get out of here before someone gets hurt."

This was the closest I had come to action, adventure, and drama on this trip. Now my guide was deliberately leading me away? I sighed and followed him. Any drama, any excitement, any emotional energy was always just out of my reach.

I was so protected, so safe, wherever I went that I might as well have stayed home, I thought, impatiently waiting in a line at the airport that didn't seem to move. I could have found more drama on the streets of Los Angeles. I had traveled again to some of the most potentially turbulent spots on the globe. And wherever I had ventured, seeking action and excitement, a peace had fallen gracefully over the land—at least wherever I stood.

Finally, the line I was standing in began to move. A few people in front of me suddenly moved away. They must have changed their minds, decided to wait in another line. Good. That made me first in line. I lugged my bags up to the counter. Just as I started to open my mouth to speak, the man behind the counter shoved a Closed sign in front of my face and walked away.

"What's going on?" I thought. If I didn't check my bags soon, I would miss my plane. As I stood there confused, the man in the beret, the annoying one, came back again. This time he was shouting in my face, and pushing me with his hands.

"Passez! Passez! Maintenant!" Then he began waving a gun in my face. What in the hell was going on?

I had traveled across the world searching for drama and I couldn't find any excitement. Couldn't find my story. Now I couldn't get on my plane to get home. I was getting angry.

I tried to explain to this man in the beret that I had a plane to catch, an extremely limited time in which to catch it, that I had been standing in this line for most of that time, and I didn't know where to go next.

He didn't want to hear anything I had to say.

"Passez! Passez! Passez!" He was screaming at me, rudely screaming. Then he pushed me away from the counters and the place where there used to be a line. Suddenly I came out of my reverie and saw where I was and what was going on. Every counter in the ticket lines for as far as I could see had been closed. All the lines had disbursed. All the people that had been standing in line were now grouped together, like a herd of cattle, a long way across the room. The walking area in front of the ticket counters had been cordoned off. Lots of men with berets and guns were standing around the room. What was going on?

I could now clearly see I was supposed to move across the room, probably to where all the other people stood. I started dragging my bags over there, then noticed that even the security entrance to the gates at the airport had closed. I didn't understand what was going on, but I sure hoped I could somehow get on my plane in time to get home.

I walked, dragging my bags, about another hundred feet when it happened.

Bang!

An explosion shattered and echoed through the halls. The floor shook. The counters shook. It looked like the windows lining the other side of the corridor were ready to break. I froze in place. Held my breath in shock. It sounded like a bomb had gone off.

I ran up to a gentleman huddled in the crowd. "What's going on?" I asked, praying he wouldn't answer in French.

"I guess they found a suspicious bag left in the hallway down there. They suspected it might hold a bomb. Instead of removing it, they blew it up."

So that's what the guard was trying to tell me. He was telling me to get going and move quickly. Now.

The moral of this story is simple and sweet. When we're looking too hard for action, adventure, and drama in our lives, when we're trying to create emotions and adrenaline instead of going with the flow, we may not see the story, the drama, and the lesson unfolding directly under our nose.

რ

"Isn't tranquillity great," the Babalawo said during our conversation together, my date with destiny that lasted many hours.

I said yes. But internally, I wasn't sure. I liked emotional energy. Sometimes I even convinced myself that some drama—whether it was getting into trouble or watching closely while other people did it to themselves saved me from what I considered a boring and sometimes mundane life. It was almost like the Babalawo could see right through me, read my mind. He reminded me of a lesson, an important one about power and manifesting what we wanted and desired.

"When we're tranquil and in a state of peace," he said, "we have the power to draw to ourselves what we want and need."

Sometimes I forget things that I know. Sometimes I forget that letting go has more power than holding on, and then I forget to let go. Sometimes I get so focused on the other person and what they need and want that I forget how I feel, what's important to me, and what I need and want too. Sometimes I forget that no matter what situation I find myself in, I do have powers available to me, even when I feel overpowered. I have the power to think, to feel, to pray for guidance, the power to let go, and take care of myself no matter what's coming down on my head. And sometimes I forget that the temporary hit of power from drama addiction wanes in comparison to the real power we can connect to when we're at peace with the world and with ourselves.

∽

Here's another hitting story, told to me by a friend. A Zen master used to walk over to his students and hit them, for no reason. After a while, the students would spend most of their time tense, afraid, expecting to get hit, and ready to ward off the next blow even before it came. After they got themselves all worked up, spending their time in class running around feeling fearful, tense, and dreading the next blow, the Zen master would tell them they were ready to learn the lesson.

"You can either spend all your time tense, anticipating and dreading the pain, trying to control and deal with it before it arrives, or you can stay peaceful and serene, knowing a certain amount of pain will always be present in life. Then wait until it happens and trust yourself to deal with the pain as it comes up."

∽

It came to me in the middle of the night, weeks after I returned home from my trip to New Mexico, when I saw Scotty, saw that he was deteriorating, the trip when my destiny bracelet broke. Each bead on the bracelet I'd been wearing represented a different story in my life. All of us are wearing a destiny bracelet, whether we know it or not. Some of our stories have already been written; some haven't yet taken place. Each bead leads to the next. All are connected and come full circle, held together by a single strand we call *fate*. One tiny bead on our bracelets represents the story we're living now.

People frequently ask how their lives would be different if that hadn't happened, if this had happened, if I had made a different choice, or if this person hadn't come along. Could I have done differently? How can I do differently, or better, in the future? Or worse, we may look at our life and think this whole thing has been a huge, tragic, pitiful waste. Why didn't I know then what I do now? I could have saved myself a lot of time and pain.

Know that it took each bead on the bracelet to weave the destiny of your life, even those choices we call *mistakes*. And if your bracelet breaks—if death is near, if loss is imminent, if someone important is about to leave—that destiny is about to change. It may be a wake-up call, a reminder to protect, love, and take care of ourselves while the next bead, the next lesson, the next story begins to unfold.

ℰ

"You're on a spiritual quest," a friend once commented to me, after learning all the places I'd visited, everything I'd done and seen. My friend was partially right. But more than being a spiritual quest, it felt like a treasure hunt.

You don't have to travel across the world to begin to seek the good in life, understand some of its mysteries, and begin playing connect the dots. We can begin our treasure hunt by valuing what we're learning right now, who and where we are, and figuring out in the specifics of that particular situation exactly what it means to own our power.

"It doesn't take as much faith to believe that everything happens for a reason as it does to embrace the belief that I am who and where I am now, today, for a reason, even if I don't know what that reason is and even if I don't particularly like who or where I am today," a friend said to me. "When I can take that in, my dissatisfaction and negativity disappear, and I can proceed calmly and gratefully with my life. To me," he said, "that's what spirituality is all about."

When I sat in front of the Babalawo that day, and he began working in the sand, praying, and cleansing my life, I had no idea how deep the cleansing would go, or what healing the past really meant. For much of my life, I had preferred to cut off and ignore parts of my past. It's over and done with. It's history. Why remember that now?

People say everything happens for a reason and God has a Plan for it all. I believe things do happen for a reason. And God does have a Plan. But if we don't learn the lesson from the circumstance and let ourselves completely heal from it—whether it is the past or today— the things that happen for a reason will just keep happening over and over again. And we'll end up on a talk show talking about what keeps happening to us and wondering why.

We can go back and see how, why, and where we gave up our power. Then we can take our power back.

By releasing our emotions, we can get clear enough to align with the power that's already there, already ours. There's a valuable lesson in every story we've lived through, and the one we're living now. By looking at our stories clearly and closely, we'll understand what that lesson is. By trusting, we'll eventually see what we're learning now.

With the millennium, time is of the essence. Everything's being magnified. Events can easily feel bigger than life. This is so we'll look at things, see things, feel things, correct our path, do what we need to do because everything we do helps shape the universe and affects the world.

As above, so below, or so people say. Maybe the war in the heavens, the one that's been going on for a long, long time, is also being acted out in its counterpart right here on earth—the ancient battle between Darkness and Light.

Sometimes it takes just the slightest bit of consciousness to help ourselves heal from the past. We can do it whenever an uncomfortable situation arises, propelling and causing us to react. How do you feel? What do you think? What are you telling yourself about how you feel, what you think, and what happened? How have you decided life, love, or work has to be? Go as far back as you're able. Then go a step further. Are they your emotions and beliefs, or something passed on to you from someone else? Sometimes the slightest whiff of consciousness of what we're feeling and what we're thinking—how it all started and where it came from—is all we need to set ourselves free. If we don't release emotions of fear, hatred, resentments, victimization, vindictiveness, and grudges—whether towards others or ourselves—we'll create situations that recreate those same emotions in the future. It's inevitable. We'll do it automatically, instinctively. We'll use past negativity to create the future. The problem is, it's always today. We'll be blocked from aligning with power.

On my travels around the world, I've visited many holy sites. What I've noticed about holy sites is that the reason they're holy is usually because after a terrible tragedy occurred there, many people started coming to this site to see it and pray. When the original tragedy occurred on the spot, people often didn't know at the time that it was holy. Not then. The site became holy later on, after people saw the incident in retrospect. After people prayed.

The twists and turns in our lives that are so painful and ugly when they happen, in retrospect, can become holy spots in our lives— the twist that takes us to the next bead. And some of the things we regret most about our lives may be the very things we came here to do and learn.

When the Babalawo finished the cleansing, going back over every story in my life, he handed me the paper bag that he had used to make the sign of the cross on my body, while he prayed.

"Take this. Put it by a tree in a churchyard. Then just walk away," he said. "Don't look back."

Let destiny have its way. But do your part too. I finally began to understand what happened that day at the Babalawo's. To heal from the past, we have to go back there until we can come out and feel clear.

I've been a straight-A student, an abused child, a junkie, a sage, and a whore. I've robbed drugstores, been to jail, stayed home for years, and been to some of the most holy spots in the world. I've been to Egypt, and to Central America where I hung out of a helicopter and shot pictures of Honduras. I've been to Algeria, Barcelona, and had dinner at a prince's palace in southern France. I've been a secretary, owned a bookstore, and been a waitress. I've been to treatment, worked for a newspaper, been a mom three times. I gave up one child, buried one, and saw the other one through until she became an adult. I've had disastrous relationships, been married, been divorced, and had some fantastic breathtaking affairs. I've written books, worked hard on my recovery, and tried to help other people recover as well. I've spent years denying I had a body or caring if I did. Now I'm going for a black belt, taking a kayak out on the ocean, running, and can tell you exactly where my liver and spleen are and not only how I, but they, also feel.

I went through years where I refused to acknowledge or believe in God. I've had moments where I've heard the angels whisper in my ear.

I've been so poor that I had no car, no phone, and sometimes lived on the streets. Other times I've had enough money to make other people mad.

I've eaten peanut butter sandwiches with homeless people on a bench on the streets and found a common ground. I've had dinner with movie stars and been on panels with the president of the United States and his wife, talking about what we had in common too.

I've been through two fires, a hurricane, a tornado, a flood, and one earthquake so far.

I've almost had it all, lost it, then got it—or at least parts of it—back again. Then I've lost it and had to scramble to put it all together one more time. I've been on the top of the *New York Times* best-seller list. I've had long periods where I thought I'd never write again.

I've had best friends and worst enemies, and sometimes the same person was both.

I've hated myself and loved myself, sometimes in the same day.

I've been written about in prominent national magazines. I've been stabbed at in the rags.

I've made good business decisions, and some that at best, were poor.

I've been lonely and brokenhearted, swearing I'd never give or receive love again. I've also had my life so full of love I've felt like the luckiest woman in the world.

I've gone from being the poster girl for drug addicts, to the poster girl for codependents, to living in Malibu and having people I used to watch on television come banging on my door.

I've lived so far inland the wind didn't blow for months at a time. Now on my worst days, I can look out the back door and think, *I might have taken the long, hard road to get there, but what the hell, at least I live at the beach.*

Now there's at least two ways I can look at all of this. I can say look at everything I've had to go through. Or I can stand back and say *wow.* Look at everything I got to experience, feel, and see. And as much as I've resisted and struggled each step of the way, maybe that's why I am here: to go through all of this and see from my point of view exactly how all these things feel.

I was talking to my friend Kyle on the phone one day. I told him everything I'd been through, seen, done, and felt. "I've done everything I've judged, held in contempt, and in the final analysis, I've done everything I've wanted to do. It's been an interesting trip, but I can't see that there's much left."

"I know something that you've wanted to do but haven't done yet," he said.

"What?" I asked.

Kyle was quiet for a long, long time. For a while, I thought he had hung up the phone.

"I'm thinking, I'm thinking," he said. "I've got it. You've never jumped out of a plane."

Jump Again

Once, when I was in Las Vegas watching a friend who was a comedian perform, I wandered into a magic store in the lobby of my hotel. I liked magic. I liked watching it, and I wanted to buy some tricks. Now, I had the perfect excuse. I was looking for birthday presents for my godson, Blake. He was about to turn nine.

The store owner performed several tricks—a card placed in the middle of the deck that magically appears on the top; a dollar bill that appears to levitate in midair; a scarf that disappears and then reappears in the magician's hand. When I agreed to buy them, the store manager, a magician himself, shut down the store and sent away all the customers except for me. You were only told the secrets when you were ready to put your cash on the table and pay the price to learn how things really worked. I felt excited. Like a child. I wanted to know the secrets. But in a way I didn't. It was like peeking at your Christmas presents before Christmas Day. I wanted to believe in magic too. I liked the suspension of disbelief.

He showed me the secrets of how each trick worked. Each trick was so simply and unmagically explained—such a gimmick. So that's how tricks were done! Everything was rigged. I preferred to believe in magic. It made life more interesting. It helped me maintain my sense of wonder and awe.

I thanked him, took my tricks, then started to leave the store. I had a plane to catch. I was on my way back home. Then I turned around. "Magic is a lot like relationships, isn't it," I said. "You get the person to think one thing is happening, get his attention focused somewhere else, so he doesn't look too hard at what's really taking place. We look, but we only see what we want, hope, and imagine. But it's all an illusion, isn't it? Isn't there any real magic in this world anymore?"

"Come back when you have more time," he said. "I'll close the store and show you some more. Most of the tricks are simple illusions, things easy to do and easier to explain. But some of the tricks really do border on magic. They take you right to the edge. . . ."

Many of us want to believe in the magic in life.

Most of us have dreams or fantasies—at least one and sometimes more—hidden in our heart, about things we'd like to do and things we'd like to have happen in our lives. Fantasies and dreams are good, especially the ones in our heart. They're the stuff that this thing called fulfilling our destiny is all about. But sometimes, bringing fantasies from the dream world, from our imagination, from the realm of the spiritual down into the world of the physical is an entirely different thing. It becomes cold reality, and it takes hard work.

"Don't get me wrong," I explained to a friend one day, when I was trying to describe my process in completing a particular task. "There are moments when it's wonderful, magical beyond belief. But there are a lot of moments, many of them, when it's tedious, painful, frustrating, frightening, confusing, and difficult beyond belief."

"Who said magic doesn't take hard work?" he said.

Once our illusions are shattered, that's when the real magic begins.

That's what this story is about: doing the hard work, then getting right up to that edge where magic touches ordinary life and letting the show begin.

☌

The video man stuck the camera in front of my face. "Got anything to say to the folks back home?"

I mumbled something about the will being in the second drawer on the left in the office, then followed Andy, a six-foot-two blond hunk from Texas with a wide grin and just the slightest hint of a southern drawl, up the metal stairs and into the fuselage of the *Twin Otter*. The other twenty-one passengers piled in behind us.

The plane was the size of one of those small puddle jumpers you take when you fly from Minneapolis to Rochester, Minnesota, or Des Moines, Iowa. One continuous bench of padded seats lined each side of the plane.

I took a deep breath, as deep as a person can breathe when they're hyperventilating, sat down next to Andy, and strapped myself in. The other passengers, in a hubbub of clamoring noise and high-fives, immediately buckled up too. The engines roared noisily away. The plane took off down the short runway at the drop zone in Lake Elsinore, California. We lifted off the ground.

The passengers on this plane came from all walks of life. They included a policeman, a cook, a high-tech engineer, and a secretary. We had one thing in common. We were flying in this plane, but we weren't going to land in it. When the plane reached an altitude of 12,500 feet, we were each going to walk to the back of the plane and roll out that door.

We were going skydiving.

The phone had rung within days after my friend Kyle had reminded me that skydiving was at least one thing I had always wanted to do, but hadn't yet done. A voice I vaguely recognized was on the other end of the line. It was the lighting designer and electrician who had done some work on my home months before. He said I had mentioned to him, too, that jumping out of a plane was something I had always wanted to do. Now, he was inviting me to come with him and try it. He was a skydiver too.

Talk about coming out of the blue. The timing on this had been too close to dismiss as coincidence. *Oh*, I thought, happily agreeing to go. *It must be God's will.*

The video man stuck the camera in front of my face again. "Who's your best friend?" he asked.

I pointed to Andy. "Him," I said.

For the next half-hour, Andy was the man of the moment. When it was my turn to jump out of the plane, I would do it strapped, attached, to him. This was my first jump, and I was going tandem instead of solo. This smiling, blonde-haired boy with a slight Texas drawl would hold my life in his hands.

I would have to completely and utterly trust him—a man. I smiled, and told Andy how much I liked him.

Thank God, Andy smiled back.

The skydiver sitting across from me, a man, was wearing a white T-shirt embossed with these words: *If you're living on the edge, it's probably because you're too chicken to jump.* Another was wearing one that read: *I'm not chasing my inner child. I'm just trying to catch up with it.* Another man's shirt offered this little skydiving quip: *Risk is relative.*

I wasn't too chicken to jump, but during the beginner's skydiving safety course, called the A.F.F. Level One (Accelerated Free Fall), it became excruciatingly clear to me that risk is risk. Checking altimeters, checking the chute for safety, holding your body properly, knowing emergency procedures—what to do if the chute doesn't open or if it opens all tangled—and landing somewhere other than on an electrical wire, on top of a tree, or in the middle of the highway all sounded too complicated to me. There was much more to think about than I had anticipated when I had fantasized about doing this.

Initially, I had wanted to jump solo. Being attached to a man wasn't my forte. But after taking the course, learning about all the risks of skydiving, and meeting Andy, maybe being attached wouldn't be that bad.

In the wee hours of the morning, before I got out of bed and headed for the drop zone, reality had begun to interfere with my dream about jumping out of a plane. Stepping out of a plane? Falling through the air? It seemed a little more terrifying in reality than it was in the fantasy. But then, that's often how fantasies are. The course brought reality the rest of the way in, until it crashed down on my head. You had to exit a certain way. You had to hold your body a certain way. It's physics, I learned—by arching your back, the lowest point (your hips) will travel first through the air, and the arch will hold you steady while you fall. It has to happen. It's how gravity works. You had to watch your altitude, practice touching the rip cord, then check your stability and altitude again. When you hit six thousand feet, you had to glue your eyes to your altimeter, strapped like a watch around your wrist. When you hit five thousand feet, it was time to pull the rip cord.

Hopefully, the chute would open.

If it did, you had to check that too. Is it a rectangle? Is it smooth or twisting in circles in the air? Are you floating, or still speeding down quickly at one hundred forty miles an hour toward the ground? If it opened, then you still had a five-point check to do. Are the lines tangled? Do the toggles, the little handles near your head that steer the chute, work? Are they still attached or did they somehow fall off? Do they stop the chute? Turn it left? Turn it right? Did the slider, the piece of fabric that aligns the lines and sets a little over your head, come down, or is it tangled in the lines? Are the end cells open, the last little cells in the silky parachute? And finally when you look up, do you see a parachute or do you see blue sky—in other words, does your parachute have rips, holes, or tears? If any answers on this checklist weren't quite right, then you had to correct the problem or cut away that chute—then open your reserve.

Before you hit the ground.

The list went on and there was a lot to think about. Steering to the drop zone, downwind at one thousand feet, upwind at five hundred, centered on the target and facing into the wind by three hundred feet; landing by flying into the wind, and flaring—stopping—three feet from the ground. More than following all the instructions, I saw death, the grim reaper, sitting on my shoulder at every turn.

Do it right or die is what I got out of that course. And you only get one chance.

"When most people hear you're going skydiving, they act like there are only five skydivers in the world including you—and the other four are dead," one skydiver had said to me.

That's how I felt after the course. Consciousness is its own punishment and reward.

There was more, much more, to this jumping out of a plane thing than I thought. If I forgot to do a necessary step or if something went wrong, Andy would be there to help—right there. He would be attached to my harness, or rather I would be attached to him—by four large metal clips, one of which would be enough to keep me secured to him.

At least that's what he said.

The man sitting on the other side of me, my left side, the video man, stuck the camera in my face again. "Going skydiving?" he asked.

That seemed to be the cue for the others to join in. "Yay! Hooray! Going skydiving! Good for you!" People were slapping my hands, cheering me on. It looked like a happy thing. It didn't feel that way. Their faces began to distort, turning long, with eyes bugging out. Their cheering comments felt more like, well, torturous jibes.

I leaned back against the wall and unlike the other times I had flown in a plane, hoped that this flight would last a long time. Some of the other skydivers were engaged in lively conversations with each other. Some were jumping out with a team to do points, or moves, in harmony in the air; they were rehearsing the free fall moves they were going to make, their routine, in their minds, slightly moving their hands in the air, eyes rolled back as if they were already flying, or more appropriately dropping, at approximately 140 miles an hour toward the ground.

I felt hot, sick, excited, exhilarated, and slightly nauseated. I felt like I was going to have a heart attack or an anxiety attack, or both.

One thing I noticed.

I definitely felt alive.

ℭ

At fifteen hundred feet Andy nudged me. "You can unbuckle your seat belt now," he said.

I did.

"What does this mean," he asked, curling two fingers.

"Arch," I said.

"What does this mean?" he asked, pointing one finger directly at me.

I couldn't remember. My mind was blank. "I don't know," I finally said.

"Pull," he said. "It means pull the rip cord so the chute will open."

"Got it," I said.

My hands were sweating. My body felt numb. The other passengers looked hot too. One of the skydivers got up, ran to the door, pulled it halfway open, and let in the fresh air.

I could see down through the open door, see the colors of the earth, and the beginning of the little neat squares of land, that different way the earth looks from a plane. I checked the altimeter strapped around my wrist. We were at two thousand feet. Opening the door and letting in the fresh air didn't help. Everything, everything I had learned up until now told me that door should be shut and should stay that way until we were safely on the ground.

The hubbub of the skydivers around me turned into a drone, a sound that matched my blood pressure and the pounding of my heart. I turned to Andy. "I think I'm going to pass out."

"You'll be fine," he said. "Turn around with your back to me so I can fasten these clips."

I leaned back toward and into him. He attached the clips on our right and left hips, and tightened the belts on the lower part of our harnesses. Then he fastened the clips attaching our left shoulders, then our right. "There," he said. "It's done."

Suddenly, a buzzing noise went off in the plane. A green light flashed by the door. One of the skydivers rolled the door fully open, then jumped out of the plane.

Another, and another, and another leapt out of that plane. Like little trained monkeys, they just jumped right out that door. In moments, the only people left in the plane were the video cameraman, Andy, and me. And the pilot. *And he gets to stay inside the plane,* I thought.

The cameraman crawled outside, hanging onto the bar at the top of the door.

Andy stood up, which instantly stood me up too because we were attached. We weren't standing fully upright. We were in a crouched, kind of standing position on the floor in the aisle of the plane. Andy started shoving, pushing me toward the door. I started pushing him back toward the cockpit from where we had come. Andy was bigger, weighed more than me.

Moments later, attached by four clips, we stood at the edge of the door. I looked down. The wind was rushing past the open door, hitting my goggles, whipping onto my face. The noise from the wind and the engines was loud, hurting my ears.

Andy and I had practiced; we had rehearsed the drill. I would cross my arms in front of me. When he said *ready,* we'd lean forward, on *set* we'd lean back. *Go* would take us out the door. Then I'd arch my body and we'd fly through the air.

"Ready . . ." We rocked forward to the edge of the door. I couldn't breathe.

"You're thinking that it's supposed to be a big daredevil thing, an adrenaline rush, an overcoming of fear. That's not what skydiving is about, at least not for me," one skydiver had said. "It's really a meditation, a meditative process. You stay calm, focused, and serene, and just let the flow, the force, take you out that door. When it's time to move toward it and go out, you just calmly do the next thing. Focus on what's essential, and forget what's not." Good idea. But right now, my fear seemed like an essential thing.

I'm afraid of heights.

"Set . . ." We rocked backward, away from the door, building up steam, momentum, pressure, to push ourselves out the door.

I have been told that everything in our lives happens for a reason. And all that we go through prepares us for what's coming next. I not only think this is true, I believe it with all my heart. Everything in my life, every single thing I had been through and learned up to this point prepared me for what I did next.

I mustered up all the courage, all the force, and all the energy I could.

"Go . . ."

And I hurled myself right back down the aisle from where we had come, pulling 185 pounds of instructor on my back. Thank God, I had learned about points of no return. This wasn't destiny, coincidence, fate, or God's will. It was another opportunity for me, a recovering codependent, to learn to say no!

I had gotten myself into this mess, but it still wasn't too late to get myself out. I might be slightly embarrassed, but after this long I could speak up and say how I felt and what I needed. It wasn't too late to back out, but I had to do it now. Thank God, Andy was a sensitive, caring, and gentle kind of guy. I knew he would understand.

"I changed my mind." I said. "I don't mean to disappoint you. I know we've spent all day training and working up to this. But I'm not going to jump. I'm not going out that door. I'm sorry," I said, scratching and crawling my way back to the cockpit. "I just can't."

What happened in the next second happened so swiftly that I didn't have time to register it. "Oh, yes, you can," Andy said gently and compassionately while simultaneously pulling me back down that aisle and out the door.

One second later we were falling through the air.

I miscalculated that point of return. There was no turning back now. I was strapped in and along for this ride. *I might as well make the best of it,* I thought next. *And if the very worst happens, at least I'll get to see Shane.*

I went on automatic pilot. The wind was loud, rushing past my face. I was falling through the air faster than normal, because I had 185 extra pounds strapped on my back. Thank God, I wasn't alone.

I remembered to arch. I could see mountaintops and the sun. All I could feel was my fear. I checked my altimeter. Andy gave me a thumbs up.

I did three practice touches on the rip cord, throwing us off balance with each rigid, fearful touch.

I checked my altimeter again. I was so frightened I couldn't read it anyway. Andy gave me another thumb's up.

Now, it was time to fly.

Together, on cue, we lowered our left arms, just like angels lowering their wings. We spun in a circle 360 degrees all the way around to the left. Then we raised our left arms, until our right and left arms were even. That brought us to a stop.

Then we lowered our right arms, and spun in a circle all the way to the right.

For a moment I just giggled and smiled and forgot to be afraid. So this is what it feels like to have the power of angels and the free will of man. We entered that space where heaven touches earth.

Andy tapped on my altimeter.

Six thousand feet. Our time as angels was done. Now it was almost time to pull. I was supposed to wait until five thousand feet. I couldn't hold back. The suspense was driving me nuts. I had to find out whether this parachute was going to open. Or not.

I reached my right hand back, located the orange wooden knob, and I pulled.

In seconds, with the force of a gentle explosion, instead of slamming toward the ground, we popped back up, propelled toward the sun. All the fear came rushing back. I closed my eyes. Held my body rigid. I couldn't bear to look. "Did it open?" I yelled at Andy, squinting my eyes shut behind my goggles.

"Look up over your head," he said.

"I'm afraid to open my eyes," I said. "Just tell me if it's okay."

"No," he said. "Look. Check things out. Then you tell me."

I looked up. A little. I didn't want to move around too much. So far so good. No use rocking this boat. I told Andy everything looked fine, as much as I could see. He agreed. Then he handed me the toggles and told me to steer the chute.

My fingers were clenched so tightly around the ends of the toggles my arms and hands went numb. All I wanted, all I wanted in the world, was for my feet to be touching the ground. My body was stiff as a board.

The treetops, the houses, the roads looked so tiny from up here. "You steer. I can't hang on anymore. It scares me too much."

He took the straps from my hands, then started turning right, then left. "Don't do that," I screamed. "You're making me more afraid."

"I have to steer to get us where we're going," he said. "Besides, it's what parachutes were meant to do."

That's when I noticed it, intact around my wrist. I had gone back to see the Babalawo. My new destiny bracelet was there. It was fine. Maybe I'd be okay.

I began to giggle again. Under canopy time, it's called. Suddenly I wasn't afraid anymore. Falling had turned into flying. Now we were floating through the air. It was like being on a gigantic roller coaster. Instead of feeling so full of fear and dread, maybe it was time to enjoy the ride.

Nichole was fine. She had a good job and a good life in New York. I missed her living at home, but we had each begun a new time in our lives.

Her dad was well. He had been sober for almost three years now and had worked hard on his relationship with his daughter. Then he had a near-death experience. The call had come in the middle of the week. He needed heart surgery. They had to bypass in five places; they weren't certain it would work. The surgery turned out beautifully. As much as anyone can guarantee life on this planet, the doctors told him he had at least another ten years.

"Isn't Daddy sweet and wonderful and smart?" Nichole had said to me one day, shortly after the surgery took place. I had to swallow back, just for a moment, any grief I had about that marriage not working out. I had second-guessed myself a lot after that divorce, especially when my son had died, wondering if I had done the right thing. Maybe David needed the experiences that came to him as much as I needed what had come to me. I cared about him and always would. All I could say to Nichole was this: "I'm glad you finally got to see a what a wonderful man, brilliant therapist, and kind-hearted person I fell in love with and married. That's who your father really is."

And Scotty? In an odd way, I knew he was all right too. He had called me the week past. From time to time I had thought about calling him, but I was afraid to look too closely there. I didn't know from day to day if he'd be dead or alive. "Hey, kiddo, how are you doing?" he said.

"Okay, how about you?" I said back.

There was a long, long pause. "Honey," he said, "I'm not doing too well. I was on dialysis last week. It's getting pretty hard. That leads me to this call and what I want to say to you next. You told me how important I was in your life. I don't think you have any idea how much I love you. And I just want to apologize for ever having caused you any pain. I try to help you out, whether we're together or not, by sending you positive energy and thoughts. I know that after Shane died, you needed me a lot. I'm just calling to see if you'll be all right, and if you're willing to let me go. I'm getting tired."

"Remember what I asked you when you came back into my life, after Shane died?" I said. "I asked you to teach me about magic. That's when you told me to remember what I already knew. You've taught me a lot," I said. "But you still haven't taught me everything *you* know."

"Do you remember what Yoda said right before he died?" Scotty asked, reminding me of one of the *Star Wars* movies that we had watched a lot together. I knew the scene he was talking about. Luke Skywalker, in training to be a Jedi, had gone to Yoda for help. But Yoda was lying on his deathbed by then. He was sick, old, and tired. Skywalker told Yoda he couldn't die, he needed to stay around and train him. Yoda said he was strong with the force, but not that strong. He said death was the way of things, the way of the force. He told Luke that he had already learned all he needed to become a warrior.

"You've been a good student," Scotty said. "Remember, a warrior's strength flows from the force. And beware the dark side," Scotty said, parroting Yoda. "For once you start down the dark path, forever will it dominate your destiny."

"Just remember this," Scotty said. "You're the most beautiful when you're running around in love. Not in love with a man, but glowing because you're in love with life. I've taken you to the edge of the universe, then back again. You know that wherever life leads you, whatever happens, and wherever you go, you'll be okay. And if I'm doing things right, if I'm staying in the flow and doing the next thing, even death won't be that hard. It'll be the next moment in time."

There was a long pause. I was silent.

"Well," Scotty said. "I'm waiting for your answer."

"I'll be okay," I said. "You can go."

Maybe, I thought, floating down toward the earth, *this is what it feels like to really let go.*

"I'm going to unfasten our hip clips now," Andy said. I felt him reaching for the left clip.

"Don't do that!" I screamed. "What if I fall off?"

"You won't," he said. "Put your knees up. Lift them high in the air. The wind is blowing strong. I don't know what kind of a landing we're going to make. We might have to slide in."

The ground was getting closer. Gravity was having its way. The ride had felt excruciatingly long—especially when I was afraid. Suddenly I realized what a short time we had actually been in the air. My shoes touched the earth at the same time as Andy's did. We walked forward a few steps. The chute fell behind us in a clumped bunch.

As gently as taking the next step, we landed on our feet. *So this is what it feels like to come to earth,* I thought.

The video cameraman was waiting for us. He ran up. Stuck the camera in my face. I had wanted this whole thing recorded, so I could review it later on. I hoped he hadn't taped my little episode at the door.

"Congratulations!" he said. "You did it. You jumped."

I ran my hands through my hair. "Not exactly," I said, turning and pointing at Andy. "I didn't jump. He pulled me out the door."

"I didn't pull you," Andy said. "I pushed."

"How do you feel?" the cameraman asked.

I took a deep breath.

"I want to jump again."

༄

"Remember not to second-guess yourself," the Babalawo said when he tied the new destiny bracelet around my wrist. "Don't live from your head. Only do what you feel in your heart." He pointed to some file cabinets in the room. "All the secrets of destiny that have been gathered through the years are in these files," he said, opening a drawer. "They've been passed down to me. I've got a feeling that some day soon you're going to be writing about these. You're going to share some of these secrets with the world."

I shrugged and didn't respond. Write about destiny? I didn't have plans to do that. Oh well, even destiny could be wrong.

Hazelden Information and Educational Services is a division of the Hazelden Foundation, a not-for-profit organization. Since 1949, Hazelden has been a leader in promoting the dignity and treatment of people afflicted with the disease of chemical dependency.

The mission of the foundation is to improve the quality of life for individuals, families, and communities by providing a national continuum of information, education, and recovery services that are widely accessible; to advance the field through research and training; and to improve our quality and effectiveness through continuous improvement and innovation.

Stemming from that, the mission of this division is to provide quality information and support to people wherever they may be in their personal journey—from education and early intervention, through treatment and recovery, to personal and spiritual growth.

Although our treatment programs do not necessarily use everything Hazelden publishes, our bibliotherapeutic materials support our mission and the Twelve Step philosophy upon which it is based. We encourage your comments and feedback.

The headquarters of the Hazelden Foundation is in Center City, Minnesota. Additional treatment facilities are located in Chicago, Illinois; New York, New York; Plymouth, Minnesota; St. Paul, Minnesota; and West Palm Beach, Florida. At these sites, we provide a continuum of care for men and women of all ages. Our Plymouth facility is designed specifically for youth and families.

For more information on Hazelden, please call **1-800-257-7800.** Or you may access our World Wide Web site on the Internet at **www.hazelden.org.**